# History by HBO

# History by HBO

## Televising the American Past

Rebecca Weeks

UNIVERSITY PRESS OF KENTUCKY

Scholarly publisher for the Commonwealth,
serving Bellarmine University, Berea College, Centre
College of Kentucky, Eastern Kentucky University,
The Filson Historical Society, Georgetown College,
Kentucky Historical Society, Kentucky State University,
Morehead State University, Murray State University,
Northern Kentucky University, Spalding University,
Transylvania University, University of Kentucky, University
of Louisville, and Western Kentucky University.


*Editorial and Sales Offices:* The University Press of Kentucky
663 South Limestone Street, Lexington, Kentucky 40508-4008
www.kentuckypress.com

Library of Congress Cataloging-in-Publication Data

Names: Weeks, Rebecca, author.
Title: History by HBO : televising the American past / Rebecca Weeks.
Description: Lexington : The University Press of Kentucky, [2022] | Includes index.
Identifiers: LCCN 2022004943 | ISBN 9780813195308 (hardcover) | ISBN 9780813195322 (pdf) | ISBN 9780813195315 (epub)
Subjects: LCSH: Home Box Office (Firm) | Historical television programs—United States—History. | Television and history—United States.
Classification: LCC PN1992.92.H66 W44 2022 | DDC 384.55/54—dc23/eng/20220308
LC record available at https://lccn.loc.gov/2022004943

This book is printed on acid-free paper meeting
the requirements of the American National Standard
for Permanence in Paper for Printed Library Materials.

Manufactured in the United States of America

Member of the Association
of University Presses

# Contents

# Introduction

"It's not TV. It's HBO."

This was the tagline of Home Box Office (HBO) from 1996 to 2009. The declaration epitomized HBO's marketing strategy to differentiate its programming, and especially its original content, from traditional broadcast fare, but the tagline's validity continues to be a topic for debate by TV scholars and critics.[1] The now iconic tagline (since changed several times, including to the abbreviated version "It's HBO") speaks not only to HBO's branding strategy but also to the changing nature of television itself. Indeed, defining just what television is, beyond a piece of furniture, is becoming increasingly difficult. As media and television scholar Lynn Spigel points out, "Television—once the most familiar of everyday objects—is now transforming at such rapid speeds that we no longer really know what 'TV' is at all."[2] How we watch and what we watch is evolving at an accelerated rate, leading people to ask, "How is this still television?"[3] The ambiguous state of TV makes the straightforward topic of "history on television" a more complicated prospect than it may at first seem. However, it is precisely the shifting and maturing nature of television and the TV industry that makes it a rich medium for crafting and telling historical stories.

No longer confined by rigid viewing schedules and large, boxy technology, watching TV has become a more flexible and accessible activity. People still gather in front of the traditional family TV and have sets switched on in kitchens, bedrooms, and home theater rooms, but many also carry laptops, tablets, and mobile phones that allow them to access the same content on these portable devices. "Platform mobility" gives viewers "mobile access to a wide range of entertainment choices."[4] For example, a viewer may start watching an episode of *Westworld* (HBO, 2016–) on a TV in the bedroom, fall asleep, and finish it the next day on a tablet on the way to work. That episode of *Westworld* originally aired on HBO at 9:00 p.m. on Sunday, but the viewer was busy at that time so elected to start watching it at 11:30 p.m. the next night, a practice known as "time-shifting." After catching up on *Westworld,* the viewer decided to "binge-watch" all available seasons of *Vikings* (History [previously the History Channel], 2013–20) on Netflix, after the streaming service recommended the series based on prior viewing choices, watching the first three seasons, a total of twenty-nine episodes, over the space of two weeks. After *Vikings,* the viewer decided to revisit an old favorite on Blu-ray, *True Blood* (HBO, 2008–14), and engaged in "transmedia" storytelling by watching "minisodes" via the *True Blood* season three Facebook page. These viewing habits, and the new media buzzwords they exemplify, start to only scratch the surface of how the practice of watching TV has mutated.[5] These changes do not signal the end (or death) of TV; "instead," Amanda D. Lotz argues, "they are revolutionizing television."[6]

The shows that viewers are watching via these new platforms are changing too. Rather than airing approximately twenty-two episodes per season (the typical length of TV series), the standard cable and streaming season generally runs only eight to sixteen episodes.[7] Violence, profanity, and nudity often feature heavily, and storylines, especially in dramatic serials, are becoming increasingly complex, demanding viewers' concentration to follow the complicated story threads. This is not to say that this is what *all* TV currently looks like; standard network procedurals and sitcoms are still on offer. What has changed is the variety of shows available. This is, as John Ellis has put it, the age of "plenty" in TV.[8] American viewers are not limited to broadcast networks and their output; people also have access to basic and premium cable and streaming providers, as well as the internet, which offers an international assortment of TV shows to be downloaded.[9] Rather than aiming to appeal to the widest possible audience by producing the least offensive programming, many shows target niche audiences without fear of alienating certain viewers. *Narrow*casting rather than *broad*casting is the name of the game in TV, especially for cable and streaming services. "Once the prime medium of mass communication," Graeme Turner and Jinna Tay argue, television "can now also be discussed as a highly personal medium of individualized, privatized consumption."[10] Despite the effects of fragmentation, scholars such as Spigel, Lotz, Ethan Thompson, and Jason Mittell maintain that TV remains a vital and central aspect of everyday life, albeit in an altered form.[11]

Indeed, it is the ubiquity of TV and its function as a "cultural hearth" that warrant a closer examination of how it tells historical stories.[12] Since its inception, television has drawn individuals, families, and nations to its brightly glowing screens to watch stories about people, places, and times that are both familiar and unknown. Much scholarship has been dedicated to analyzing and understanding historical feature and documentary films, but TV, and the long-form drama in particular, has received scant attention. This is unsurprising, perhaps, given that television has long been considered an inferior medium. TV is often denigrated as a rushed production line of cheaply produced passive entertainment, while film has, at least to an extent, been acknowledged as an artist's medium.[13]

Long-form drama, though, which in my classification includes both TV miniseries (series with a limited number of episodes that tell a closed story) and TV serials (ongoing multiseason series), has unique capabilities and possibilities for engaging with history. This potential has been amplified by the intertwined technological, industrial, and cultural developments outlined above. The changes to viewing habits, content, and technology have shaped the kinds of historical stories that can be told on the small screen, as well as the way they are told. This book examines how these changes to the television industry, coupled with the longer running time and unique structure of long-form dramas, shape how historical stories are created and told on TV. The case studies chosen for this exploration of how TV "does" history are all HBO original content. While the premium cable channel claims to be "not TV," HBO's original programming has become a template for other broadcast and cable channels, as well as streaming services. Because HBO has been at the forefront of many television industry advances, it makes sense to study its historical programming as an entryway to examining how history is presented in "quality TV" dramas during the current "golden age" of television.

## HBO and the "Golden Age" of TV

This is not the first golden age of TV; nor are HBO's shows, and the many others they have inspired, the first to be called "quality TV." The history of American television programming can be broken down into roughly three periods. TVI, or "the network era," lasted from the early 1950s to the early to mid 1980s and was dominated by the Big Three networks, ABC, CBS, and NBC.[14] TVII, the period from the early to mid 1980s through the late 1990s and early 2000s, is the era of "multi-channel transition." The advent of remote controls, VCRs, and increased channel options changed the way the industry operated and the way viewers engaged with television. Finally, TVIII, or the "post-network era," is characterized by "proliferating digital platforms."[15] Within each of these periods there has been a so-called golden age of television that is linked to "quality" programming. The live anthology dramas of the late 1940s and 1950s, which "carried the cachet of the 'legitimate theatre,'" were the first to embody these concepts.[16] Many of these teleplays were adaptations of classic theater and recent Broadway plays, before the networks themselves began commissioning original works from notable playwrights.[17] The second golden age occurred during the multichannel transition, and it was during this period that critics and scholars began to explicitly discuss quality TV.[18] Robert J. Thompson identifies quality TV of the TVII period as possessing "thoughtful dramatic treatments of contemporary issues, striking visual styles, complex literary dialogue, and sophisticated comedy."[19] However, he also notes that an exact definition is "elusive," and that quality TV of this period was "best defined by what it was not . . . 'regular' TV."[20] While quality TV shows of the TVII period such as *Hill Street Blues* (NBC, 1981–87), *St. Elsewhere* (CBS, 1982–88), and *Twin Peaks* (ABC, 1990–91) were initially few and far between, in the 1990s quality TV shows proliferated and became commonplace on network TV.

The third golden age is again closely linked to quality TV serial dramas, although the characteristics of quality have evolved and the current crop is produced not by the Big Three networks but by cable (and, more recently, streaming) channels. The third golden age of TV began in 1999 at the start of the TVIII period, and whether or not it has ended is a constant issue of contention. John Caughie states that "Golden Ages only exist in retrospect" and it is through hindsight that they are constructed. In the current world of TV programming, the advent of every TV season and release of almost every new high-profile drama generates a discussion of whether or not it signals the end of the current golden age. Golden ages and quality TV are, as Caughie states, ideas that are perpetually cloaked in quotation marks.[21] "There can never be a judgement of quality in an absolute sense," Jane Feuer reminds us. Instead, "quality" means something different to every group, or what Feuer calls interpretive communities. For the TV industry quality is determined by demographics, for religious and activist groups quality TV promotes their own viewpoints, and "for academic television studies, 'quality' is a descriptive term that identifies a television genre called quality drama."[22] When I refer to quality TV, I do so in this final sense—not as a marker of value or as a judgment of quality, but as a descriptive term or category for drama serials of the postnetwork era that exhibit certain traits. As Dean DeFino outlines, postnetwork quality TV shares many characteristics with quality serials from the previous golden age, such as multiepisode story arcs and complex characterization. He also identifies new elements, including "verisimilitude, moral ambiguity, psychological realism, and narrative irresolution," which were pioneered in HBO serial dramas.[23]

HBO has become synonymous with quality TV in the third golden age but has long been a leader in the TV industry, not only in terms of original content but in regard to technology and business model. HBO was launched in 1972 and in 1975 became the first pay TV channel to broadcast via satellite with the "Thrilla in Manila" boxing match. Eleven years later HBO led the way in guarding against unauthorized access to its channel by digitally encrypting its signal, thereby securing revenue. HBO was also one of the first to build up its services, adding Cinemax to its package in 1980, which was followed in subsequent years by the inclusion of many more channels, such as HBO Comedy, HBO Family, and HBO Latino.[24] HBO continued to remain competitive by entering the streaming market, introducing HBO Go in 2010, a service allowing subscribers to access HBO's current catalog and stream content on unlimited devices. This was followed by HBO Now in 2015, a standalone service that bypassed the need for viewers to have a traditional cable subscription. In 2020 both services were superseded by HBO Max, a streaming platform offering all of HBO's original content, as well as access to WarnerMedia's catalog. As Trisha Dunleavy argues, throughout its history HBO has proved itself to be a "first mover," adeptly able to take advantage of new technologies and changes within the industry.[25]

HBO's complex historical dramas are, in part, a result of the company tailoring content to attract and maintain educated and affluent audiences. As a pay-service provider, HBO relies on monthly subscription fees rather than revenue from advertisers. This means that HBO is "free of commercial interruption and uncontaminated by the demands of advertisers" but is consequently completely reliant on subscription fees and needs to work constantly to maintain and build its subscriber base.[26] The audience that HBO actively targets is middle to upper class and educated, as they are the ones with the disposable income to spend on luxuries such as monthly subscription fees. HBO originally branded itself as a first-run movie and sporting event service, but it soon added in-house documentaries and stand-up comedy specials. HBO produced its first film, *The Terry Fox Story*, in 1983 and continued making films and miniseries before increasing its original programming output in force in the mid-1990s. Producing weekly original content that would require viewers to tune in regularly was a way to combat "churn," the practice of viewers canceling their subscriptions.[27] To engage its target audience, this original programming needed to distinguish itself from the more traditional broadcast fare, which HBO achieved by crafting smart, sophisticated, and risqué material. Viewers who now subscribe to HBO expect what its intense brand marketing promises: bold, innovative, and groundbreaking dramas, rather than the "comfort food" procedurals common to broadcast networks.[28] As John Mack Faragher points out, understanding HBO's audience is crucial to understanding the programming it produces.[29] Subscribers expect and demand a level of sophistication and complexity in HBO's original programming, not only in its contemporary dramas but in its historical dramas too. With viewers that are unlikely to be satisfied with cookie-cutter master narratives, HBO has an incentive to produce challenging historical series that will appeal to its core audience.

What initially set HBO apart from other networks (and still does, to an extent) was its risk-taking on unusual and unique projects, as well as its willingness to give creators creative freedom. The generous budgets HBO provides, along with authorial freedom and lack of network interference, continue to draw top creative personnel in the film and TV industry.[30] David Chase, creator of *The Sopranos* (HBO, 1999–2007), is adamant that the show could not have been made for network TV and could have been made only at HBO.[31] From the beginning, HBO decided to self-finance many of its shows, meaning there are no investors or advertisers to appease. Tom Fontana, a veteran TV writer and one of the showrunners behind *Oz* (1997–2003), HBO's first original drama, remembers being surprised at the lack of notes from HBO and the encouragement to do what he wanted with the show.[32] This hands-off approach with creative talent and the quest to rack up awards buzz, critical acclaim, and cultural capital have resulted in an environment that fosters diverse visions of history. There is no trademark HBO approach to history; instead it invests in individuals who craft unique and varied histories. This is the strength of history by HBO.

HBO's approach to the long-form drama (and consequently to historical drama series) profoundly influenced the programming of other cable and broadcast networks and streaming services. Taking note of the critical and commercial success of *The Sopranos,* many other networks followed suit within the confines of their own budget constraints and content restrictions. "Other networks," note Leverette et al., "have begun to imitate the HBO formula in terms of style and content, the 'HBO effect' if you will."[33] In fact, by the mid-2000s, HBO itself was seen to be flagging in the drama category, with other cable networks such as AMC, FX, and Showtime arguably outdoing HBO at producing HBO-style quality dramas. *Mad Men* (AMC, 2007–15), *Hell on Wheels* (AMC,

2011–16), *Masters of Sex* (Showtime, 2013–16), and *Manhattan* (WGN, 2014–15) are a few examples of historical TV series shaped by the HBO effect.

HBO's impact on the long-format series makes it the perfect case study, and its vast array of historical programming exemplifies the possibilities of crafting history on-screen. The shows selected for consideration are set during different periods in US history and include one miniseries, *Band of Brothers* (HBO, 2001), and three serials: *Deadwood* (HBO, 2004–6), *Boardwalk Empire* (HBO, 2010–14), and *Treme* (HBO, 2010–13). These are by no means the only (or, indeed, the "best") examples of history on television; series from other networks, cable companies, and streaming services, as well as those set in other historical periods, are equally worthy of similar analysis and, hopefully, will be explored in the future. However, given that this is the first study of how history is constructed in quality dramas of the current golden age, HBO series provide a useful, logical starting point.

Based on Stephen Ambrose's book of the same name, *Band of Brothers* follows the men of Easy Company, 101st Airborne Division, from their basic training in the United States and then throughout their various campaigns across Europe during World War Two. *Deadwood* tells the story of a rough-and-tumble mining camp in the Dakota Black Hills in the 1870s and focuses on the schemes, machinations, and negotiations that preceded the territory's entry into the United States. *Boardwalk Empire,* set largely in Atlantic City, charts the rise and fall of various bootleggers, both real and fictional, who sought power and money during the era of Prohibition. Finally, *Treme* engages with a much more recent period in US history, the aftermath of Hurricane Katrina in New Orleans, Louisiana. On the surface, each series is easily categorized; there is a war series, a western and gangster series, and a traditional drama. But no film or television series can be reduced to just one genre. All four are dramas. *Treme* could be classified under musical, and *Band of Brothers* under action. The more controversial question is, Are these historical series? Clearly, all four are set in the past, but are they historical in the sense that they seriously engage with history and have something meaningful to say about the past? Much like the word "television," defining exactly what is meant by "history" in the study of "history on television" is less than straightforward.

## The Form and Function of History on TV

The question of how to categorize different types of films and TV shows set in the past has long occupied scholars, with two broad categories often being employed: historical films and costume dramas. Sue Harper provides a clear-cut definition: "Historical films deal with real people or events: Henry VIII, the Battle of Waterloo, Lady Hamilton. Costume film uses the mythic and symbolic aspects of the past as a means of providing pleasure, rather than instruction."[34] This basic description, however, does not adequately cover the various approaches to history on-screen. If it were applied to the series under review, only *Band of Brothers* would be considered a historical TV series, as it focuses predominantly on real people and follows a documented timeline. *Deadwood* and *Boardwalk Empire,* with their blend of real and invented characters and incidents, are impossible to place in either category. *Treme,* which has a central cast of invented characters, would, strictly speaking, belong in the costume drama category, although it clearly provides instruction as well as pleasure. As James Chapman argues, history on film "is an imprecise genre," and he points to the difficulty of classifying films and trying to assess the "relative balance of fictional and historical elements."[35]

Other scholars have been more flexible in their attempts to define historical film and television. Natalie Zemon Davis describes historical films as "those having as their central plot documentable events, such as a person's life or war or revolution, and those with a fictional plot but with a historical setting intrinsic to the action."[36] If Davis's definition is used, *Deadwood, Boardwalk Empire,* and *Treme* could be categorized as historical series alongside *Band of Brothers,* as the historical settings are intrinsic to the action of each show. Alison Landsberg goes one step further, identifying a specific subset of historical TV series as "historically conscious dramas." This subset arguably provides the best explanation and definition of shows like *Deadwood* and *Boardwalk Empire,* which are, at first glance, quite difficult to define. These series "do not aim first and foremost to re-create historical events. Rather, they aim to reconstruct the lived contours of a particular historical moment."[37] The focus is not on documenting major historical events (which may occur on the periphery) but instead on generating the mood, atmosphere, and mentality of a given period. The characters are not necessarily real historical figures in these shows but are "people who *could have existed.*"[38] In his study of Hollywood historical films, David Eldridge considers any film with a setting predating the year of release by five years to be a historical film. "This label," he explains, "is founded on the hypothesis that all films which utilise the past contain and reflect ideas about history, whether or not they are explicitly conceived of as 'historical.'"[39] While Eldridge's interpretation of historical film is very inclusive, it is, perhaps, too open and not selective enough. For a TV series or a film to be considered historical—a form of history—it must be, as Landsberg puts it, historically conscious and must attempt to say something meaningful about the past. *Band of Brothers, Deadwood, Boardwalk Empire,* and *Treme* approach the past in a variety of ways and ultimately represent different types of TV history, but undoubtedly all contribute something meaningful about the past.

The histories HBO and other network, cable, and streaming channels produce are important because it is through television that many people encounter the past. From its inception, TV has mined historical records, both ancient and recent, for stories to attract and entertain audiences. Practically every TV format has told stories that are rooted in history. The live anthology dramas of the 1940s and 1950s regularly drew upon history with episodes like *Playhouse 90*'s "Bomber's Moon" (CBS, 1958) and *Studio One*'s "The Trial of John Peter Zenger" (CBS, 1953). Short-format historical stories continued to be told in made-for-TV movies such as *The Execution of Private Slovik* (NBC, 1974) and *Hiroshima: Out of the Ashes* (NBC, 1990). Even sitcoms, a format not traditionally associated with history, have woven history into the settings and comedy of shows like *Hogan's Heroes* (CBS, 1965–71) and *Goodtime Girls* (ABC, 1980). Miniseries, including *Holocaust* (NBC, 1978) and *The Winds of War* (ABC, 1983), have been a particularly high-profile vehicle for history on TV, drawing well-known talent, attracting huge audiences, and sweeping TV awards. Primetime dramas like *Gunsmoke* (CBS, 1955–75), as well as more unconventional series like the science fiction show *Quantum Leap* (NBC, 1989–93), have brought history into people's homes week after week over the course of years.[40] And this, of course, is without taking nonfiction and reality programming into consideration. Gary R. Edgerton surmises that films and TV shows provide the primary frame of reference for understanding historical events and periods.[41] For example, what many people know about slavery in the US comes from watching the TV miniseries *Roots* (the original ABC 1977 version and/or the 2016 History remake), *Underground* (WGN, 2016–17), and the films *Amistad* (Spielberg, 1997) and *12 Years a Slave* (McQueen, 2013), seen either in movie theaters or on TV.

Roy Rosenzweig and David Thelen's study from the 1990s supports Edgerton's point by illuminating how often people engage with the past through film and TV.[42] Although the nature of TV and how people watch it has changed greatly since the 1990s, the broad findings are still revealing. Of the approximately 1,500 Americans surveyed for the study, 81 percent had watched a TV show or movie about the past in the last twelve months (the second most popular activity to engage with the past, behind looking at photographs with friends and family), while only 53 percent had read any books about the past in the same time frame. Respondents were also asked to rank the "trustworthiness" of the sources under review: for this, film and TV received a mean score of 5.0, the lowest of all the categories, while nonfiction books generated a mean score of 6.4. When asked about why they viewed film and TV as the least trustworthy, many interviewees cited the economic imperatives of the entertainment industry. However, many also stressed that it was impossible to judge the trustworthiness of all films and TV shows. Instead, respondents said "they'd found ways to screen distortions introduced by commerce, entertainment, ideology and prejudice. They chose both individual texts and genres of sources to meet changing tastes and needs and then engaged those sources on their own terms."[43] They would seek opinions from family, friends, and coworkers and discuss and debate with those around them what they had watched. This finding dispenses with the notion that viewers are passive, showing that they actively seek out what kind of history they want to watch and continue to think about it after the fact. This ongoing engagement with historical texts is even easier today, as people do not have to physically find others who have watched the show; they can simply go online and join one of the thousands of online forums.

For people to understand who they are and where they come from and gain a sense of personal and family identity, they pursue family history; in order to gain a sense of national identity, however, people turn to sources like TV, films, books, and museums. As Rosenzweig and Thelen's study shows, the survey respondents deemed history more trustworthy when coming directly from family members and other people they knew. This method of learning, of course, provides only limited access to the past. Television and movies (and books) "offered respondents the most accessible wide-ranging pasts to reach into."[44] Family history is personal and necessarily narrow, whereas film and TV offer a much larger scope. Indeed, many scholars have emphasized the role that film and TV play in shaping national identity.[45] James Chapman argues that "the theme of identity is central" to the historical film and, by implication, TV. In fact, TV, even more so than film, is a medium that historically has been targeted at a national rather than an international audience.[46] Chapman asserts that history on-screen "is not merely offering a representation of the past; in most instances it is offering a representation of a specifically national past."[47] Screen histories interpret key periods and events in a nation's history, potentially influencing both individual and collective ideas of nationhood.[48]

However, history on-screen transcends and has influence beyond national borders, especially as content becomes more accessible beyond national boundaries. HBO original programming, for example, is sold in 155 countries and is available to illegally download almost anywhere across the globe. As Tessa Morris-Suzuki points out, the myths created by Hollywood movies, and likewise by HBO, "are important not just because they are national myths, but also because they are global myths."[49] Audiences these days have far greater access to televisual histories of other nations via downloading, purchasing DVDs, and streaming, and are limited only by the content that has been produced. The act of viewing history on-screen can produce a connection between viewers in the present and the historical narrative they witness on-screen—what Landsberg calls "prosthetic memory." Prosthetic memory "emerges at the interface between a person and a historical narrative about the past, at an experiential site such as a movie theatre or a museum." "The person does not simply apprehend a historical narrative," she explains, "but takes on a more personal, deeply felt memory of a past event through which he or she did not live." This means that historical memories are not confined to a single group or geographic location; memories of traumatic events such as the Holocaust and slavery can be shared by any person regardless of nationality, class, or ethnicity. This is significant because these prosthetic memories can "have a profound effect on our politics."[50] Film and TV, then, not only have the potential to shape and influence national identities; they can also inform and influence viewers' attitudes toward other nations, international politics, and world affairs. History on-screen matters on a number of levels.

Clearly, HBO is not the first network to engage with history or to produce rich and complex televisual histories, but it does provide a snapshot of what is currently possible in the changing medium. For example, contemporary television shows may not have the cultural power to create "mythic" histories that dominate popular memory, but this is arguably an advantage of contemporary TV. A historical TV series aired today is unlikely to garner the ratings of an "event series" like *Roots* or *Holocaust*, the latter having been seen by an estimated 120 million viewers worldwide. These shows had a significant cultural impact, bringing attention to controversial and taboo historical topics. They are undoubtedly important histories because of the awareness they generated and public discussion they provoked.[51] Today, due to audience fragmentation, it would be incredibly unusual if a television show had the same impact. Rather, what is exciting about history on TV at the moment is not the influence and dominance of one "event series" but the sheer variety of shows and the flexibility of the medium.

Fragmentation of the audience and the industry's focus on narrowcasting resulted in a TV environment that is producing more challenging televisual histories and more history programming in general. Viewers have the opportunity to seek out lesser-known histories as well as multiple interpretations of the same event or period. Morris-Suzuki argues that written texts, being much cheaper to produce, are far more prolific and offer readers a variety of interpretations on the same historical event. Film, on the other hand, "creates a single, unforgettable, widely influential narrative."[52] Once a film is made on a subject, it is unlikely the film industry will revisit it again anytime soon (Morris-Suzuki's example is the mutiny of the slave ship *La Amistad* and the film version *Amistad*). While Morris-Suzuki's point is true to an extent, there are film and TV shows that cover similar ground, if not exactly the same, offering audiences a variety of interpretations on a given subject. *Band of Brothers* may be the only TV miniseries focusing on Easy Company, 101st Airborne Division, but it certainly can and should be viewed alongside other films, documentaries, and TV series that depict US involvement in the European Theater in World War Two. AMC's *Hell on Wheels* presents a different approach to the post–Civil War American West than *Deadwood,* while English gangster series *Peaky Blinders* (BBC, 2013–) shares a focus with *Boardwalk Empire* on the traumas suffered by young men in the Great War. HBO alone has produced not only *Treme* but two Spike Lee documentary series on Hurricane Katrina: *When the Levees Broke* (2006) and *If God Is Willing and da Creek Don't Rise* (2010). Fragmentation makes room for a wide spectrum of narratives and interpretations, of which dramatic TV series compose only one element. History on TV also consists of documentaries, telemovies, travelogues, reality shows, and feature films, which together provide vast and varied histories.

## Debating History On-Screen

Over the past forty years an expansive scholarship concerning history on-screen has emerged. As already suggested, this scholarship seeks to understand the role that film and TV play in shaping popular memory and national identity, as well as how history on film influences the general public and their understanding of history more generally. Perhaps most significantly, scholars still struggle to come to terms with the legitimacy of history on-screen and debate where its value lies. Should film (because most of the scholarship focuses on film rather than on television) be regarded, first and foremost, as a primary document, valuable for what it can tell historians about the people, society, and culture that created it? Or is film a legitimate *form* of history, capable of conveying valid historical interpretations and engaging in historical discourse? If it is a legitimate form of history, where should the line be drawn between "serious" on-screen histories and costume dramas? While debates about the legitimacy of the medium as a valid object of study for historians may be considered settled, there is no emerging consensus regarding these other central questions, despite the volume of work that has been produced and continues to appear.[53]

The debates over history on-screen rose to prominence in the late 1970s and into the 1980s, just as many other academic disciplines began to seriously address visual media.[54] Two French scholars, Marc Ferro and Pierre Sorlin, were among the first to produce book-length studies of history on-screen, both of which are still regarded as key texts in the field.[55] Importantly, in the foreword to *The Film in History: Restaging the Past,* which was published in 1980, Sorlin asserted his intention to shift focus away from "fact" (documentary film), which had previously been the focus of British scholars, toward "fiction" (dramatic feature films), broadening the scope of studies into history on-screen. After examining films on a number of historical topics, including the American Civil War, the French and Russian Revolutions, the Italian *Risorgimento,* and Italian resistance during World War Two, Sorlin stated that films are most valuable not as works of history but as documents that reflect the time in which they were made. In summarizing his findings about their historical content, Sorlin concluded that "most of the films have revealed rather poor material . . . and we have realized that specialists and non-specialists have very different notions of history."[56] Ferro, although skeptical, acknowledged a different potential of history on film. In the final chapter of *Cinema and History* (published in French in 1977, translated and released in English in 1988), Ferro tentatively suggested that film can, in fact, make "an original contribution to the understanding of past phenomena and their relation to the present."[57] Many traditional historians have since accepted Sorlin's claims and are willing to consider films as primary sources of the societies that created them. But, despite numerous scholars continuing to expand upon Ferro's ideas, the idea that film can *do* history, particularly dramatic feature films, remains a far more controversial proposition.

The forum on history on film in the 1988 *American Historical Review* (*AHR*) brought together a range of Anglo-American scholars with differing views of the place of film in history. Of the five participants, David Herlihy, with his article, "Am I a Camera? Other Reflections on Films and History," provided the most conservative argument, which is useful as a window into the mindset of more traditional historians. While Herlihy conceded that film can represent the "visual styles and textures of the past," he fretted over what he saw as its limitations. Historical films, he argued, "make history seem too easy and our knowledge of the past too certain." Film cannot incorporate footnotes, provide warnings to viewers, or convey doubt to audiences about the veracity of some aspect of the past; it cannot "easily explore beneath surfaces and illuminate the desires or motives that drive behaviour" or generate an understanding of the complex social, political, and cultural forces that shape society. Furthermore, as film requires thick description, filmmakers rely on their imaginations to construct a filmic world that may or may not be accurate. Ultimately, Herlihy considered historical films to be one-dimensional illusions that "cannot serve as independent statements regarding the past."[58]

Robert Rosenstone, John E. O'Connor, Robert Brent Toplin, and Hayden White, on the other hand, all presented articles that were much more positive and open to viewing film as a legitimate form of history.[59] To varying degrees, these scholars stressed the fact that film must be read, evaluated, and judged as a work of history in a way that is very different from what is required for written history. "The representation of historical events, agents and processes in visual images," White argued, "presupposes the mastery of a lexicon, grammar, and syntax—in other words a language and a discursive mode—quite different from that conventionally used for their representation in verbal discourse alone."[60] Rosenstone, O'Connor, Toplin, and White collectively lamented that in 1988 historians were ill-prepared to read and analyze historical films in a productive way. White coined the term "historiophoty," meaning "the representation of history and our thought about it in visual images and filmic discourse," and in doing so proposed a new category that liberated the visual from confines of traditional historiography.[61] Across these articles, a wide selection of films were discussed, although the scholars identified documentary and experimental films as offering the greatest possibilities for presenting history on-screen.

Although not part of the *AHR* forum, Natalie Zemon Davis's article "'Any Resemblance to Persons Living or Dead': Film and the Challenge of Authenticity," published the same year, also made a strong contribution to the history-on-film debate. Using the disclaimers that often appear at the beginning and end of historical films as a jumping-off point, Davis explored the concept of authenticity in historical films and concluded that dramatic features can render a "good telling" of the past. She highlighted what she considered to be crucial elements of a historical film capable of warding off common critiques by historians: suggesting multiple historical interpretations, incorporating ways of showing where knowledge of the past comes from, and maintaining distance between the audience in the present and the narrative in the past.[62] In 2000, Davis followed up her article with the book *Slaves on Screen: Film and Historical Vision,* focusing on five feature films from Hollywood and beyond over a span of forty years.[63] Once again Davis argued for the place of the historical film alongside written history, seeing it as "a source of valuable and even innovative historical vision. . . . Rather than being poachers on the historian's preserve, filmmakers can be artists for whom history matters."[64]

Of all the contributors to the *AHR* forum and early scholars of history on film, Robert Rosenstone emerged as the most vocal and persistent champion. William Guynn credits Rosenstone for "much of the impetus for the reconsideration of the history film," and describes Rosenstone's 1988 article for the *AHR* as "the first attempt by an American historian to construct a positive theoretical position from which to consider the legitimacy of historical film."[65] As well as editing two collections on the topic—*Revisioning History: Film and the Construction of a New Past* (1995) and *A Companion to the Historical Film* (with Constantin Parvulescu, 2012)—Rosenstone has contributed to a number of journals and collections on the subject and produced two book-length studies, *Visions of the Past: The Challenge of Film to Our Idea of History* (1995) and *History on Film / Film on History* (2006).[66] Of course, Rosenstone's ideas have evolved, as he has written on the topic for over thirty-five years. In a 2012 essay, Rosenstone returned to a 1982 essay he published on *Reds* (Beatty, 1981), a film he worked on as a historical consultant.[67] Rosenstone in 2012 expressed frustration at the Rosenstone of 1982 for dwelling too much on data and facts and on how the film version of the American socialist John Reed differed from his own biography of the man. In the years between 1981 and 2012, Rosenstone came to appreciate that *Reds,* and film more generally, can be a work of history, albeit "with its own rules of engagement with the past."[68]

Across his body of work, Rosenstone attempts to break down what he perceives as the artificial differences between traditional written history and history on film. He acknowledges that history on film and written history have very different strengths and capabilities, but he also stresses that both are shaped by their creators and influenced by the present, and that neither has the ability to mirror reality. In particular, Rosenstone takes issue with scholars like Sorlin who see historical films as being not about the past at all but about the present. He accepts that this view is true to an extent, but points out that exactly the same is true for academic historians: they, too, write "inevitably looking toward both the past and the present." Rosenstone suggests written history and historical films should be treated the same way: "looking for what they say both about the past they describe and about the present in which that past has been created."[69] Perhaps most importantly, Rosenstone suggests concepts for thinking about and analyzing historical film, such as the necessity and ability of film to condense, compress, alter, and invent.

Rosenstone's approach to history on-screen continues to influence scholars from a wide range of disciplines, including film, history, literary studies, and cultural studies, who have expanded and continue to build upon his core ideas.[70] Although a number of books continue to be published that focus primarily on "historical accuracy" and righting the perceived wrongs of history portrayed in film, history-on-film scholarship has diversified and offers a rich array of approaches to understanding how history on film operates.[71] Furthermore, the proliferation of studies has resulted in greater attention being paid to a wide variety of dramatic feature films, such as Hollywood blockbusters, independent films, experimental cinema, and foreign films spanning the course of cinema history. J. E. Smyth's *Reconstructing American Historical Cinema* is a particularly persuasive and innovative contribution to the field. Smyth focuses on historical films from the classic Hollywood period, examining films from *The Public Enemy* (Wellman, 1931) to *Citizen Kane* (Welles, 1941). Drawing upon close readings of the films, as well as memos, reviews, research notes, and scripts, Smyth argues that writers and producers of these Hollywood films consciously sought to reinterpret American history, and that they placed this imperative above considerations of box office success. Such films, she contends, are evidence that a filmic writing of history exists.[72] Approaching the topic from a completely different angle is film and English scholar Marcia Landy, who, rather than questioning the legitimacy of history presented on-screen, pushes the boundary of what constitutes history. In *Cinema and Counter-History,* focusing on European, Asian, and African films, Landy uses cinema "to think counter-historically," examining texts that "offer versions of the past and future that run *counter* to received views about historicity."[73] Marnie Hughes-Warrington, in both *History Goes to the Movies* and her edited collection, *The History on Film Reader,* pays particular attention to reception, the role of the viewer, and the possibility of multiple readings.[74]

And, in a recent study, Julia Erhart explores the distinctive, but often disparaged, contributions of female filmmakers in crafting historical films.[75] These scholars—and many more—explore how film meaningfully engages with the past, often utilizing both exemplary and flawed examples to provide a rounded inquiry.

Another related area that has generated significant scholarship, although it is rarely discussed in conjunction with historical film, is British heritage cinema, also commonly referred to as period film and costume drama. Scholars working in the field, such as Andrew Higson, Belén Vidal, Claire Monk, and Julianne Pidduck, explore similar and interconnected concerns to those working in the field of history and film.[76] While Higson is often critical of heritage film, with its overwhelming visual sumptuousness, which he sees as generating nostalgia and commodification, Vidal offers a very different perspective. In *Heritage Film,* Vidal considers both British and European heritage film, exploring how the conditions of production have shaped representations of the past, as well as acknowledging the evolution of the genre which has resulted in historically complex narratives that challenge the viewer. Alongside British heritage film, there are countless subgenres focusing on particular geographic regions, events, and periods that have expanded the broader field of history-on-film studies.[77]

Many of the arguments made and conclusions drawn in studying the legitimacy and possibility of putting history into film apply to television, and a few ambitious works address both, or history in the media more generally.[78] The edited collections *History and the Media, The Historical Film, Americanization of History, The Persistence of History,* and *Histories on Screen* provide a variety of approaches to the study of history on-screen from established and up-and-coming scholars. Quite often, however, TV continues to take a back seat to film in these collections.[79] The study that makes the most cohesive and persuasive argument for the place of history on-screen is Alison Landsberg's *Engaging the Past.* Building on concepts from her previous work, *Prosthetic Memories,* Landsberg considers interactive history websites, feature films, reality TV shows, and dramatic TV serials. She tackles common criticisms of history on-screen, namely that these types of history foster facile identification and rely heavily upon emotion. Over the course of the book Landsberg contends that audiovisual history should not be so easily dismissed and argues that affective engagement can lead to cognitive thinking on the part of the audience and provides a framework for evaluating new and popular forms of history.[80] Landsberg is not the only scholar working in this area; the affective element of history in popular media is a topic that is currently generating exciting new scholarship.[81]

The majority of the literature dedicated to history on television focuses on documentaries aired on networks such as PBS and BBC or basic cable channels like History. Ann Gray and Erin Bell's *History on Television* and their edited collection *Televising History* examine what they see as a boom in history programming in Britain and Europe since the mid to late 1990s.[82] Both books stress the importance of history on television and the role it plays for the public, but they focus primarily on nonfiction or "factual" shows, rather than dramatic series. A key concern driving the texts is the production context, how and why history programs are produced and who has the power to shape the history presented on-screen. Likewise, *Television Histories*, edited by Gary R. Edgerton and Peter C. Rollins, shares similar approaches and concerns while providing more US-based examples.[83]

Within these edited collections, individual essays on fiction programming can be found, but they tend to focus on how TV informs collective memory and privilege the role of the present in shaping the past, rather than exploring how shows seriously engage with history. For example, in his study of Flemish period serials, Alexander Dhoest states that *Wij, Heren van Zichem* (1969–72) "does not offer much in terms of 'proper' history," although he does concede that the show makes an effort to get the surface details right. What Dhoest does start to identify are the advantages of presenting history on TV. He notes that TV has room for "digressions and elaborations" and the time to create a truly fleshed-out world that can linger on the seemingly inconsequential aspects of everyday life.[84] Steve Anderson's article "History TV and Popular Memory" considers series that "raise questions of historical representation in unexpected ways."[85] Refreshingly, rather than dwelling on historical accuracy, Anderson looks at shows such as *You Are There* (CBS, 1953–57), *Meeting of Minds* (PBS, 1977–81), and *Quantum Leap*, which engage with history in creative and experimental ways.

Ultimately, only one thing is for certain: there is no one way of analyzing and engaging with history on-screen. Despite the vast number of books, articles, and essays that continue to be published on the subject (only a comparatively small selection of which has been discussed here), there is no consensus on the best way of approaching and evaluating history on-screen. Scholars continue to disagree on what is of central importance, be it production context, reception, or close reading. Even the definition of history itself has been challenged and contested in history-on-screen studies to the point where postmodern historians are uncomfortable.[86] Postmodern historians recognize that there is no absolute historical truth, that the past as it actually was can never be recovered, and that history can never be objective, as it is always shaped by the historian who creates it. Rather than reconstructing the past, historical interpretation is understood as "an act of linguistic and literary creation."[87] Such postmodern views helped open the door to exploring new forms of history, such as film and TV, but the advent of postmodern history does not mean that the core concepts of traditional empiricist history—fact, truth, and objectivity—have been completely abandoned. Far from being a shortcoming of the existing literature, these ongoing debates over the nature of history, and history on-screen, are one of its strengths, as scholars from a range of disciplines with differing central concerns challenge others to constantly reevaluate their own understanding of history on-screen.

This study attempts to add to this ongoing discussion, not to provide any concrete or definitive answers. Besides, screen texts and technology are evolving far too rapidly for any decisive conclusions to be reached. Recently, Rosenstone stressed the need to properly "understand the historying done by the history film." To do this, he argues, "the history film cannot be judged through the current canons either of written history or of the genre analysis of film studies, but by combining the two."[88] This is precisely what I will be doing in each of the chapters, using concepts and methods of analysis from history and film and television studies and examining TV industry contexts to explore *how* history in HBO's serials is constructed and *why* it is constructed that way. The focus is not on identifying or judging the historical arguments and interpretations presented in each of the shows or on how social and political contexts influenced the interpretations and their reception. These are valid ways of approaching and assessing history on-screen but are outside the scope and aims of *History by HBO.*

While some of the arguments I proffer are relevant to both TV and feature film, the book focuses on exploring the unique capabilities of the long-form series as a vehicle for history, as well as identifying its limitations. It considers how changing production practices and developments in technology have shaped and affected modern historical series and engages in close reading of scenes, characters, mise-en-scène, and sound. For the historical periods depicted in the series, I draw upon the historiography—not because written history should be privileged above the audiovisual, but because no work of history can, or should, be judged in isolation. While I firmly believe that TV has great potential to tell historical stories and is not inferior to the written word—simply different—I also maintain a belief in the discipline of history as it has evolved over the centuries. The question "What is history?" needs to be expanded, rather than abandoned completely.

Central to this book is the role invention plays in the creation of historical television. Invention is difficult for many historians to come to terms with, because on the surface it upends the traditional empirical approach to history. "To take history on film seriously," Rosenstone muses, "is to accept the notion that the empirical is but one way of thinking about the meaning of the past."[89] Rosenstone has spent considerable time identifying the different types of fiction that history on-screen necessarily engages in. As he sees it, invention is a strength of the medium rather than a weakness, as without it history on-screen "would not be dramatic, but a loose, sprawling form far less able to make the past interesting, comprehensible, and meaningful."[90] "Fictional moves" he identifies include compression, condensation, alteration, and metaphor. These fictions compress and condense time, space, and characters to fit within the demands of the medium, alter historical facts in order to express larger historical truths, and engage in metaphors to convey historical ideas. "Filmic literalism is impossible," he reminds us. "The camera's need to fill out the specifics of a particular historical scene, or to create a coherent (and moving) visual sequence, will always ensure large doses of invention in the historical film."[91] Inventions do not render history on-screen *unhistorical* or invalid; instead, they are precisely what make history on-screen possible.

Rosenstone's concept of invention does not, however, allow for carte blanche creation of historical people, events, and arguments. Of central importance is that the inventions crafted for the screen are inventions of truth. This means they should engage the discourse of history and not ignore it. "Like any work of history," he argues, "a film must be judged in terms of the knowledge of the past that we already possess. Like any work of history, it must situate itself within a body of other works."[92] Bruno Ramirez, a historian who has worked as a screenwriter on several historical films, makes a similar argument to Rosenstone's, suggesting that "fiction can be put to the service of history" but that the inventions need to be "historically plausible." Central to achieving this, according to Ramirez, is serious research on the part of all filmmaking personnel involved. When historically truthful inventions are crafted, they can "exploit the narrative potential of filmic language to the utmost and thus enhance the understanding of the story that is being recounted."[93] Of course, historical inventions do not always fit into the category of truthful inventions. Rosenstone offers *Mississippi Burning* (Parker, 1988) as an example of a film that engages in false invention—that is, its focus on two white FBI agents as champions of the civil rights movement goes against the discourse of history. Davis, too, is leery of unnecessary inventions that add nothing to the historical narrative and those that are tailored to create a link between past and present.[94] Historical invention, then, comes in many shapes and forms, and it is difficult to make sweeping generalizations about how it is employed across film and TV.

The HBO series chosen for this study all engage with invention in unique ways and to varying extents, shaped by the vision of the showrunners and the stories they wished to tell. Trevor McCrisken and Andrew Pepper pose a pertinent question in the introduction to their work on history on film: "Do any distortions or uses of fiction . . . actually strengthen the argument being made and add to the viewer's ability to learn something about the historical period in question?"[95] The answer that this book presents is yes: invention in history on TV is more effective at conveying historical truths than is "fact." Each of the chapters explores why and how each of the shows engage in invention and judges the appropriateness of the inventions and the consequences for the story being told. The study goes beyond typical considerations of invention in character and incident by also exploring the many types of invention practiced in the more technical areas of TV production, such as sound, production design, and costume design.

The following chapters focus on one HBO series and one element of televisual language, as well as related historical concepts. Chapter 1 addresses an often cited yet underexplored aspect of history on-screen: its ability to create the "look and feel" of the past. Like most historical shows, *Deadwood*'s "look and feel" is generated primarily through the mise-en-scène: the sets, costumes, props, lighting, staging, and performances captured and framed by the camera. HBO's generous budgets and willingness to expend a large amount of cash per episode results in mise-en-scène with relatively few limitations, meaning that mise-en-scène enriches, rather than hampers, the creation of the historical narrative. Indeed, this has been a core facet of HBO's business model: investing more money per episode but reducing the number of episodes in a season overall. Quality, rather than quantity, is the name of the game in HBO serials, and this is reflected in the mise-en-scène. Focusing on *Deadwood*'s sets and costumes reveals that these overlooked practicalities convey considerable historical information that adds to the historical narrative and plays a significant role in engaging viewers. Moreover, by recognizing the individuals and production teams responsible for researching and creating the physical historical world, this chapter highlights the complex and collaborative nature of history on-screen. Often, in history-on-screen studies, scant attention is paid to the issue of authorship, which this chapter seeks to redress.

The extended running time of the serial creates significant implications for the creation of complex historical characters, which is the subject of the second chapter, on *Boardwalk Empire.* Showrunner Terence Winter sought to maintain mystery and drama in his story of Prohibition by constructing and inventing some characters that did not exist in the history books. The result is three clear character types: real historical figures, like Al Capone; characters inspired by historical figures, such as Nucky Thompson (who is based on the real-life figure Nucky Johnson); and completely invented characters, like Jimmy Darmody. Capone, Thompson, and Darmody are all "difficult" characters—complicated, flawed, and tempestuous.[96] Without the need to satisfy advertisers, HBO was an early pioneer of the difficult character, which has become a celebrated staple of postnetwork quality TV. The chapter provides an in-depth case study of each of the three characters in order to assess the possibilities and limitations of each character type for transmitting history.

*Treme* is the focus of chapter 3, which considers how TV narratives are constructed at the level of the episode, the season, and the box set series as a whole. It is not only the longer running time of the TV serial that sets it apart from film; developments in style and technology, coupled with changes in industry and audience expectations, have resulted in intriguing new ways of telling stories, including historical ones, on the small screen. *Treme* is an example of what media scholar Jason Mittell calls narratively complex TV—television shows that employ elaborate storytelling techniques and balance serial and episodic storytelling. Indeed, Mittell sees HBO as having "built its reputation on narratively complex shows" like *Treme,* a series that demands audiences' full attention to follow the myriad of storylines and puzzle out the references to New Orleans culture.[97] Many of the criticisms leveled at history on-screen—the closed, linear narrative that presents a single interpretation, its inability to footnote and reference—are challenged in the analysis of *Treme*'s three and a half seasons.

The final chapter, on *Band of Brothers,* brings to light an area that has received scant attention in history-on-screen studies: sound. Just as the scripts and mise-en-scène for historical TV series are meticulously researched and crafted, so too is the sound. Imagine attempting to watch a historical TV show without the sound on: the narrative would likely become incomprehensible and its historical value greatly diminished. The value of sound, though, goes beyond dialogue, which is often employed to provide context, assign meaning, and explain complex plot points. The music in *Band of Brothers,* for example, reflects and reinforces the series' overarching historical argument, while the sound effects form their own kind of history, an aural interpretation of the past. This chapter breaks down the three elements of screen sound—music, sound effects, and voice—and explores what each contributes to history on-screen. The ability of sound to add to the history-on-screen experience has been bolstered by developments in home theater technology that allow for increasingly complex and multilayered soundscapes that engage viewers, thus linking back to the "feel" of the past discussed in chapter 1.

Almost any pairing of show and topic would have been possible and would have resulted in similar (but not identical) findings. All of the series, for example, are narratively complex and feature a wide array of characters and in-depth storylines. However, certain shows do lend themselves to particular topics. The different character types on *Boardwalk Empire* are more clearly defined and easily categorized than are the real and invented characters in *Deadwood,* and offered more precise examples through which to explore the issue of character in historical television. The intense and at times almost overwhelming soundtrack of *Band of Brothers,* especially in the battle sequences, made it an obvious choice for the study of sound, although *Treme,* with its rich use of music, would have also been a strong case study.

Each of the body chapters remains tightly focused on the topic at hand: mise-en-scène, character, narrative, and sound. The conclusion, however, will attempt to briefly judge the historical value of the shows, returning to the central question of what makes a historical TV series. Here, at the outset, it is fair to state that I do not believe all historical TV series are created equal (as is true for written histories). But all these shows do have historical value if only we open our minds and expand our horizons to see what TV, with all of its sights and sounds and moving parts, is truly capable of.

# 1

# Building a Historical World

## *Deadwood*

Viewers first see the mining camp of Deadwood in an extreme long shot just over ten minutes into the pilot episode. They view it from the perspective of Calamity Jane, standing high in the Black Hills in the Dakota Territory, watching the slow progress of the wagon train as it winds its way down into Deadwood. The short main thoroughfare is lined on both sides by wooden structures no more than two stories tall and is dwarfed by the endless mountains and tall dark pines that surround it. From this establishing shot, which situates Deadwood in its wild and isolated environs, the scene cuts to Seth Bullock at the front of the wagon train as he first experiences Deadwood's hustling and bustling Main Street. The camera alternates between a number of positions over this fifty-second sequence: it is positioned behind Bullock's head, allowing the audience a clear view of the road in front; it zooms in on Bullock's face from the front and side as he takes in sights and sounds around him; and it tracks along the left and right side of the street, mimicking Bullock's progress down the road. Bullock and the viewers are overwhelmed with the activity on the street. Men work away on various construction tasks while others loiter and pass a bottle, small dirty tents crowding the promenade; vendors peddle whiskey shots, guns, and live chickens while a butcher empties out the entrails of a dead animal. There is so much to take in: the buildings, the myriad of people populating the street, each with different guns, tools, and clothes, the countless signs (for a music hall, a meat market, and even a miners' assay office and chemical laboratory), the horses and horse troughs, and the lines of washing hanging out to dry. The scene is awash with visual clutter.

This is Deadwood circa July 1876 or, more accurately, a representation of the mining camp. The series, created by David Milch, ran for three seasons on HBO from 2004 to 2006. Milch originally pitched a show to HBO about

Seth Bullock arrives in Deadwood.

criminals and cops and law and order set in ancient Rome at the time of Nero. HBO was interested in working with Milch, but as there was already a series in development with a similar setting (*Rome,* 2005–7), HBO asked him whether he could find a new time and place that would allow him to explore the same themes. Although not a fan of the western genre, Milch decided on the American West and the mining camp of Deadwood, "a locale famous for its brazen, flagrant, and unrepentant illegality."[1] The characters that populate the narrative are a mixture of real Deadwood residents (Bullock, Al Swearengen, Sol Star) and fictional types often found in westerns. Milch uses the setting of Deadwood to explore the themes of law and lawlessness, order and chaos, and individuality and community. Hints of these themes can even be seen in the scene described above: the general chaos of the street, the omnipresence of firearms, the entrepreneurs hawking their wares, the construction of community spaces.

It is not cheap or easy to re-create the aesthetics of the past, and it is evident from this early scene in the pilot episode that HBO spared no expense in re-creating Deadwood. HBO's business model and approach to original programming have allowed the company to lavish both time and money on its series, an important practical consideration for historical series. A big budget does not translate into "good history," but it is undoubtedly advantageous given the practicalities of having to build/source/design the physical world of the past. Broadcast networks rely on revenue from advertisers, and "as each hour within primetime schedules is a source of advertiser revenue, networks are pressured to divide their budget on an array of different content so as to ensure diversity across each of their schedules."[2] As a subscription service, HBO does not have the same considerations or the high volume of original programming and long seasons consisting of twenty or more episodes. HBO's decision to limit the number of episodes per season allows it to invest greater funds into fewer episodes while also giving showrunners more time to craft each installment.[3] *Deadwood* cost, on average, $5 million (US dollars) an episode, an extremely high cost, even for HBO (*Rome, Boardwalk Empire,* and *Game of Thrones* [2011–19] would have a higher cost per episode in the future). For audiences, the promise of convincing sets, lavish costumes, and spectacular set pieces is part of the allure of HBO historical series.

As Bullock arrives in Deadwood, there is so much visual detail in this one scene alone that it is impossible to do it justice in written form. Indeed, this is a key difference between written history and history on-screen. The former, as William Guynn points out, has weak descriptive powers, while the latter has much stronger ones.[4] The written word can be as vague as it pleases, whereas film, by its very nature, must include a great amount of detail to fill the frame. A writer can paint a broad picture of a particular scene with words—much like the one provided above—and let the reader's imagination do the rest. In contrast, in a televisual representation of the past, the historical world must generally be created (either physically or digitally) down to the finest detail.[5] Discussing the creation and composition of film shots, Ed Sikov states that "every detail matters. Every detail is a statement of meaning, whether you want it to be or not."[6] This is precisely part of what makes creating screen history a difficult endeavor. Every detail within the frame has meaning, and in a historical television series that detail has historical meaning—something to say about the past. This challenge is, however, a potential benefit of the medium. The longer running time of TV serials means that rather than relying on easily recognizable historical signifiers, TV serials can incorporate multidimensional historical signifiers across seasons. *Deadwood*'s sets and costumes, for example, go beyond the standard signifiers of the western genre and contribute to the creation of a complex and nuanced historical representation.

That history on-screen can, with seeming effortlessness, evoke the "look and feel of the past" is an issue that is at once regularly critiqued by scholars and critics while also remaining underexplored and generally overlooked. In Pierre Sorlin's seminal examination of the historical film, for example, he does not even mention set or decor. For C. S. Tashiro this is a serious omission because to "pretend somehow the viewer (or critic) does not take surfaces as an *integral part* of the historical message is self-deceiving."[7] When the physicality of the historical world does garner mention, historians tend to berate filmmakers for being less concerned with getting the historical narrative right than perfecting the costumes, props, and settings that generate an aura of authenticity. The visual details that make up the world on-screen give the impression of historical authenticity while masking inconsistencies and inaccuracies in the content. Focusing specifically on the Hollywood feature film, Jonathan Stubbs articulates some of these reservations: "In many historical films, the past is embodied in their abundance of realistic, visible details, rather than by social relations, ideology, or other essentially invisible forces."[8] The spectacular settings and period clutter are viewed as "something to be gotten past in order to get the 'really important' material—history."[9]

Furthermore, history on-screen is critiqued not only for focusing on the surfaces of the past at the expense of serious historical content but for incorrectly representing those historical surfaces. Historical details may "correspond to popular conceptions about what the past looked like and not necessarily to historical records."[10] The "insistent fringe" identified by Roland Barthes in 1957 is but one example of a sign commonly employed in Hollywood historical films. These short fringes with curls laid flat against the forehead bring with them the "label of Romanness," and no matter what the characters do in the narrative, this "frontal lock overwhelms one with evidence, no one can doubt that he is in Ancient Rome."[11] These fringes, and many other signs, are often used to evoke a historical period and indicate historical authenticity regardless of whether they are historically accurate. Contemporary aesthetics also shape the historical representations on-screen, seen in the modern clothes, hairstyles, and makeup trends that appear alongside historically accurate representations. Historical films are regularly found guilty of "leaving out any unpalatable bits of historical gear and adjusting the attractive elements into a slightly more modern shape to gratify the unconscious cravings of contemporary eyes."[12] These are, of course, all valid criticisms that can be found to varying degrees across historical film and TV series, but this does not mean the visual elements of history on-screen should be ignored or considered only when they ignite the ire of historians.

Historians' mistrust of the visually rendered past is not particularly surprising given their general reluctance to utilize the visual in their own histories. Peter Burke and Michael L. Wilson point out that, on the whole, historians have been slow to embrace images as a source of historical evidence equal to the written word and to utilize images to their fullest potential in their own published work.[13] Historians prefer to ground their research and historical narratives in written sources, with images playing an ancillary role at best. Wilson contends that "pictorial sources have value only to the degree that they *add* to the main work of historical knowledge. . . . The visual remains an addendum to the linguistic."[14] This may, in part, be because many historians feel ill-equipped to fully analyze and "read" visual sources. Burke suggests that to address this, historians need to develop new forms of "source criticism" relevant to visual evidence and teach these methods within the discipline.[15] The inadequate use of images also extends to their appearance in published historical monographs. Although historians now regularly include images in their work—photographs, paintings, engravings, cartoons, etc.—the use of these images is largely supplemental, and they often appear embedded in the text with little or no comment. They are treated as "merely decorative, showing what a person or place 'actually' looked like or adding a period 'flavor.'"[16] Historians themselves, then, are not above reproach for the way they make use of and present images.

There are scholars already working within the field of history-on-screen studies who specifically address the potential advantage and power of the image track. Robert Rosenstone readily acknowledges that film can slide into "false historicity," relying on a period look and nothing more to convey history, but he also appreciates what it can offer. "Film," he states, "provides a sense of how common objects appeared when they were in use."[17] Rather than appearing obscure and inanimate in a museum case or photograph, the tools, weapons, clothes, and everyday objects of the past are brought to life, animated by activity and use. "Because they tell us much about the people, processes, and times, 'reality effects' in film become facts under description, important elements in the creation of historical meaning," he argues.[18] Alison Landsberg likewise views as a benefit the ability of film and TV to create the look and feel of the past. The authentic props and costumes "have the effect of reminding viewers that the past *was* different," helping to maintain the distance between audience and narrative necessary for cognitive thinking.[19] For these scholars, achieving a "period look" is not sufficient to transform a film or television series into a work of history; the visual details must serve the historical narrative. In a way, they should function like puzzle pieces, providing little pieces of information and filling in small gaps, helping to produce a larger historical picture that is bigger than the sum of its parts.

This chapter seeks to further this line of inquiry, exploring how the look and feel of the past is actually crafted and what it contributes to the representation of history on-screen. Contrary to common criticisms of historians, history on-screen does not always mean the visual spectacle of the historical world is privileged over the actual plot, characters, and historical interpretation. Inadequate time has been devoted to understanding how the material past is rendered on-screen, what it offers on its own, and what it adds to the historical narrative. This chapter, then, primarily focuses on how history is conveyed by the mise-en-scène, rather than the script. None of the shows examined in this book could be analyzed by looking merely at the scripts, which are simply words on paper. One could get a sense of the history portrayed from the script, but when analyzing the actual TV series, with all of its sights and sounds, a much richer and more powerful history is revealed. The script is undoubtedly important, yet it is only one element that will contribute to the history on-screen. There are the more "practical" aspects to consider, like the settings and locations, costumes and props, the performances and the sound (explored later in its own chapter). Many of these elements come under the broad heading in film studies of mise-en-scène. John Gibbs and Ed Sikov argue that an understanding of mise-en-scène is the "first step in understanding how films produce and reflect meaning."[20] This is precisely why mise-en-scène is a good place to start this examination of history in serial form, looking not only at how style creates meaning but at how style creates *historical* meaning.

"Mise-en-scène" itself is a complex term that requires some examination. As Adrian Martin points out, the phrase has meant different things to different people in different parts of the world over the course of its history. It is not a fixed concept, but one constantly in flux.[21] The French term has its origin in the theater and literally means "to put on stage," and has been used in English since the late nineteenth century.[22] Early attempts to define mise-en-scène in relation to cinema were vague, "gestures towards an aesthetic, rather than a careful or patient inventory of its component parts."[23] Since then, however, many have sought to provide a more concrete definition. In their seminal film studies text, David Bordwell, Kristin Thompson, and Jeff Smith explain that "mise-en-scène includes those aspects of film that overlap with the art of theatre: setting, lighting, costume and makeup, and staging and performance."[24] All of the details described in this chapter's opening paragraph of Bullock's arrival at Deadwood, all of the individual elements that created such a vivid representation of the past—the buildings, the props, the costumes, the actors—can be grouped together under the heading of mise-en-scène. This chapter focuses primarily on the aspects of mise-en-scène directly under the purview of the show's production designer—specifically, the sets, props, costumes, and makeup. To create the *Deadwood* set, a large team headed by production designer Maria Caso researched, planned, built, sourced, and arranged every single element captured by the camera.

The production design is the overall look of a TV series or film; it provides a sense of time and place and contributes to the psychology of the characters and the progression of the narrative. On *Deadwood* this visual design was created by Caso and the art department in close collaboration with other crew and departments, particularly the directors of photography and showrunner David Milch. Costume and hair and makeup are separate departments under the supervision of the production designer. The production designer must be intimately acquainted with the characters, the story, and, for a historical production, the history and construct a complete on-screen world that reflects and enhances the story. The production designer is, therefore, a visual storyteller, rewriting "the script in visual terms," although this individual's contribution to the narrative often flies under the radar.[25] The ultimate aim for a production designer is to achieve these goals while having the work remain invisible to the audience. When something looks wrong or attracts attention to itself, it pulls viewers out of the narrative. This is a particularly tricky balance to achieve on a historical production. The production design must express a specific historical time and place, as well as the characters and the narrative, while also maintaining an "invisible neutrality."[26] On *Deadwood,* Caso's goal was to "tell the richest story and be of service to the characters with realistic looking sets as well as visually interesting locations to suit the script and give the show a unique ground breaking visual distinction. On a budget, of course!"[27]

Production design for historical film and television often requires a balance between adhering to the expected visual style of the genre and achieving period authenticity through research. Production designers regularly draw upon a variety of "visual texts," ranging from past films and TV series to paintings and photographs. Employing signs familiar to a genre helps to quickly build and establish the historical world for the audience.[28] However, competent production designers also carry out extensive research and do not rely exclusively on what Sue Harper calls "deeply rooted cultural topoi."[29] Research forms a "base of knowledge" for the production designer. As production designer Eve Stewart (*The King's Speech,* Hooper, 2010; *Les Misérables,* Hooper, 2012) explains, rigorous research means "you end up with an inherent understanding of the period—so if you need to do something quickly, which you often have to do, and for not very much money," decisions can be made on the spot.[30] Changes may be made to the look of the past for dramatic or narrative reasons, but production designers stress the importance of solid historical groundwork. "You might decide to change things," states Antxón Gómez (*Che,* Soderbergh, 2008), but what is crucial is that "you're doing it from a base of knowledge."[31]

A film's or a TV series' production design is not only something that is overlooked by history-on-film scholarship but is also an area that is not well understood or appreciated outside of the industry, or even inside it. Key texts on production design lament that, although crucial to the success of a film or television series, the concept of production design and the role of the production designer are only hazily understood outside of the art department. Much like the area of sound (discussed in chapter 4), production design has been ill-represented in general film studies texts. As Tim Bergfelder, Sue Harris, and Sarah Street point out, one reason for the scarcity of scholarship may be the temporary nature of set design—erected and shot, then dismantled or destroyed—making it "a decidedly slippery target" of study for the scholar, with only limited resources (the film or TV series itself, concept drawings) available.[32] Production designers themselves were amongst the first to study and explore what their profession brought to screen narratives. Léon Barsacq applied his hands-on knowledge in the early foundational text *Caligari's Cabinet and Other Grand Illusions* (originally published in French in 1970), charting the development of production design from George Méliès and the early days of cinema through European cinema of the 1920s and 1930s and Hollywood cinema of the 1950s.[33] Other influential texts followed, including Charles Affron and Mirella Jona Affron's *Sets in Motion,* although they were relatively few and far between.[34] More recently though, since the 2000s, there have been an increasing number of texts dedicated specifically to production design, including edited collections of interviews, case studies of specific periods in set design, and general overviews of the topic.[35] Further contributing to confusion over production design are the myriad terms employed over the course of film history, as well as the evolving roles and duties of those in charge of production design and those on their team.[36]

The first section of this chapter focuses on the mining camp itself, particularly the communal spaces that provide the backdrop for the actors and the stories that play out. The camp is more than this, though; it is a character in itself, and like all good human characters it changes and evolves as the show progresses. The sets help tell the history of the camp as new permanent buildings replace temporary structures, as new and repurposed buildings are used for community spaces, and as the footprint of the camp grows. As well as helping to chart the progress of the camp, sets reveal the social history of these structures. Al Swearengen's Gem Saloon, the heart of the camp, demonstrates the multiple roles and functions that spaces could have and how such structures were experienced and utilized. The second section zeroes in on the finer details within the set, particularly the costumes designed by Janie Bryant.[37] While the previous section focuses primarily on the "look" of the past, this section centers on the "feel" of the past, in terms of both the tactile sensations and the emotions that the series evokes. It also considers issues of authenticity and invention in mise-en-scène. While props and costumes in historical dramas are primarily judged in terms of their authenticity, most are not authentic in the sense that they date from the period but are instead usually crafted using modern methods and materials. This is another type of invention which history on-screen engages in that can, in fact, work to the benefit of the production. Of course, there are too many individual elements that make up mise-en-scène to do them all justice in this chapter, which is why aspects of mise-en-scène will continue to be discussed throughout the book.

Once one is aware of what the various departments, including art and costume, bring to the construction of history on-screen, questions over authorship naturally arise, which the third section of this chapter addresses. A key strategy of HBO has been to promote its showrunners/creators as authors and artists. This strategy has contributed to a wider discussion of authorship on TV while also enhancing the value of the HBO brand by foregrounding the talent and "genius" it employs. Milch was (and, with the release of *Deadwood: The Movie* in 2019, still is) one of HBO's celebrated auteurs. However, by recognizing the individuals and production teams responsible for researching and creating the physical historical world, this chapter highlights the complex and collaborative nature of history on-screen.

## The Look of the Past: Sets

For several years in the 2000s it was possible to walk three streets of 1876 Deadwood, totaling the length of about two football fields. Given permission, you could stroll through the upscale Bella Union, check out Utter Freight, and visit the Number 10 Saloon, where Wild Bill Hickok was shot and killed. To get to this Deadwood, South Dakota, you needed to travel thirty miles north of Los Angeles, California, to Melody Ranch. Deadwood was constructed on the same movie studio ranch where classic westerns like *The Cisco Kid* (syndicated, 1950–56) and *Hopalong Cassidy* (NBC, 1952–54) were filmed, and the vast majority of the series takes place on these three specially constructed streets. Unlike many traditional westerns that divide their time between the wide-open spaces and natural wonders of the West and the community spaces of the settlement, *Deadwood* only occasionally strays beyond the camp and its hillside cemetery into mining operations in the Black Hills.[38] HBO's hefty budgets, and the research and dedication of the production team, brought this iteration of Deadwood to life, with the aim of capturing the look and feel of the historic settlement.

While it is admittedly convenient to use the phrase "look and feel of the past" as a shorthand for the complete on-screen visual world, it is overly simplistic and ultimately inadequate.[39] This is especially true for the first half of the equation—the look of the past. A painted backdrop depicting the western camp or a photograph of Deadwood could potentially provide information about what the place looked like at a particular point in time. The *Deadwood* set does more than this; it creates historical *space.* Of course, as Bergfelder, Harris, and Street point out, "sets on their own do not create space on the screen." Sets assume the appearance of three-dimensionality "in conjunction with the work of the cinematographer, who through framing and lighting devices animates the fragmentary construction and imbues it with an imaginary wholeness, and the editor, who during post-production adds a temporal dimension to spatial relationships."[40] In the finished product viewers get to see not only how the past looked—the furniture, the decor, the clothing, and the architecture of the buildings—but also how the public and private spaces of the past were experienced and utilized. The creation of historical space effectively allows viewers to see the look of the past in action, conveying significantly more historical information than the look of the past alone.

The historical narrative that *Deadwood* presents must be first identified in order to assess and appreciate the role production design plays. A real mining camp, Deadwood was located on land ceded to the Lakota (called the "Sioux" by settlers) in the 1868 Fort Laramie Treaty. As part of the treaty, whites were to keep off the Lakota reservation and the US Army was tasked with enforcing this. Rumors of gold in the Black Hills soon spread, however, and these rumors, in addition to a nationwide depression starting in 1873, prompted thousands of prospectors to illegally flock to the area. The mining camp of Deadwood was established in April 1876 and within a few months was populated by approximately seven thousand whites. As it was located on the Great Sioux Reservation, it was not initially subject to any rules or laws of the United States government; it was outside US sovereignty. A provisional municipal government was set up early on in the camp (provisional because there could be no official government without it being treasonous) and business exploded, with 173 businesses operating by the end of summer 1876.[41] The US government quickly moved to annex the Black Hills, including Deadwood, from the Great Sioux Reservation and created three new counties in the Dakota Territory. By February 1877, Deadwood was officially part of the United States and legal settlement began. Due in large part to its unlawful origins, the initial mining camp of Deadwood and the town it quickly grew into had a rough-and-tumble reputation. Deadwood historian Watson Parker argues that, contrary to popular myth, the town actually ran fairly smoothly from the outset. A "judicious combination of force and judgement" ran "the town with less conflict and excitement than the dime novelists have portrayed."[42] The appearance of notorious western figures such as Calamity Jane and Wild Bill Hickok, as well as notable violent events such as Hickok's death, mean that Deadwood continues to stand out from other similar mining camps.

Even though the series takes this specific place as its name and follows its general chronology, *Deadwood* is not a history of its namesake. Milch uses "a combination of sheer invention and interpretation of historical events to create a place that, while it has some grounding in historical reality, is never confined by it."[43] The series takes Deadwood, along with its inhabitants, and *knowingly* manipulates the events and individuals associated with the camp's history in order to explore more general themes relating to individuality, community, and law and order on the western frontier. There is a universal element to these themes Milch is exploring, evidenced by how he was able to adapt his initial pitch to HBO by changing the setting from ancient Rome to Deadwood. Once he made this decision, however, he undertook two years of research, grounding these themes in a very specific historical context.[44] Steven Peacock astutely summarizes Milch's focus: "*Deadwood* is concerned with the fundamental theme of settlement, exploring the creation and closure of the frontier as a line between urbanised, civilised society and an untamed wilderness and wildness."[45] Regardless of its name, *Deadwood* is not a history of a particular mining town, but a history of the formation of community in the West.

The show's approach to history can be seen in the treatment of the Gem Theatre, adapted to the Gem Saloon in *Deadwood*, a significant historical space in the series. The Gem Saloon built for *Deadwood* is not an exact replica of an 1876 saloon, nor is it an architecturally sound building. Indeed, as Juan Antonio Ramírez points out, there are key differences between real-world architecture and screen architecture. Not only are sets temporary, flexible, and adaptable (often repurposed for multiple productions), but they are fragmentary, with only what the filmmaker needs designed and built due to money and time constraints. As well as being stylized, set design often alters the size and proportions of real spaces to enhance a desired mood, exaggerating certain elements and abolishing others in order to maximize the intended message and best serve the narrative.[46] *Deadwood*'s Gem exhibits many of these properties. Although the viewer becomes familiar with many spaces within the saloon, others remain hidden. The main space that the viewer sees in the Gem is the large open barroom with a double-height ceiling. It is furnished with a bar, piano, and tables and chairs for drinking and gambling and is accessible through the large double doors that lead directly to the Main Street promenade. Leading off from the large room towards a back entrance is a short hallway lined with doorways. Behind one of these doors is the prostitutes' communal room, where Doc Cochran regularly examines the girls. Otherwise, viewers do not see behind the other closed doors, and it is more than likely they were not built at all. Back in the main saloon area, a staircase ascends to a gallery overlooking the bar area and another row of doors. Up here is Swearengen's office and adjoining private rooms, and presumably more brothel rooms. The Gem set was not structurally sound either; its exterior and Swearengen's porch were located on the Main Street set, but its interior was actually located about fifty yards north on a soundstage.

Inspired by the real Gem Theatre and its owner/operator, the Gem Saloon of *Deadwood* has a seedy reputation. "Of all the low spots the longest-lived and the most continuously notorious was the 'dissolute and degraded' Al Swearengen's Gem Theatre," explains Parker. Descriptions of the Gem paint a vivid picture of an "'everlasting shame of Deadwood,' a 'vicious institution,' a 'defiler of youth, a destroyer of home ties, and a veritable abomination.'"[47] To call the Gem a theater would not be incorrect; it put on a variety of theatrical amusements and hosted traveling theater companies, as well as Indian troupes later in its history. The major source of the Gem's income, though—reportedly up to $5,000 a night—was the women, who not only performed on the stage but joined the men in between and after acts, encouraging them to drink and retire with them to the curtained boxes for privacy. The Gem Theatre was first and foremost a "hurdy gurdy" house, a brothel.

Many of the traits of the historic Gem Theatre are carried over into the Gem Saloon of *Deadwood;* it is a brothel, a bar, and a gambling den operated by Swearengen, although the theater element has been removed completely—except for a piano. The Gem Saloon, though, transcends its forebear by taking on numerous other roles within the community. Just as many other frontier mining saloons did, the Gem Saloon becomes a multipurpose hub, highlighting the significance of these spaces in the evolution of the American West.

First and foremost, the Gem Saloon is a place where the men of the camp come together to relax and find company, both male and female. Although often empty of patrons during the daylight hours, the Gem comes to life at night. After long solitary days spent working gold claims, the men convene in the Gem to drink, gamble, and converse. The saloons of the "Wild West" have a particularly seedy and violent reputation in popular culture, but as Kelly J. Dixon argues, they were mainly "public places where people went to relax and socialize as opposed to places where people sought brawls and certain death."[48] While some sudden and vicious acts of violence do take place at the Gem, it is, for the most part, a place of leisure and entertainment for the majority of miners who frequent it.

During the quiet daylight hours, the Gem often transforms into a community space. The Gem swiftly converts from barroom to courtroom in episode 5 of season 1 when Swearengen offers up his saloon as a venue for the trial of Jack McCall. His barmen Dan Dority and Johnny Burns dutifully prepare the room, covering deer antlers on the wall with cloth and rearranging tables and chairs for the jury, judge, lawyers, and accused. Such uses of saloons were not unusual according to Elliott West, who has studied frontier saloons in the Rocky Mountains. Given the lack of official public buildings, and the roominess and availability of saloons during the day, courts often convened in saloons.[49] Furthermore, "early residents came together in drinking places to solve other common problems," and saloons often "served as midwives at the birth of the first governments."[50] The Gem serves these functions too, with the first meeting of the town's notables being held in episode 6 when cases of smallpox are reported. Swearengen invites the men to the Gem, and as they sit together around one large table, they devise a plan of action to procure a vaccine and tend to the sick. Three episodes later, as Swearengen's fears over annexation grow, he organizes another meeting. "Be at my joint in two hours," he tells E. B. Farnum. "We're forming a fucking government." Within the confines of the Gem, Swearengen suggests the formation of an informal municipal government, and those assembled volunteer themselves for posts. Over

The Gem Saloon is transformed into a courtroom for the trial of Jack McCall.

the course of the rest of the series, the Gem continues to function as the meeting space for official and unofficial town meetings. "As a base of operations you cannot beat a fucking saloon," Swearengen tells Dan, and he is right. The saloon was "the mining camp's most versatile social institution, particularly in the early days."[51]

As a community space the Gem Saloon also provides insights into the cultural norms and social mores of the frontier mining town. Although the Gem is a flexible community space, it is not open equally to all and reveals a social hierarchy. When Mr. Wu, a Chinese businessman and Swearengen's dope supplier, enters the Gem through the front door in episode 6, it causes a stir amongst all those who see. Wu and Swearengen have, beneath the very humorous surface, a strong and mutually respectful relationship.[52] Nonetheless, when their business is complete, Swearengen tells Wu: "Get the fuck out of here, Wu, the back way—understand? The back way or we'll start getting people having the wrong fucking idea of things around here." "Celestials," as Chinese immigrants were often called, lived in segregated Chinatowns in western frontier towns, and indeed Deadwood had a comparatively large Chinatown. These immigrants' relationship with the white inhabitants was complex. They provided essential goods and services and were a cultural source of fascination. However, a strong anti-Chinese sentiment existed in most camps, as they were perceived to be barbarous, overly sensuous, and a threat to white men's jobs, perceptions that often resulted in violence.[53] Wu's second-class standing in Deadwood is illustrated by how he is not permitted to enter through the Gem's front door.

Even though the Gem Saloon set is not a historical building in any strict sense, the way it is constructed, shot, and edited communicates the historical importance of saloons in frontier mining camps. "Increasingly," states William Whyte, historians have "come to accept the value of the built environment as historical evidence," and studies of town halls, schools, factories, and hospitals have appeared, seeking to explore the meaning these structures held. As Whyte points out, uncovering the meanings of historical buildings and architecture is an incredibly complex task that requires examining many stages in a building's history.[54] One crucial element in understanding the significance of buildings, whether they are carefully planned and designed or hastily assembled and functional, is how inhabitants experienced those buildings and utilized the space. This is an area that history on-screen can address and communicate exceptionally well. Through "holding" the action, the Gem Saloon *shows,* rather than *tells,* why the saloon was so central to frontier camps and towns. Of course, the Gem was not the only saloon in Deadwood, and "no camp was worth its name unless it could boast of several."[55]

*Deadwood* offers up a variety of saloon sets and in doing so complicates the architectural typologies of the western saloon. Just as shows and movies set in ancient Rome use Barthes's insistent fringe as a sign of Romanness, the western also employs a number of signs, ranging from small props (the cowboy hat, the sheriff's badge) to a codified set with specific buildings (the saloon, jail, Main Street, etc.).[56] Within this schema, the filmic saloon has its own signifiers: the rough wooden bar and furniture, dim lighting, and, most notably, the swinging saloon doors through which "trouble" enters the establishment. *Deadwood* does employ some of these familiar signs but, importantly, supplies viewers with a spectrum of saloons. As West points out, once frontier mining camps were established and became more permanent, "different categories of drinking spots that catered to the diverse needs of the townspeople and reflected the economic, social, and even ethnic components of the town began to appear."[57] There were as many as twenty-seven saloons operating in Deadwood by September 1876.[58] To present such a large number would have been impossible, even with *Deadwood*'s sprawling cast and numerous storylines. Instead, the series presents three distinctly different saloons: the Number 10, the Gem, and the Bella Union.

Aided by the extended running time of the series, *Deadwood* allows viewers to become intimately acquainted with all three saloons and thus demonstrates that there was no archetypal saloon. The Number 10 Saloon is a single-story structure far more crude in its construction than the Gem. Canvas stretched tight over a wooden frame serves as the roof, while large gaps in the rough cladding are visible as the camera captures patrons gambling around card tables. The walls are heavily adorned with deer antlers and hand-printed signs proclaiming "50 Cent Whiskey Shots" and "No Spitting on the Floor." It is always incredibly dim inside the Number 10 Saloon at night as there is no overhead lighting. Indeed, the lighting fixtures in each of the three saloons perfectly illustrate their differing aesthetics. In the Gem the main lighting is supplied by two rough wooden chandeliers, along with wall lamps and candles. In the Bella Union, the more upscale saloon, lighting is provided by proper brass chandeliers and lamps. Instead of rough wood, the walls are covered in green patterned wallpaper and the wood is rich and dark and polished. *Deadwood*'s saloon sets communicate the standing of their proprietors, their target clientele, and their various offerings of entertainment and amusement. While the Number 10 offers up booze and simple tables for poker games, the Bella Union showcases professional craps tables, a cashier cage, and decidedly cleaner-looking prostitutes than those at the Gem. The Bella Union, Number 10 Saloon, and Gem Saloon sets demonstrate not only the centrality (and ubiquity) of the saloon in camp life but also the incredible diversity of saloons, which came in various shapes and sizes.

The saloon sets are just three of many spaces created by Caso and her team; as a whole, the *Deadwood* set charts the progress of the camp and contributes to the historical narrative at the heart of the show, about how "order arises out of the mud."[59] Frontier mining camps either died or thrived and evolved quickly, the latter of which is witnessed over the course of *Deadwood*'s three seasons. The show actually opens in the Montana Territory in May 1876 and moves to Deadwood ten minutes into the first episode. This opening sequence in Montana is vital for establishing key characteristics of Bullock but is also significant for providing a counterpoint to Deadwood. There is already a level of "order" to Montana; the streets are flat and even, the buildings complete and solid, the sidewalks empty of clutter. This picture contrasts sharply with Bullock's first experience of Deadwood's muddy and chaotic Main Street. Bullock and Star arrive in Deadwood in July, and from this point on most episodes in each season cover one consecutive day in the camp, although there are a few exceptions to this rule.[60] This means that season 1, for example, covers only about two to two and a half weeks of time in the camp. The time in between seasons is ambiguous, as no firm dates are supplied, and Milch does not strictly adhere to the historic camp's chronology. Season 2 takes place months after the end of season 1, sometime in early 1877, and season 3 picks up approximately six weeks after that. *Deadwood,* then, only covers roughly a year in the camp's history, but it is a time of intense development and change. Within the space of a year the real Deadwood was illegally settled, had formed its own government, had thousands of inhabitants and hundreds of businesses, and was incorporated into the United States.

The *Deadwood* set contributes to the larger narrative of the camp evolving from an impromptu settlement full of individuals seeking a fortune to a community coming together and establishing permanent roots. Permanent buildings expand the footprint of the town and replace provisional structures. Initially, boards, canvas, and logs were used to construct cheap and hastily built dwellings. But then, states Duane A. Smith, "as the camp matured, the architecture reflected its growth and change."[61] Substantial wooden buildings and even brick and stone replaced the crude domiciles as people decided to settle. Such changes are particularly evident in season 3. As Swearengen takes the newly arrived theater manager, Jack Langrishe, on a tour of the residential area in episode 3 of season 3, he explains, "This is new, the entire area is recent," pointing out the Bullock and Ellsworth homes made of brick and stone.[62] Opposite the houses is a rough, grassy area with tree stumps and makeshift park benches, populated by milling townspeople. "And who does this fucking belong to?" Langrishe asks. "Well, I guess this belongs to fucking everybody," Swearengen replies, lingering a moment and looking happily surprised at this revelation.

Swearengen may be bemused by the realization of a neighborhood park, but community spaces and institutions have been appearing since season 2, contributing to the show's evolution narrative. As both Smith and Parker point out, real communities began to form when people organized to create social institutions that drew even more people together.[63] Citizens "organized to promote their common interest," Smith explains. When they joined these institutions, they often realized "they had common aspirations and even plans for their camp. When this occurred, something intangible happened to the entire community; it became more than just a temporary working habitation."[64] Creating certain types of institutions and establishments, such as schools and banks, was considered an outward sign of progress for a mining camp. These particular spaces are added to the *Deadwood* set throughout season 3. An assembled crowd applauds as Alma Garret opens the doors of Deadwood's first bank; the Chez Ami, a former brothel, is repurposed as a school in the first few episodes; and a new schoolhouse is acquired midway through the season. The transformation of the larger set structures is buttressed by the introduction of new props. In the season 2 opening episode a stagecoach arrives in Deadwood (the first the audience has seen) and a telegraph wire is erected, both signaling the town's progress and increased connectivity to the rest of the United States.

It is difficult to overstate that these are but a very few examples of the *Deadwood* set and what it is capable of: on-screen there is a complete historical world. When watching, spectators see an illusion that this world extends far beyond what their eyes can see. Of course, there was a limit to the physical spaces that could be specially created—a boundary to the set. The way the camera moves and the way the action is staged, though, give the impression that the camera provides a window into a much bigger world. This is especially true of the scenes that take place on *Deadwood*'s streets. During the season 1 finale, there is a particularly tense sequence when many of the show's characters come out onto the street and move from building to building, giving the viewer a sense of the geography of the camp. Bullock moves along Main Street from his hardware store to the Grand Central Hotel, crosses the street, and heads back down to the Bella Union. After entering the Bella Union, he exits and turns left down a side street and then right into Chinese Alley, where he has heard a gunshot. Along this course the camera also captures the arriving General Crook and his army parading into camp down Main Street, Johnny Burns dragging Reverend Smith on a stretcher from Doc Cochran's to the Gem, and Alma, Sol, Farnum, Charlie Utter, Joanie Stubbs, and Cy Tolliver all crisscrossing and moving along Main Street. The result is the impression that this is a living and breathing camp, that the camera could move into any one of the tents or shanties on Chinese Alley (which the viewer never does really see) and it would be complete.

As well as the physical structures and objects captured on-screen, the "look of the past" can refer to the overall visual style of the production. As Michelle Pierson points out, the creators of historical films often re-create the past by giving them "the look of having been made at an earlier time." "The colour and grain of old techniques of photographic and cinematographic reproduction" are employed to create a "period look" and accentuate the historical setting for the audience.[65] This can be achieved by manipulating the image digitally (the desaturated color palette of *Band of Brothers* is an obvious example of the practice) and can be crafted manually. Of course, the past was not sepia tinted or grainy, but these techniques serve a number of potential functions. They highlight and enhance the mediated nature of history on-screen, contribute to the historical narrative (the subdued palette of *Band of Brothers,* for example, reflects the grim experiences of war), and help "root the story within a specific historical micro-universe."[66] *Deadwood*'s sepia-toned color palette was achieved not only through color grading but through the work of Caso and her team.[67] The choice of color palette was influenced by the sepia tones of old photographs, as well as the historical realities of life in a mining camp. "We used quiet colors (compound hues, neutral tints, browns, blacks and grays) with touches of jewel tones," Caso explains. Buildings and furnishings in Deadwood were built with the abundant supply of lumber from the Black Hills, but there was no paint available. Caso remembers being told that having a plethora of plain wooden structures "would all run together and look terrible" on camera, but she pushed forward with the idea, staining buildings various shades of brown and aging the sets with wax and glaze.[68] The end result is a color palette reminiscent of sepia photographs that also communicates the rough and provisional nature of the camp.

The "look of the past," in its various forms, is clearly capable of conveying a wealth of historical information, even if its ability to do so is often left unacknowledged. Rosenstone, addressing the debate over the "information load" of historical film and whether or not it is impoverished or rich—specifically the visual detail and specificity required by the medium—proposed his own question. The question is "not whether film can carry enough information but whether that information can be absorbed from quickly moving images, is worth knowing, and can add up to 'history.'"[69] The first part of the question is the hardest to answer definitively. Attentive, thoughtful, and highly visually literate viewers will likely pick up on the visual nuances of the historical narrative or may seek out further information and clarification from the many insightful weekly reviews and recaps available on websites like HitFix and the AV Club.[70] On the other hand, there will always be more-casual, less-involved audiences who may completely miss out on and overlook the finer visual details (or who may require a second viewing to appreciate them). Varying levels of engagement and understanding are to be expected of any text, written or visual. It is easier to respond in the affirmative to the other parts of Rosenstone's question, even focusing solely on the visual elements of on-screen history. The *Deadwood* sets "add up to history."

## Authentic Invention and the Feel of the Past: Costumes

Even more so than the "look of the past," the "feel of the past" is a vague and undefined phrase. What exactly is the feel of the past, and what does it consist of? Rosenstone and Landsberg identify both experiential and emotional components, elements that are often intertwined and difficult to separate. Sounds and visuals vividly re-create the historical world, creating an impression of what it might have *felt* like to be there, encouraging the audience to feel and care deeply about that past. Film utilizes its unique audiovisual language—editing, camera angles/movement, music, etc.—"to heighten and intensify the feelings of the audience about the events depicted on the screen."[71] Audiences become invested in the characters and storylines, leading them to identify with the emotions experienced by the historical actors. Indeed, it is the distinctive experiential powers of history on-screen and the resulting emotions they provoke in viewers that scholars often find particularly troubling. As Landsberg points out, "The proper mode of historical engagement is analytical and distanced, cognitive rather than emotional."[72] Landsberg's proposed theory of affective engagement, however, persuasively demonstrates that history on-screen does not necessarily foster a seamless identification with the past. Instead, film can encourage mental and cognitive activity in viewers that results in historical thinking. The viewers may become emotionally invested in the past, but they do so as themselves: there remains a distance between audience and narrative that stimulates cognitive thinking.[73]

The emotional and experiential connection to the past is, of course, built up through narrative and character, but mise-en-scène also plays a significant role in encouraging this aspect of feeling. Scenes from episode 10, season 2, as Seth and Martha Bullock watch over their unconscious and dying son, demonstrate how mise-en-scène is employed to heighten emotion. Undoubtedly they are an emotional set of scenes anyway, given the storyline, but the emotions are intensified by the performances, staging, and lighting. Taking place at night, the scenes are shot with a particularly low light, eliminating any background details beyond the close-ups of Seth's and Martha's faces. Their skin is bathed in a golden-orange glow, highlighting their tears and anguished expressions. The camera alternates between close-ups of the two but sometimes pulls back enough for a shot of all three together: William lying prostrate in front, Seth and Martha sitting over him, the small fractured family finally brought together by tragedy. The audience is invited close into the family circle when no one else in the camp is; they witness the Bullocks' suffering in close proximity.[74]

Feeling can also refer to the knowledge and understanding developed by the viewer of a historical period or event. Landsberg states that film can "create and convey something like period truths, a sense of the different texture and contours of everyday life at a specific moment of the past." In other words, the viewer gets the feel of the past, becoming familiar with its day-to-day rhythms. This is especially true for television series given their extended running times. The long duration of a series "enables the construction of a place that feels enduring, to which one returns again and again."[75] Over thirty-six hours the audience gets a feel for life in the camp, from the general harshness of life on the frontier to the power structures that govern the camp. This feel for the camp (which requires a level of dedicated viewing) eventually helps the audience to follow the complex storylines and often opaque actions of the characters. They get a feel for how things are done in the televisual version of Deadwood. Mise-en-scène once again plays an important role in cultivating this particular feeling for the past. The *Deadwood* saloon sets, as already noted, become familiar spaces with recognizable patterns of quiet days and raucous nights. The Gem quickly establishes itself as the central hub of the camp, playing host to a variety of events and serving dual roles in the community. Swearengen, the Gem's owner and the camp's puppet master, rules from the balcony of the Gem. When George Hearst arrives in Deadwood and challenges Swearengen's dominant position (and takes a sledgehammer to the wall of the Grand Central Hotel to create his own mirror balcony and seat of power), he threatens to disrupt the feel for *Deadwood* that the audience has settled into.

The explanation thus far of the "feel of the past" covers several aspects of what it means to feel, which is "to have a sensation, impression, perception or emotion." History on-screen creates a vivid visual and aural impression of the past, inciting emotion in viewers and allowing them to perceive and understand what it may have been like in the past. But what of sensation? "To feel" can mean to have a bodily sensation of heat, cold, or pain caused by an external stimulus and also to be affected through touch, a sensation of the skin.[76] Although television is a visual and aural medium, it can stimulate senses beyond sight and sound in the viewer. This discussion will focus specifically on how the carefully crafted surfaces of the sets, props, and costumes create the tactile sensations of the past. Surfaces are often overlooked in favor of what lies beneath. Binary oppositions such as surface/depth suggest, as

Victoria Kelley argues, "that the real value of interest lies in the second half of the pairing, not the *superficial*, but the *in-depth*."[77] This is the attitude often applied to history on-screen: undervaluing the physical world in favor of the historical narratives played out against (sets) and within (costumes) these physical surfaces.

These surfaces and their varied textures contribute to the feel of the past, affecting the viewer in a bodily way. As Vivian Sobchack summarizes, "We do not experience any movie only through our eyes. We see and comprehend and feel films with our entire bodily being, informed by the full history and carnal knowledge of our acculturated sensorium."[78] The exploration of embodied spectatorship, or how cinema affects and engages the body of the viewer, has been taken up by scholars such as Sobchack, Laura U. Marks, and Jennifer Barker, especially since the 2000s. Marks is particularly interested in what she terms "haptic visuality," in which "the eyes themselves function like organs of touch."[79] Marks's definition of haptic visuality is rather narrow, but her idea of the eye as an organ of touch is a useful one.[80] In this discussion of *Deadwood* it is more useful to employ the related term "haptically charged surfaces" to denote shots (and not always necessarily close-ups) that feature "conspicuous and evocative" textures.[81] These surface textures provoke a response or recognition from the spectator's own body; they encourage the viewer to feel with his or her body, which in turn contributes to the experiential and emotional components of the feel of the past.

Human skin is a familiar surface on-screen, but its regular look and texture can be manipulated to stimulate responses of desire and, as in *Deadwood*, repulsion. Typically makeup has been exempt from attempts at historical accuracy. While costume—and, to an extent, hair—is designed and styled to match the historical period, contemporary standards of beauty and makeup are regularly employed in historical productions.[82] An attempt at period-appropriate makeup on *Deadwood*'s female characters is evident: Calamity Jane is constantly covered in dirt, Trixie's complexion gives the impression of no makeup at all, and Alma, as the wealthiest woman in town, is generally the most polished looking. But it is not the skin of *Deadwood*'s healthy female or male inhabitants that prompts a strong bodily response. In season 1 smallpox appears and soon spreads through the camp, resulting in the establishment of a pest tent. The viewer sees dense coverings of pustules over faces and limbs, and infected skin pink and shiny with fever as Doc, Jane, and Reverend White minister to the ill. In episode 7 Jane and White are both seen bringing their healthy, unblemished skin into close contact with an infected patient as they

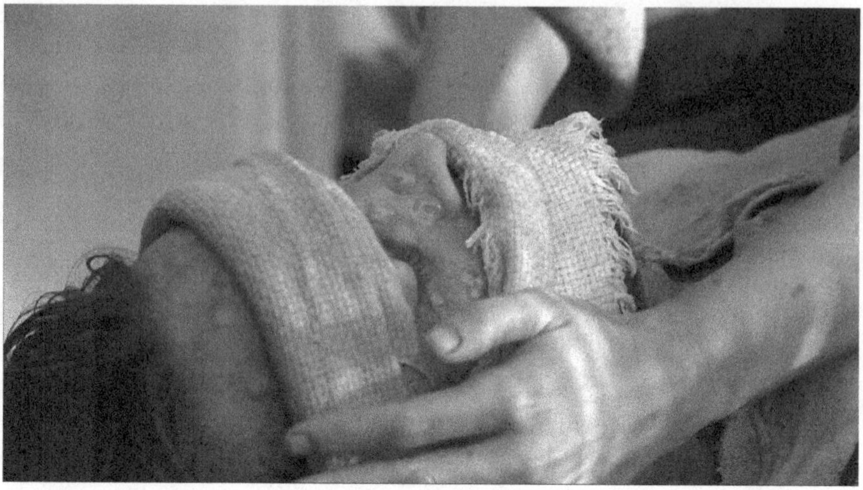

Calamity Jane comes into close contact with the skin of a smallpox victim.

lay wet cloths over his forehead and lips. The haptically charged surface of the man's face, covered in nubbly inflamed pustules, prompts the viewer's body to recoil and provokes a feeling of dread and revulsion.

The surfaces of the camp itself and its inhabitants generate a sensuous feel for how dirty and grimy life on the frontier was. The hair of *Deadwood*'s residents (again, except for the more genteel and respectable characters, such as Alma and Martha) often appears slick and greasy and unwashed. Their clothes, especially those of the men, are dirty and distressed. Janie Bryant and her team took to using wire brushes and sandpaper to wear and age the textiles' surfaces, also coating them in fuller's earth (a clay material often used in film production) to create layers of dirt. Bryant wanted the "costumes to feel and smell and seem as dirty as they really were during that period."[83] *Deadwood*'s muddy main thoroughfare is, perhaps, the surface that most evocatively conveys the dirtiness of the camp. The streets of historic Deadwood in its early years were "a reeking cesspool of rottenness" made up of mud, garbage, and manure from a menagerie of different animals.[84] To re-create this, Caso and her team used eighty truckloads of dirt and kept the streets constantly wet and muddy.[85] The textured surface of the mud is foregrounded throughout an epic five-minute fight between Dan and one of George Hearst's men. The camera is often positioned low to the ground, at the same level as the men. The viewer can see in exquisite detail their bodies slipping and sliding in the muck, their clothes and skin becoming saturated in dirt and blood.

Dan Dority slips, slides, and almost drowns in Deadwood's mud.

Then, when the camera pulls back to a high-angle shot, the viewer sees the complete vista, with smooth and rough patches of mud and puddles dotted across the surface. In another scene in season 1 Alma rushes through the street with her ward, Sofia Metz, in her arms. The camera closes in on her legs, the mud itself taking up the full bottom half of the screen, the hem of her long skirt dragging, and her dainty boots squelching and sucking in the mud. Viewers do not just see the thick, rich Deadwood mud, especially when it comes into contact with the bodies of the characters; they can almost touch and feel it with their own bodies too.

The clothes that adorn Deadwood's inhabitants, made from various materials and textures, likewise contribute to the feel of the past. "Screen costume," Sarah Gilligan summarizes, "functions as a crucial 'storytelling' element of mise-en-scène, supporting our understanding of characters' traits, emotions and motivations through a 'dress plot' of changing garments and appearances."[86] Consider the style of three of *Deadwood*'s female characters—Jane, Trixie, and Alma—particularly in season 1. Jane's loose-fitting trousers, coat, and hat, Trixie's revealing work attire, and Alma's prim and proper Victorian gowns help to establish character, providing the audience with clues about the women's socioeconomic standing and place in society. However, this is achieved not only through design—the cut, shape, and color of the fabrics—but through the actual materials used. Jane's masculine attire is fashioned from worn brown leather, moleskin, and tweed. Trixie's worn, flimsy camisoles and her plain corset contrast sharply with Alma's luxuriant satins, velvets, and lace. These various materials and textures function as "storytelling devices" but are also recognizable to many viewers.[87] Clothing is a human's second skin, and we are all intimately familiar with the feel of different textures against our flesh. Our bodies know the touch and sensation of the fabrics captured on camera, although the styles are foreign. Naturally, some textiles are more haptically charged than others. Joanie's and Alma's jewel-toned velvet ensembles are particularly evocative, the deep, soft fibers of the material contrasting with and pulling the attention of the viewer away from the rough, hard world around them.

These surface textures provide practical information about what things looked like while also stimulating sensations and contributing to the other "feelings" of the past previously discussed. Viewers cannot fully touch the infected skin, the mud, or the luxurious textiles, but they do still "have a partially fulfilled sensory experience of these things which make them intelligible . . . and meaningful."[88] It is useful here to return to Landsberg's idea of affective engagement. Affective engagement "draws the viewer into proximity of an event or person in the past, fostering a sense of intimacy or closeness but not straightforwardly through the eyes of someone living at that time." History on-screen can touch, move, and provoke the spectator's body, but what is of central importance to Landsberg is that the past remains a foreign country. "Accepting this claim," Landsberg argues, "is epistemologically important to the project of history, for it is the first step in acknowledging that any attempt to represent the past is inevitably imaginative work, a construction."[89]

The haptically charged surfaces of *Deadwood* provoke bodily responses in the viewer while retaining a sense of difference. We most likely have memories of caressing a soft, tactile fabric and of squishing through mud. Even if we have never touched a sick, infected body, we can imagine, in part through our comprehensive set of touch memories, what it might be like. Our bodies remember and imagine the feel of these surfaces. The sensation provoked in viewers is thus immediate and close—they sense it in their own bodies—yet it is distant too. They are familiar sensations in an unfamiliar world. Although viewers are responding in an affective way, it does not mean they lose sight of the past as a foreign country. Instead, the bodily response can generate cognitive thinking. We are repulsed and panicked by the infected skin, which prompts us to think about the realities of life on the 1870s frontier. The smallpox vaccine is many days' ride away, and the facilities for caring for the sick are crude by modern Western standards. Likewise, Alma's long, heavy gowns do not just dazzle the audience with their beauty and rich fabrics but also invite viewers (and I think particularly female ones) to consider the restriction of movement and the impracticalities experienced by women who had to conform to such a code of dress, especially on the frontier.

Alma's dresses and, indeed, all of *Deadwood*'s costumes are crucial in the creation of the historical world and play an "authenticating role."[90] Costumes are "a key ingredient in surface realism"; they "convince us of the historical or cultural authenticity of the period or place on offer."[91] The idea that historical authenticity—"what makes a cinematic account seem real and worthy of belief"—is often secured with surface detail is a point made by numerous scholars, including historians who have worked on historical films. For Natalie Zemon Davis, authenticity is most frequently conceived of as "a matter of the 'look' of the past, or rather 'the period look,' 'period props' and 'period costume.'"[92] Hannah Greig agrees, arguing that while the representation of material culture is rigorously researched, filmmakers are much more flexible in their manipulation and shaping of historical events, timelines, and persons.[93] Film studios during the classical Hollywood era would often stress in press releases and marketing materials the lengths their costume (and set design) departments had gone to in order to achieve historical accuracy.[94] Jane Gaines and Charlotte Herzog surmise that this focus on authenticity in the physical details served a particular purpose: "If viewers can be convinced that historical detail is accurate, the narrative may be liberated to a degree from any obligation to follow pre-existing historical accounts."[95]

However, this focus on the sets, props, and costumes providing a mask of authenticity for the "inauthentic" narrative ignores that authenticity in mise-en-scène is not realistic, achievable, or, indeed, particularly desirable. Authenticity in costuming is impossible, as the costumes are always shaped by the designer's modern aesthetics and influences beyond the historical record. What we see on-screen is a mix of old and new; period-appropriate styles and fabrics that have been constructed and fitted with a modern eye. Edward Maeder argues that the costume designer, "like the sculptor, painter, or even the historian, works within physical, social, and aesthetic limits to make a creation acceptable and comprehensible by contemporary standards." While costume designers may endeavor to faithfully re-create historical clothing, their "vision is so influenced by contemporary style that [they] cannot be objective, and the result is always an interpretation."[96] Furthermore, as already noted, in film and TV every genre has an expected visual style, and for the art and costume departments there is a tension between striving for period authenticity and adhering to visual styles of the genre.[97] Bryant not only researched 1870s fashions and the clothing of real-life historical figures like Calamity Jane and Wild Bill Hickok but was also influenced by other western films. *McCabe and Mrs. Miller* (Altman, 1971) immediately came to mind when Bryant read the script, and it continued to be a major influence on her as she designed the costumes for *Deadwood.*[98]

It is more productive to think of mise-en-scène as another type of invention that history on-screen necessarily engages in. While Caso, Bryant, and their staffs strove to create historically accurate sets and costumes that resembled what they had found in the archives, what they produced is ultimately still an invention. Rosenstone's categories of true and false invention—invention that either engages or ignores the discourse of history—can also be usefully applied to the physical invention of the historical world. Since the concept of historical authenticity is already so closely associated with mise-en-scène, it makes sense to adapt Rosenstone's terms slightly when discussing this particular aspect of history on-screen. Authentic invention "engages the discourse of history," is rooted in research, and, while never replicating the past exactly, contributes to the historical narrative in a multitude of ways. On the other hand, inauthentic invention "ignores the discourse of history," adds nothing to the historical narrative, is primarily concerned with visual spectacle, and unwittingly presents the audience with visual falsehoods (as opposed to films and TV shows that do this knowingly to create a particular effect).[99] Recognizing the invented nature of the historical world does not undermine it; in fact, being able to make the physical world from scratch, and to alter, edit, and destroy it, is a benefit.

Re-creating historical costumes has a number of advantages, especially since clothing is a vulnerable remnant of the past. Textiles are incredibly difficult to preserve: they "suffer from exposure to light, damp and insect infestation . . . become faded and discoloured. Fibres break down, shatter, and eventually disintegrate."[100] An outfit displayed in a museum needs to be carefully mounted on conservation-friendly materials, illuminated by a low light, rotated in and out of display, and, of course, kept static, hung on an inanimate mannequin (the last is true for both historic objects and replicas).[101] Chances are the outfit will only be partial, "dependent on accidents of survival," and what survives will likely reflect only a section of society, usually the wealthy or elite.[102] History on-screen gives viewers the opportunity to see all manner of clothes in their proper environment and to see how they move and sit on the human body. As Philippe Perrot notes, clothing can condition gait, posture, and behavior: "one does not stand or act the same way with or without a corset, with or without a tie."[103] Bryant made sure that the female actors were always wearing the appropriate undergarments, such as camisoles, bloomers, petticoats, and bustle cages. These undergarments, along with the cut of their clothes, gives the actors a certain posture and a limited range of motion authentic to the period. The clothing on *Deadwood* has no historical value except as it is captured on-screen. In contrast to real historical textiles, they can be worn, dragged through the mud, removed hastily, and torn as is required by the script, with little to no concern for their well-being.[104]

Bryant and her team employed modern materials and techniques to construct *Deadwood*'s costumes, but these ahistorical methods do not translate to the screen.[105] Due to time and money constraints, the clothing for the extras was rented and bought, a common practice on historical film and TV sets, while the clothing for the principal characters was "built" from scratch. As Maeder points out, "Finding authentic fabric and materials is always a problem. . . . In such situations the designer is forced to improvise, to adapt available materials and techniques to imitate historic ones."[106] For *Deadwood*'s costumes Bryant utilized a range of textile suppliers, including upholstery stores, across the United States. Even so, she admits that sometimes she had to compromise on the materials, as there simply was not the quality of cloth available that there would have been in Victorian times, although this was not an insurmountable problem. "You can find things," she explains, "that are close enough and that will photograph beautifully."[107] All these costumes—rented, purchased, specially crafted—were constructed with the aid of modern devices such as sewing machines and over lockers, very different to the technology available in the 1870s. Ultimately, though, these inventions have no effect on the history presented on-screen. The audience cannot tell from the image or from the haptic response it elicits that what they see, from the material to the seams, are not authentic.

One of the added benefits of building mise-en-scène from scratch, particularly sets and costumes, is that the art and costume departments can take all the details from the vast research they have conducted and create their own heightened interpretations. They can choose the elements they believe best serve the historical narrative and employ them in their designs. Rather than being viewed as something negative, the ability to select and edit is an advantage. There is only so much time in a TV series and only so much visual information that can be captured on camera. What is captured, then, needs to be as effective as possible at conveying a clear message. Authentic invention can convey information to the audience, potentially more clearly than even the "real." However, it is worth keeping in mind that incorporating the real—actual clothes from the period, on-location shooting at historic sites—does not necessarily make something more authentic. Choices are still made about which vintage outfits will work for the show and which will not and how buildings and locations will be shot, lit, and edited. What matters, of course, is that when designing and building mise-en-scène, those responsible engage in authentic invention.

## Collaboration and Screen History: Authorship

Clearly, mise-en-scène plays an important role in the construction of history on-screen, creating a multidimensional, sensuous world that is integral to the historical narrative. The art and costume departments on *Deadwood* are responsible for the structures and surfaces that create the look and feel of the past, contributing to the history and shaping the audience's engagement with the past.[108] Although Milch oversaw the production in his role as showrunner, he did not research, conceive, plan, or build the sets, props, and costumes that form *Deadwood*'s historical world. Part of the reason, perhaps, why mise-en-scène is overlooked and dismissed by scholars is they do not take the time to consider the people behind its creation and the full extent of the work that goes into it. Now that the contributions of the art and costume departments have been identified, a discussion of authorship cannot, and indeed should not, be avoided.

Caso, Bryant, and their teams clearly played a significant role in crafting the history on-screen, but it is a role that is rarely acknowledged. Instead, the focus is typically on the director (in film) and the showrunner (in TV) as the central authorial figure. In the realm of TV, HBO has itself played a part in developing this discourse by actively promoting its showrunners as independent authors.[109] This is a key marketing strategy designed to help HBO stand apart from other cable and broadcast networks. HBO developed this approach "to cultivate a 'high culture' status for its brand," Trisha Dunleavy explains. "The effect was to entice 'upscale' viewers seeking to align themselves with programming whose 'art television' reputation offered an elitist contrast to universally available 'ordinary' television."[110] In the process of seriously examining mise-en-scène in a historical TV series, a number of questions regarding authorship naturally arise. Who is responsible for the historical interpretation presented on-screen? In the case of *Deadwood*, it can be argued that Milch functioned as a kind of "head historian," almost like the editor of an edited collection. He selected the key personnel, provided direction, and was ultimately responsible for the focus and approach of the series and its overarching historical narrative. However, many individuals and departments made his vision possible and enriched and influenced his narrative. Assigning authorship in history on-screen is an incredibly complex proposition but is also a potentially rewarding path to follow.

Whether presented on-screen or in written form, all history is authored, and knowing the identity of the author-historian is of central importance to any serious student of history. According to Alun Munslow, most historians tend not to think of themselves as authors, as they are not "free to create, invent or design their own stories." But as Munslow bluntly puts it: "No author, no history." Although scholarly historians aim to report the facts and construct a truthful interpretation of history based on historical sources, they still make a "vast range of 'literary decisions.'" Historians make choices about what facts are included and excluded, whom or what events are focused on, the chosen time frame of their study, and the authorial voice they employ in the act of writing. "The historian-as-author," Munslow explains, "relies on precisely the same authorial mechanisms, manoeuvres, strategies and schemas as all authors."[111] E. H. Carr makes a related argument in *What Is History?* and underscores why, when reading a work of history, the reader's first "concern should be not with the facts which it contains but with the historian who wrote it." "The facts are really not at all like fish on a fishmonger's slab," he explains. "They are like fish swimming about in a vast and sometimes inaccessible ocean; and what the historian catches will depend, partly on chance, but mainly on what part of the ocean he chooses to fish in and what tackle he chooses to use. . . . By and large, the historian will get the kind of facts he wants. History means interpretation."[112] Identifying the author of a written work of history is fairly straightforward, as the author is named on the opening page. For a historical film or television series, coming to terms with authorship is far more difficult.

Although clearly central to the study of history, the issue of authorship has received surprisingly little attention from history-on-screen scholars. There are, of course, a number of works that focus on particular filmmakers who have made a name for themselves in historical film, with Oliver Stone providing a notable example.[113] The correlation is implicit: it is the director who functions as the author-historian in historical film. But, as Davis argues, decisions about how the look and feel of the past are rendered on-screen are made by a myriad of people, and therefore assigning authorial responsibility to any one person is problematic. "In films," she explains, "the processes of research, interpretation, and communication are widely dispersed, even if directors put their stamp on the product along the way and in the final editing." Research is undertaken by each of the film's departments (art, sound, music, etc.), and the finished product will ultimately be shaped by small decisions made by all those involved—from the actors to the directors of photography, editors, costumers, and set dressers (to name but a few)—during preproduction, during on-set shooting, and in postproduction. "Such collective creation contrasts with historical book writing," she concludes, "whose cast of characters would extend at most to a few co-authors, student research assistants, an editor and copy editor, and a book designer."[114] Bruno Ramirez, who has also worked on historical films, likewise acknowledges the contributions of the various film departments in crafting on-screen narratives. In fact, Ramirez is one of the few scholars to recognize the "crucial contribution" of the art department in creating history on-screen, and stresses the close coordination between each of the departments vital to producing coherent and nuanced histories.[115] Both Ramirez's and Davis's comments illuminate the complicated and collaborative nature of history-on-screen authorship. Using *Deadwood* as a case study, and by focusing specifically on Milch's role alongside the art and costume departments, their ideas and observations can be developed further to fully explore the question of authorship in history on-screen. Ramirez's and Davis's discussions were centered on feature film; TV authorship, although similar in some respects, presents quite a different model.

The central figure that has emerged in cable television shows is not the director, as it is in film, but the showrunner. Television has long been viewed as a commercial enterprise rather than an art form authored by individuals, but with the rise in popularity and critical acclaim of scripted serial dramas in the late 1980s and early 1990s, the position of the showrunner increasingly came to the fore. First appearing in trade publications in 1990, the term is now a common part of TV parlance.[116] Even so, "showrunner" is an ambiguous and unofficial title that is perhaps not fully understood outside of the industry. Quite often a series is conceived and created by a writer or writers who pitch the show to network executives. Once the project is green-lit and has gone through several stages of approval, the creator "assembles a team of writers and producers to undertake the ongoing creative process, while the creator steps into the role of executive producer to function as head writer via the unofficial title of 'showrunner.'"[117] Showrunners are most commonly "hyphenates"—writer-producers.

During production they serve dual functions: they are "in charge of the production and the creative content of a television show" and have both creative and managerial duties.[118] The showrunner typically supervises the writers' room, works on the set day-to-day to liaise with directors, actors, and the rest of the production crew, and has final authority over the editing process. Milch's influence as showrunner over the production of *Deadwood* provides a clear example. Milch is not credited as the director of a single episode (a role many showrunners dabble in) and is credited as the solo writer of three episodes and co-writer of two episodes. Yet, as cast comments and an in-depth profile of Milch for the *New Yorker* revealed, he was intimately involved in all aspects of production. Milch's routine was to lie in the living room of a trailer, staff writers present, dictating thoughts and lines of dialogue to an amanuensis.[119] Milch was present at rehearsals and during shooting, setting the scene for cast and crew with his "spiels" and providing insights into the larger significance of the scene in the show's narrative. He could also be found in the editing trailer working on the final cuts.

As the head writer, one of the key roles of the showrunner is to maintain a consistency of voice, a major factor for *Deadwood*'s completely unique language, which mixes ornate prose and profanity in almost equal measure. The showrunner maintains control over all the scripts even though, episode to episode, he or she is not explicitly credited. As Brett Martin explains, most TV series have a writers' room and follow a similar procedure: six to twelve writers work together to produce detailed season and episode outlines. The individual episodes are then assigned to one or two writers, who pen the script. Once they are finished, however, the showrunner reviews and amends the script, often changing it significantly and making sure the language is consistent from episode to episode. Common practice is for the staff writer to retain sole credit for the script, even with significant rewriting by the showrunner.[120] Milch would write and rewrite constantly, changing dialogue at the very last minute and even improvising on set. Sean Bridgers, who played Johnny Burns, stated that with Milch "you have to have faith in the way he works, that you might not get your lines until you're about to shoot the scene."[121] Actor W. Earl Brown, who played Dan Dority, was given a writing credit for episode 10 of season 3. Brown stated that while he was proud of "my episode," he could not take credit for much of the script. One scene was conceived and penned by regular *Deadwood* writer Regina Corrado, another scene was of completely unknown origin to him, and Milch, "the Maestro," as Brown called him, had tinkered with the script. "What I did write, initially at least, were all the scenes inside the Gem," Brown remembered. "And while they are few and far between, there are a few actual lines I wrote which survived as first written." As Brown explained it, every writer on staff "wrote on every episode" and then each episode was rewritten by Milch, who would "mold, manipulate, and mangle the words into literature."[122] Parsing out exact writing credits on *Deadwood*, then, is an impossible task.

Moreover, although he never officially directed an episode, Milch was often present on set performing tasks typically attributed to the director of a feature film. Directors on TV shows are "often hired as rotating freelancers" and, while certainly making important contributions, do not have the control or powers of oversight that the showrunner has.[123] On-set dynamics between Milch and episode 12 director Ed Bianchi can be witnessed on "The Wedding Celebration" featurette on the season 2 DVD. Bianchi and Milch discuss the particulars during prep for the night ahead of shooting, including where props will be placed and where the camera will be positioned.[124] Bianchi asks Milch numerous questions and generally defers to his authority.[125] Milch was also on hand to coach the actors through their performances, explaining the importance of the scene in the larger narrative, illuminating the psychology driving the characters, and providing feedback on the delivery of the ornate prose.[126] Not only did Milch have final authority over the scripts, but he exercised considerable control over the mise-en-scène, those areas in the production of film—setting, staging, performance, and framing—that are typically assigned to the director/author in feature films.

HBO has led the way in drawing upon traditional and familiar concepts of authorship from other media and actively cultivating the image of the showrunner to lend legitimacy to its shows.[127] Just as in feature films, auteurism in TV is promoted to elevate postnetwork quality TV above mass-produced programs, particularly those from the major broadcast networks. *Deadwood* was not just any TV western (traditionally a lowbrow genre); it was a *David Milch* western. As Horace Newcomb points out, *Deadwood* is "most often referred to as 'David Milch's *Deadwood*'" and is "all but inseparable from the authorial, or auteur, status of Milch."[128] Assigning the role of author to Milch is unsurprising given his pedigree: he has a distinguished academic career, was mentored by great American writers, such as Robert Penn Warren, has published works of fiction and poetry, won an Emmy Award for his writing on *Hill Street Blues*, and was executive producer on the critically acclaimed *NYPD Blue* (ABC, 1993–2005). "Celebrating showrunners as producers of artistically-valuable quality television," Tobias Steiner argues, "has been a particularly crucial element of cable network HBO's larger strategy of quality programming."[129] HBO did not invent the showrunner, but since the early 2000s it has employed it effectively as a branding strategy.[130] The idea of the showrunner-as-author is often developed and endorsed in prerelease marketing materials and in medias res paratexts. Many of the special features included in the *Deadwood* DVD box set do just this. "Trusting the Process with David Milch" focuses on Milch's unorthodox and unique working style. Actor Stephen Tobolowsky (Hugo Jarry) proclaims early on in the featurette, "I don't think anything goes on on this set that David doesn't affect, alter, correct, delete, add. He is sculpting this as he goes."[131]

The public is encouraged to think of *Deadwood*—and, indeed, postnetwork quality TV shows more generally—as the work of (usually) one man. However, the realities are far more complex, as this chapter has already shown. "Series television is a massively collaborative endeavor," stress Michael Z. Newman and Elana Levine. "Despite the rhetoric within production circles of respecting the vision of the showrunner-*auteur* myriad choices and decisions are made every day a TV show is in production, and many or most of them are outside the purview of even the most hands-on showrunner."[132] There are numerous leadership roles within a series, from different department heads (art, sound, casting, editing, etc.) to multiple producers. This issue of collaborative creation comes through in the limited existing literature on TV authorship and is equally relevant to this consideration of history-on-TV authorship, bringing to the forefront the tension and balance between acknowledging the centrality of the showrunner and acknowledging the contributions of the vast number of people with diverse expertise who contribute to the series. Of all the showrunners examined in this book, David Milch is the most actively involved and omnipresent, being involved, like Tobolowsky said, in every element of the show.[133] Yet, even in this most extreme of cases, the argument can still be made for the complicated nature of history-on-screen authorship. If we look at Milch and consider his own biography and previous works—or, to return to Carr's analogy, what part of the ocean he chooses to fish in and what tackle he chooses to use—we find clues to his historical interpretation and what has shaped it. But in asking questions about the authorship of history on-screen, we can delve deeper than the showrunner/director. When we do so, it becomes much clearer what the various television/film departments contribute to the construction of history on-screen, and our understanding of the work will be that much richer.

Taking only the art department, which has been the focus of this chapter, one can start to see how vast the production of *Deadwood* truly was and how many were involved in creating its look and feel of the past. Working with Milch was, of course, central, but the art department had relatively free rein within the confines of his vision. "David would give us information about the characters and he allowed us to create and design the sets for the show," Caso remembered. "Working with David is very unique because he allows us to be fearless in our designing."[134] Similarly, Bryant's conversations with Milch were not about the costumes per se but about the characters—what their lifestyle was, where they had come from—and apart from a few specific requests, costuming decisions were left up to her.[135] Both Caso and Bryant undertook their own research independent of Milch. Caso and her team, for example, traveled to Deadwood to liaise with the town's museum curator and sought out all the literature they could find that referenced the camp, as well as old photographs. Based on this research, as well as discussions with Milch, they planned, built, and maintained the *Deadwood* sets. These sets and props, as already argued, did not simply provide a one dimensional "look" of the past but actively constructed history on-screen and contributed to the larger historical narrative.

Furthermore, Caso and Bryant are just two more individuals, alongside Milch, who contributed to the production. An art department is organized as a hierarchy, with various tasks and responsibilities assigned and carried out by various groups. As production designer, Caso was head of the art department, and beneath her was the art director. The art director directly oversees the execution of the sets and manages the many craftspeople involved. These craftspeople include the construction teams, made up of construction coordinators, foremen, and assistants who build the actual structures (the exterior of the Gem Saloon, for instance) and the painters who stain and age them. The set decorator then fills these spaces and provides all the details that are found within them (the tables and chairs of the Gem, the pictures and antlers and light fittings). They work closely with the propmaster and the propmaster's assistant, who make and/or source the props. The leadman assists the set decorator as well and is in charge of the swing gang, the set dressers, and the on-set dressers, who arrange all of the furniture and props on set and maintain continuity between takes. There is also a greensman, who is a set decorator specializing in outdoor scenes featuring landscapes and foliage. These roles alone deal with only the sets themselves and do not even start to touch on the many other creative personnel employed in related departments, such as costume, hair, and makeup and visual effects. Some of these positions were held by the same people across all three seasons, while others were employed on *Deadwood* for a season or two, or perhaps only a single episode. Whether they worked there briefly in a minor role or for two seasons in a managerial position, as Caso explains, they "all collaborate[d] to achieve the look and feel that David Milch wanted."[136]

What does this mean, then, in terms of putting history on-screen? Who is ultimately responsible for the history that is presented? As Caso states, her team worked together to bring history alive from the script to the screen, from the mind of Milch into reality. *Deadwood* is Milch's interpretation of history, but his interpretation is built upon and complemented by the work of many others. To return to the earlier analogy, Milch, as the editor and overseer, employed individuals such as Bryant and Caso to apply their insights and expertise to his subject. Their contributions are significant in their own right, but, importantly, all those assembled on *Deadwood* worked together to create a cohesive historical narrative. Not all the cast and crew function as author-historians, although some individuals and teams do (see the section on sound effects in chapter 4), but they nonetheless make history on-screen possible. It is this collaborative nature that makes history on-screen an exciting area to consider, full of possibility. It is unlikely that the amount of research and practical work required for a production like *Deadwood* could be achieved by one person (in a reasonable time frame), nor is one person likely to have a profound interest, and skills, in such disparate areas. Film and TV employ people who are talented in their respective areas, and they contribute their part of the puzzle to the historical picture that is portrayed on-screen. The collaborative nature of history on-screen needs to be better understood and celebrated, rather than ignored.

## Conclusion

There is no one alive who can claim to have walked the streets of Rome in the time of Julius Caesar, to have witnessed the confrontation between American colonists and British troops in Boston, or to have arrived in 1876 Deadwood by horse-drawn wagon. There are, perhaps, a very few who could claim to have experienced warfare in the Ardennes Forest or the island of Peleliu or who may have strolled along the Atlantic City boardwalk in the 1920s. Nonetheless, many avid TV viewers do have an idea of these far-flung places and times from watching HBO's long-form dramas: *Rome, John Adams* (2008), *Deadwood, Band of Brothers, The Pacific* (2010), and *Boardwalk Empire.* These TV series and miniseries have "overcome the constraints of time and place by bringing us millions of images of diverse places, people, buildings and many otherwise unfamiliar objects."[137] This is a unique power of history on-screen: viewers do not have to imagine the look of the past or the past in motion, as it is there in their own home before their very eyes on tablet, TV, computer, and mobile screens. Individual production designers and their teams vary on nearly every TV show (and film), but with the right combination of showrunner, production designer, and art department crew, an incredibly rich and detailed past can be rendered on-screen. Creating the look and feel of the past is not an exercise in crafting empty veneers, as the case of *Deadwood* has shown. The look and feel of the past adds many more layers to history on-screen.

However, it is worth recognizing the practical constraints the production as a whole, and the art department in particular, works under. It is not always an ideal working environment, as the work is in part governed by the realities of production schedules and budgets. When he was writing the script for episode 10 of season 3, Brown was told by Milch to keep all the scenes after the attempted shooting of Alma confined to the Gem. When asked why, Milch responded, "Because we are waaay over fucking budget and it's cheaper to shoot on the stage rather than in the thoroughfare."[138] In this instance and presumably many more, the script was shaped by time and money considerations to save shooting days and production expenses. The actual timeline and logistics of production can also influence people's roles and effectiveness. In film, production designers are usually brought on at quite an early stage, but their job can be made difficult by the need to work in close consultation with the director of photography, who is often not employed until much later in the process because he or she is typically more expensive to employ. The production designer's job generally finishes at the end of the shoot and does not continue into postproduction, which is becoming a bigger issue as more and more gets added to the look of a TV series or film once shooting has concluded.

Indeed, the nature of production design is changing dramatically. "Of all the disciplines," Fionnuala Halligan opines, "production design is changing at the fastest speed. Digital advances have altered the nature of what we traditionally perceive as set design, with the finished product a complex blend of processes."[139] *Deadwood* provides just one example of production design: relying mainly on the traditional processes of physically building the sets and traveling to suitable locations to shoot the scenes outside the camp. Only occasionally were special visual effects (VSFX) employed, such as the use of a green screen for the cemetery sequences so that the camp could be appropriately positioned in the background. For other HBO shows, though, VSFX are becoming increasingly important. Terence Winter was aware that accurately depicting 1920s Atlantic City on-screen in *Boardwalk Empire* was going to be a major challenge and was particularly concerned about creating the boardwalk. It would be one of the primary locations for filming and would have to be convincingly rendered on-screen. It was while watching a behind-the-scenes featurette for the HBO miniseries *John Adams* that Terence Winter realized that with the help of computer-generated imagery (CGI) he "might actually be able to pull this off." "The special effects have really made the difference from being able to do this and not do it," Winter conceded.[140] HBO's budgets and the technology that the series makers have consequently been able to employ mean that *Boardwalk Empire* was able to reproduce the look of the 1920s in its production design. Winter is proud of the fact that, in terms of production value, *Boardwalk Empire* is on par with Hollywood movies. "We've done things as big and spectacular as feature films," he boasted.[141]

Arguably, historical TV series are placed in a precarious position by the budget needed to maintain the look and feel of the past and to compete with what big-budget historical feature films can offer. In May 2006, before the third season had even aired, HBO announced that the contracts for *Deadwood*'s ensemble cast would not be renewed for a fourth season, effectively ending the series. At the time and in the years since, there have been conflicting stories from Milch, then HBO chief executive Chris Albrecht, and subsequent HBO executives over why the show ended, and to this day no consensus has been reached. Milch's commitment to a new HBO series (*John from Cincinnati,* 2007), Paramount's partial ownership of the show (due to a previous contract Milch had signed), and the cost of the show, paired with supposedly dwindling numbers, are all cited as possible reasons.[142]

Rumors of returning to Deadwood and concluding the show on a more satisfactory note persisted for over a decade but seemed, after such a long period of time, unlikely to materialize. However, in 2018 HBO confirmed a *Deadwood* movie was in the works, with Milch and key cast and crew returning. Once again, creating the look and the feel of the past was of paramount importance to Milch, Caso, and the production team. They faced a number of difficulties given that some of the sets had been destroyed (Melody Ranch had been used for films and TV series, including HBO's *Westworld,* in the intervening years) and the original blueprints for the set were lost.[143] Caso and her team aimed to strike a balance between rebuilding the set familiar to viewers of the original series and acknowledging the reality that Deadwood changed tremendously in the years between the end of season 3 and the events of the film, which take place in 1889. "Modernity had hit Deadwood and you see the growth clearly," Caso explained.[144]

This modernity is evidenced in the first minutes of *Deadwood: The Movie* (Minahan, 2019). Mirroring the pilot episode, the audience's first view of Deadwood comes from Calamity Jane's point of view as she looks down from the Black Hills. The outlook is much changed; the footprint of the town has expanded greatly from a single main thoroughfare to a great mass of buildings of varying shapes and sizes. The changes are clearer once down amongst the inhabitants of Deadwood. The streets are still awash with visual clutter, but the buildings themselves are now made of brick and stone, and the signage is permanent and professional rather than hand painted and haphazard. Along the familiar dirt streets, pocked with muddy pools, are the Gem Saloon and Grand Central Hotel, although both have received considerable cosmetic upgrades. While *Deadwood: The Movie* does not have the same luxury of time as the previous seasons, it serves as a fitting coda—not only to the characters who populate the narrative but to the town itself—and continues to demonstrate how integral look and feel are to crafting a historical narrative on-screen.

# 2

# Constructing and Inventing Historical Characters

## *Boardwalk Empire*

Terence Winter, the showrunner of *Boardwalk Empire,* was an avid follower of *Deadwood,* but he knew from the beginning that he wanted his new historical show to be different from David Milch's western. "I was a big fan of *Deadwood,*" Winter explained, "but once I found out that all those people were real, the first thing I did was Google everybody."[1] After searching the web and discovering the fates of many of *Deadwood*'s main characters, including Al Swearengen, Seth Bullock, Wild Bill Hickok, and Calamity Jane, the experience was partly ruined for Winter. "Whenever Al Swearengen would get into trouble, I'd say, 'Well, I know this guy doesn't die until the 20th century, so he's going to be okay.' And then I said, 'Fuck, I shouldn't know that. And I bet David Milch doesn't want me to know that.'"[2] Winter decided to construct and invent characters whenever possible in *Boardwalk Empire* to prevent viewers doing just what he had done with a show he loved—jumping the gun and taking the jeopardy out of the series.

In his choice to populate the historical narrative with fictionalized characters, Winter had a great deal of freedom from HBO, a network known for its lack of interference. He was working on *The Sopranos* as a writer and executive producer when HBO approached him with *Boardwalk Empire: The Birth, High Times, and Corruption of Atlantic City,* by Nelson Johnson. The book explores the history of Atlantic City, New Jersey, from the 1850s to the present and focuses on key figures that had a hand in shaping the resort town over the decades. According to Winter, HBO simply gave him the book and said, "Find a series in here."[3] A blank check to create without constant oversight from network executives is a trademark of HBO's approach to producing original content that continues to draw creative talent. Given the loose parameters of his task, Winter quickly ruled out anything contemporary, feeling it would be "too close to Tony Soprano's world," with both shows being based in New Jersey and concerned with criminals and corruption.[4] Winter settled on the 1920s, the period "that most struck his creative fancy" and which he also felt would intrigue audiences.[5]

Winter inhabits *Boardwalk Empire* with three character types—real historical figures, characters inspired by historical figures, and completely invented characters—but it is the fictional characters that clearly dominate in an effort to circumvent what Winter felt was one of the pitfalls of *Deadwood.* The central character in the series is Enoch "Nucky" Thompson, the treasurer of Atlantic City, based loosely upon the real-life Enoch "Nucky" Johnson, who features heavily in Johnson's book. The show follows the ups and downs of Thompson's political career and affiliations, his personal relationships, and his progression as a gangster. As his invented protégé, Jimmy Darmody, tells him in the first episode, "You can't be half a gangster," an idea that continues to be a major theme throughout the subsequent seasons. While the show is grounded in Atlantic City, Thompson also negotiates with real gangsters in New York, Chicago, and Philadelphia. While viewers can "cheat" by finding out the histories of Al Capone, Lucky Luciano, and Arnold Rothstein, the fates of Thompson, his family, his business associates, and his enemies largely remain a mystery, as do the fictional relationships between Thompson and the real-life gangsters. The balance of character types on the show is evidenced by looking at the main cast listed in the opening title sequence and the characters they play. Of the fourteen actors named in the season 1 opening credits, only three play historical figures, while four play characters inspired by historical figures and the remaining seven actors play fictional characters, a balance that remains constant over all five seasons of the series.

It is through characters, as well as the sights and sounds of a TV show (see chapters 1 and 4), that audiences engage with history. In *Boardwalk Empire,* as in most mainstream film and television production, it is the characters that motivate and drive the narrative.[6] Timothy Corrigan and Patricia White explain that characters' "wishes and fears produce events that cause certain effects or other events to take place; thus, the actions, behaviours, and desires of characters create the causal logic of a film narrative, whereby one action or event leads to or 'causes' another action or event to follow."[7] It is the characters who react to historical events, who are shaped by historical circumstance, and who instigate change. The characters move the cause-effect chain of the narrative forward. Therefore, TV's ability to include a range of characters and spend an extended period of time with them is crucial when it comes to engaging with history on-screen. The main characters (and some supporting characters), each crafted with a fleshed-out backstory and desires, have the potential to develop storylines that engage with historical issues.

Characters, then, are essential factors in developing narrative and are also central to attracting and maintaining audience engagement. "Characters constitute a major entry point into our engagement with narratives," writes film scholar Murray Smith; "we look for characters; we sort major from minor characters; we seek to establish the goals and desires of such characters and we project and anticipate their destinies." While most viewers will recognize that characters are "artificial," they will still think about and respond to them as if they were real people.[8] Audiences may even develop parasocial relationships with certain characters, a type of relationship that is completely one-way between a viewer and a media figure. The viewers feel like they know the character and respond to and think about the character as a real human being.[9] Parasocial relationships are generally associated with an unhealthy or pathological attachment to characters, but as Jason Mittell points out, these relationships should "instead be viewed as an active, participatory facet of media consumption, with fans choosing to engage with a media text and extend its reach into their own lives."[10] Character construction is an important area to explore, as characters not only propel the historical narrative but are a key source of interest and investment for the audience that can make viewers think and care deeply about the past.

Of course, the construction and development of characters can vary greatly depending on the type of show on which they appear. Episodic television shows, epitomized by the sitcom, often tell a self-contained story within the show's time frame; serials, epitomized by the daytime soap opera, develop overarching storylines that require audiences to have prior knowledge of previous episodes.[11] Characters in episodic series, argues John Fiske, often do not develop or grow from episode to episode and "only appear to have life in each episode," not the "dead time" in between. Characters in serials, on the other hand, have narrative arcs that flow across episodes, and they "appear to live continuously" between shows with memories of prior events.[12] Viewers invest in the characters differently on the two types of shows; while repetition and familiarity are key to characters on sitcoms, audiences look for depth and progression in serial characters.[13] The characters in *Boardwalk Empire* fit into Fiske's latter category; their actions in one episode have consequences that ripple across subsequent episodes, and storylines continue between weekly installments, leaving the viewer to piece together what has happened to the characters in the time that has elapsed.

Multifaceted historical characters in TV dramas like *Boardwalk Empire* result from both the longer running time of serials and the TV industry's willingness to experiment with characterization—along with audiences' openness to it. Postnetwork quality TV serials are celebrated by critics and viewers for crafting complex and engaging characters. These characters are generally three-dimensional and, more often than not, can be classified as "difficult": "unhappy, morally compromised, complicated, deeply human."[14] Wholesome, likable heroes and one-dimensional bad guys, while not missing from TV, have certainly lost favor in preference to antiheroes. Media critic James Wolcott writes that TV characters, particularly those on cable, "acquire dimensions, depths, personal flaws, moral failings, and discordant quirks that seem integral and variable, not pinned on like prom corsages. They're given enough time to sit and stew, to mull over the next move, a luxury seldom extended to movie characters."[15] There is simply more time to first establish the character, the background and motivations, and for that character to evolve in a way that appears feasible and organic to the audience.

HBO did not invent complex and difficult characters, but it has excelled in crafting and filling its original programming with them. Looking back over his twenty-plus-year career, HBO chairman and CEO Richard Plepler identified the "complicated hero" as a defining part of the HBO model, although he recognized that the company inherited and embraced the trend from network writer-producers such as Steven Bochco.[16] Arguably, as a subscription service, HBO can push the boundaries on character construction even further than its network antecedents. As Anthony N. Smith notes, broadcast "networks' primary reliance on advertiser support has typically ensured that characters' failings have their limits," whereas the lack of advertiser influence on HBO's characters removes any such constraints.[17] *Boardwalk Empire*'s main characters, be they real, invented, or a mixture of the two, are exemplars of the postnetwork quality TV character traits; they are captivating, charismatic, and deeply flawed, and, importantly, they have time to develop over the seasons.

Despite the centrality of character in narrative, only a relatively small body of relevant scholarly literature exists, although since the 1980s it has become an increasingly popular subject. Disciplines such as literary studies, communication studies, film and media studies, psychology, and philosophy have produced "rival theories" for understanding and analyzing the concept of character.[18] One of the key debates centers around realist and structuralist approaches. Henriette Heidbrink succinctly sums up the opposing views: "There is a long ongoing debate between 'humanistic' positions [the realist approach] on the one hand that deal with characters on a mixed basis of phenomenology, hermeneutics and textual analysis, and on the other hand so-called formalists, structuralists and semioticians that hold the view that characters should be addressed as signs, semantic components (semes), 'bundles of differentiations'/paradigms, words, sentences, or more generally, textuality."[19] Such theoretical debates generally take place within the realm of academia, not in "everyday talk about characters." This chapter takes a similar approach to characters as that of Smith, considering characters in a more "traditional sense," wherein they "are treated as fictional analogues of human agents, basic constituents of representation embodied in a vast array of specific modes of characterization and purposes of representation."[20] As he notes, this basic concept of character forms the basis of understanding and discussing narratives. Jens Eder also appeals for openness and flexibility when looking at film (and, one can speculate, television) characters. "What is the most important, the most decisive feature of film characters?" he asks. "The answer might well be: their variety and multilayeredness. The central feature of characters in general does not exist; depending on the question asked, different features may turn out significant."[21] The questions asked in this particular chapter involve the representation of historical characters on-screen, the potential of each character type as a vehicle for history, and the consequences when a narrative contains all three. It assesses the depth and complexity of the characters on *Boardwalk Empire,* concentrating specifically on how historical discourse is embedded into the fabric of the characters and presented to the audience. *Band of Brothers, Deadwood,* and *Treme* all include what can generally be termed "historically complex characters," but what makes *Boardwalk Empire* a prime case study for the issue of characterization are the three clearly delineated character types.

Each of the three sections that follows focuses on one of *Boardwalk Empire*'s central characters, each representing one of the main character types: historical figure, partly based on a historical figure, and completely invented. The three chosen characters all occupy critical and central roles on the show but are by no means the only subjects that could have been chosen; they do, however, work well as exemplars of each character type. The first section looks at Capone (played by Stephen Graham), considers issues of historical accuracy, and situates *Boardwalk Empire*'s representation of the infamous figure in relation to other popular representations over the decades. The second centers on Thompson (Steve Buscemi) and the confluence of history and invention. It deals with how and why changes were made to the life of the real historical figure and the implications for what Smith calls alignment and allegiance. The final section focuses on Darmody (Michael Pitt) and the practical construction of character, along with the capability of completely invented characters to convey historical information.

## Reinventing the Ultimate Gangster: Al Capone

"I could never invent an Al Capone," Terence Winter conceded. "Or I could, but it would be a lot of work. Or an Arnold Rothstein. These are very colorful, very three-dimensional people who already existed. I'm starting with them as fully formed human beings as opposed to starting with a blank piece of paper. So a lot of the work is already done for me."[22] Capone and Rothstein are two of the historical figures on *Boardwalk Empire,* along with Luciano, Meyer Lansky, Johnny Torrio, and George Remus. As well as these real-life bootleggers, the show incorporates a host of political figures, including Attorney General Harry Daugherty, Secretary of the Treasury Andrew Mellon, and President Warren Harding. But it is the gangsters—Capone, Rothstein, Luciano—who are the most recognizable to audiences and who occupy more central roles on the show. Winter knew that he and the show's other writers would have to follow their well-documented paths and not stray too far from the history. In this sense, the "biggest challenges are the historically accurate characters" because with these figures there are the "least amount of parameters."[23] These characters provide events and milestones that root the show in a specific place and time and attract an audience that is drawn to these familiar figures.

The writers did not rest on their laurels by rehashing the same old Capone seen in countless films and TV shows; instead they present viewers with a new multifaceted version of Capone and use his ambiguous underworld history to their advantage. While he is a well-known legend, there are many gray areas in his life, giving *Boardwalk*'s writers the chance to mold and shape their own unique character to fulfil the needs of the narrative. Indeed, Capone offers a prime example of how Robert Rosenstone's concept of true invention can be employed when constructing an on-screen character. Changes can be made to a real historical figure in the service of the larger TV narrative—and in the service of the on-screen characterization—without radically altering or compromising the historical discourse surrounding the figure. Furthermore, the starting point of the series, along with its extended running time, allows for the creation of a more nuanced Capone character. Rather than appearing on-screen as an easily recognizable pop culture version of Capone, *Boardwalk Empire*'s version evolves slowly as the character signs that make him the familiar figure build up. Viewers are provided with a more detailed and fully rounded interpretation of Capone, one that considers aspects of his career and personal life rarely found outside of published biographies.

*Boardwalk Empire* is only the most recent show to bring Capone to life on-screen; he has been reincarnated on film and television for decades, often appearing as a one-dimensional villain. Many of the underworld protagonists of the classic gangster films of the late 1920s (Lewis Milestone's *The Racket,* 1928) and early 1930s (Mervyn LeRoy's *Little Caesar,* 1931) are associated with the figure of Capone, even though they do not share his name.[24] *Scarface* (Hawks, 1932) is the film from this period most closely linked to Capone, and while elements of the story are fictionalized, including names, locales, and the personal life of Capone (in this film called Tony Camonte), the film clearly charts his well-known rise, culminating in the St. Valentine's Day Massacre. Capone continued to be reincarnated on both the big and small screen throughout the twentieth century, but his most high-profile appearance was in Brian De Palma's silver screen remake of *The Untouchables* (1987), in which he was played by Robert De Niro.[25] The Al Capone presented in De Palma's film highlights many of the problems that biographers such as Robert J. Schoenberg have identified with the Capone seen in popular culture. Not only are the documented facts stretched almost beyond recognition, but Capone himself is a caricature, a one-dimensional thug bordering on insanity who ultimately shows no development or growth from the earliest representations that appeared in the twenties and thirties. "Capone's story is actually so little known," biographer Schoenberg contends, "that moviemakers have shown no compunction about ludicrous inventions and liberties with the facts, confident that audiences would not know enough simply to laugh at them."[26] Consequently, he has become a myth, an illusion, "a larger than life symbol of evil," in the popular imagination.[27]

The extended format of the television series, as well as the starting date of *Boardwalk Empire,* means that viewers are presented with a more complex, and at times new and unknown, portrait of Capone. By the end of its run, *Boardwalk* had five seasons to develop its Capone character.[28] Roberta E.

Pearson and Máire Messenger Davis posit that the "difference between the narrative structures of series television and the feature film" may account for differences in character construction and development between the two media. "The one-off feature film has to rapidly establish a character's defining traits," they explain; "television can accumulate defining traits in a more leisurely way across episodes, but must also maintain character consistency over a much longer narrative arc."[29] For a historical character such as Capone, it means that more elements of his personality and history can be incorporated, rather than his appearing fully developed, or worse still, as a stereotype of how people expect Capone to behave and act. Also, while a number of viewers may be familiar with the general histories of the real gangsters, by starting the show in 1920, Winter had an opportunity to present viewers with new representations of these oft-depicted lawbreakers. In the early twenties, Capone, Luciano, and Lansky were working beneath well-respected and established gangsters and were virtually unknown to the general public. They were "gangster toddlers," and audiences are not as familiar with these earlier incarnations.[30] After over eighty years of appearing in film and television, Capone is an established screen character, so *Boardwalk Empire* engages in a balancing act: exploring and adding new dimensions to his character while fulfilling viewer expectations and endowing its version of Capone with character traits already linked to the historical figure.

Capone's character is developed and revealed slowly over the seasons in both subtle and obvious ways. Externally, Capone adopts the costume associated with the classic gangster figure. Laura Beshears explains that "the image of the Prohibition-era gangster, rising through the criminal ranks in his three piece suit, fedora, tie, overcoat, and polished shoes, has become ingrained in the collective American consciousness."[31] At different points throughout season 1, Capone adds a new piece of the uniform, signifying his growth and development from a driver to a figure of authority. When we first meet Capone in the pilot episode, he is unrecognizable (apart from his scars), dressed in a sloppy suit and page-boy cap. By episode 12 he has completed his physical transformation; he stands alongside his mentor, Johnny Torrio, in his suit, overcoat, and fedora. These external changes are not merely superficial; they "become markers of other changes in the character's social and personal sense of self and ability to evaluate others."[32] Although Capone's transformation from young hood to up-and-coming gangster is relatively straightforward, other narrative strands related to Capone's character are more complex and require the audience's full attention to puzzle out the significance. When

Capone and Darmody first meet, the subject of World War One arises and Capone claims he fought as part of the Lost Battalion. Initially there is nothing to contradict Capone's story, but as season 1 progresses, his account comes under suspicion. Each time Capone references his service and the scars he received courtesy of the Germans, Darmody responds in a subdued, unconvinced manner. Finally, in episode 6, Darmody makes it clear he does not believe Capone's war story and challenges him to play "five finger fillet," a knife game played by soldiers in the trenches. The audience is misled: what was initially stated in episode 1, and what could have been another defining character trait of Capone (as service in World War One is for Darmody), is revealed to be untrue. Instead, this lie exposes another historically accurate dimension of his character: that Capone self-consciously worked to create a certain image of himself and that what he said could not always be taken at face value.

*Boardwalk Empire* provides an arena where both new and previously established aspects of Capone's character and history can be displayed side by side. In a single episode viewers get to see both the violent and intimate sides of Capone and the private and public spheres he occupies, one of which has rarely been accurately portrayed. In episode 4 of season 3, Capone is seen at home with his family as well as with business associates at the Four Deuces (a saloon and headquarters of the Torrio gang). In particular, Capone interacts with the overweight Jake Guzik, who makes collections for Torrio and passes the money on to Capone. Guzik and Capone share an easy relationship, and while Capone jokes about Guzik's obesity and lack of personal hygiene, he does so without malice. While making a collection at another bar, Guzik is first taunted and then savagely beaten by a man named Joe Miller. Upon seeing Guzik's swollen and battered face and hearing what happened, Capone promptly heads to the same bar, picks on Miller, and beats him to death in front of a room full of patrons. Capone showers the body with money and tells those around him to "pay for his funeral." This scene, though sensationalized, is based on a real incident and illustrates Capone's violent temper, a facet of his character that audiences are likely to be familiar with.[33]

A largely unseen side of Capone is presented in a narrative that parallels the Capone/Guzik/Miller storyline. Capone's wife, Mae, and his son, Sonny, have both been introduced in earlier episodes, and Sonny's hearing problems have already been established. For Winter, Sonny's deafness was a fascinating detail about Capone's life, and as he points out, "I don't know that it's ever been depicted or even mentioned in any movie about Capone."[34] Capone's

Al Capone tenderly embraces his son.

home life is often either absent in films, as in *The Untouchables,* or completely fictionalized, as in *Scarface.*[35] In this episode Capone discovers that Sonny is being bullied at school and encourages him to fight his tormentors; however, it becomes clear that Capone's son is not the type to fight back, bursting into tears when a practice boxing session with his father becomes too much. Rather than pushing the boy, Capone stops and tenderly embraces him. At the very end of the episode, just after he has beaten Miller to death, he wakes Sonny up when he arrives home and plays the song "My Buddy" on the mandolin while his son places his hands on his vocal chords and feels the vibrations of his father singing. Here, a different but also documented side of Capone is portrayed: his role as a loving and devoted father.[36]

The two Capone storylines complement and work in harmony with one another, with both revolving around bullying and Capone taking frustrations from one area of his life out on another. It is a narrative contained within that one episode; neither strand is revisited in subsequent installments, and these isolated incidents do not shape the major storylines of season 3. This narrative is, however, a character piece that continues to flesh out and reveal the figure of Capone. While the details of Capone's history are debated by his biographers, they generally agree on the type of man he was. He could be warm, charismatic, and generous with friends, family, and acquaintances, but he was also a shrewd and ambitious businessman with an imposing physique and lethal temper. In scenes consisting of just eight minutes of one episode, the two differing sides of Capone are effectively presented to the audience.[37]

As historical figures go, Capone offers an unusual and potentially advantageous set of circumstances; given the invented and ambiguous nature of Capone's known history, there is a lot of room for interpretation for the writers of *Boardwalk Empire*. As J. E. Smyth argues, the underworld of 1920s Chicago "was a world where nothing could be proved, where truth was occluded by contradictory tales, where no one saw what happened, where police, judges, newspapermen, and, by implication, popular historians all told lies. Capone and his colleagues simply defied the tools of historiography." Early biographers and historians of the period such as Fred Pasley and Walter Noble Burns faced unique challenges while researching their subjects. Smyth says these men realized that their area of study "left few opportunities for traditional research and definitive conclusions. Their work ignored footnotes and bibliography, quoted word of mouth, presented multiple perspectives on a single event, admitted gaps and unknown information, and mixed facts with metaphors."[38] Capone himself played a part in his own invention. Unlike Torrio, Capone embraced being a public figure and cultivated a positive public image, appearing at public events and establishing relationships with members of the press. Capone presented himself as a misunderstood businessman, a loving family man, and a philanthropist. Edward Behr describes Capone as a "sophisticated operator" and a "superb media manipulator" who was able to convince respected members of the press that, although he may have engaged in the illegal liquor trade, he did not believe in violence and was often unjustly fingered by the police for crimes he did not commit.[39] There are many aspects of Capone's history and criminal career that remain unknown and shrouded in uncertainty, which gave the writers of the show the opportunity to sift through the numerous interpretations and choose which version worked best to advance the show's narrative.

This potential is embraced from the pilot episode and sets the groundwork for how *Boardwalk Empire* will develop the real historical figures and employ them in the narrative. The first episode details the shifting power dynamics of the Chicago crime syndicate with the murder of the current boss, Big Jim Colosimo. There is no consensus on the murder of Colosimo, and Torrio and Capone's possible involvement in his death. Torrio, Colosimo's business manager who ran his brothels and gambling establishments, was a gifted businessman who saw the opportunities that Prohibition provided and the money that could be made from bootlegging. While Torrio was keen to move into this new area, Colosimo was wary and content with the profits generated from prostitution and gambling. Colosimo was assassinated on May 11, 1920, in the vestibule of his beloved café, shot to death by an unknown assailant. Over the years many biographers have addressed Capone and Torrio's potential involvement in the assassination. According to Schoenberg, both Torrio and Capone were directly involved in the murder; Torrio had "consulted his rising young lieutenant, Capone, on the choice of the right man to do the job, and then left him to make the arrangements."[40] In this version Capone chose Frankie Yale, a gangster whom he had worked for as a teenager in New York, to be the trigger man. John Kobler presents a similar scenario to that advocated by Schoenberg, although Laurence Bergreen challenges the notion that Torrio or Capone was involved.[41] Bergreen does identify Yale as the killer, but discounts the idea that he was hired by Torrio or Capone. He instead suggests that Yale's actions were driven by his desire to move in on the Chicago vice trade.[42] Bergreen also disregards a rumor that surfaced years after Colosimo's murder that Capone himself had hidden in the cloakroom of the café and pulled the trigger.

Winter ultimately chose the most popular explanation and account of Colosimo's death, one that would also help advance the narrative by quickly establishing two ambitious characters in Torrio and Capone. Throughout the first episode the reasons behind the hit on Colosimo are slowly revealed. As Capone and Darmody, both currently drivers, wait outside while their employers conduct a meeting, they too discuss business:

> Darmody: You guys going to get into the liquor business too?
> Capone: Colosimo says no, too much heat from the law, says there's enough money in the whorehouses.
> Darmody: But you don't agree?
> Capone: Well, I'm Johnny's muscle, who gives a fuck what I think?

Darmody and Capone soon devise a plan to hijack a carload of liquor. This is a completely fictional event, but is crucial to the major storylines that will progress throughout season 1. It is also important in advancing and explaining the Torrio/Colosimo/Capone narrative. Capone drives the hijacked liquor to Chicago, where he is met by a delighted Torrio, and it is clear that despite Colosimo's misgivings Torrio is forging ahead with his bootlegging plans. Yale is also present when Capone arrives, and we see him again a few moments later, poised behind Colosimo with a gun pointed at his head. The clear implication is that Torrio wants to get into the liquor business and so hires Yale to take Colosimo out, following the scenario that Schoenberg and Kobler present in their biographies. Because of the ambiguous nature of underworld history, there is no way of definitively stating that *Boardwalk Empire* was accurate or inaccurate in its depiction of this event. Gangster history, typified by Capone, often lacks conclusive facts and is based upon supposition. In some areas, including the date of Colosimo's death, the history presented on-screen is clearly inaccurate, but Winter felt it was acceptable to take artistic license "because the spirit of why he was killed was correct" and, ultimately, "it didn't matter really that it happened a few months later."[43]

While all the details of Capone's history may not be correct, it was crucial to Winter that the show stayed "true to the spirit of who the people were" and what happened. "I'm not going to kill Capone off in 1925," Winter explained. "He had his rise through the ranks in Chicago, and being, basically, the king of that world and I won't deviate from that."[44] Staying true to the spirit of the period applies to all three types of characters on *Boardwalk Empire.* For the real historical figures, that means capturing the personalities of the gangsters as closely as possible, even in invented scenarios.[45] Although Winter's statements about staying true to the spirit of history are quite broad, his ideas are closely aligned with Rosenstone's concept of true invention. History on-screen, Rosenstone contends, "cannot exist in a state of historical innocence, cannot engage in capricious invention, cannot ignore the findings and assertions and arguments of what we already know from other sources."[46] Staying true to the spirit of Capone essentially means that the writers did not violate the discourse of history—either by radically altering Capone's documented record or by presenting him in a completely contrary fashion. The writers used what has been written and reported about Capone to inform how the character acts and responds to situations.

The general trajectory of the gangsters' careers and the major documented events of their lives must be adhered to; however, Winter was willing to play around with timelines and relationships in order to work within the format of the show and advance the story. Traditional written history, too, is concerned with more than just the accurate plotting of time or chronicling of events. What distinguishes history is the "self-conscious organization of arguments, interpretations, or narratives," which we can see taking place in the construction of Capone's character, regardless of the shifting of some dates.[47] Colosimo's death came in May 1920, not January 1920, when the pilot is set, but in terms of the show's structure it needed to be included in that first episode, when the major figures of each city—Thompson and Darmody in Atlantic City, Capone and Torrio in Chicago, and Rothstein and Luciano in New York—were being established. It would not have served any purpose to include Colosimo in a few more episodes only to have him killed off and be left with the same dynamic after the delay.[48] True invention is also practiced in designing Capone's interactions with the completely invented characters and those inspired by historical figures. Capone and Torrio did not have the friendly relationship with Nucky Johnson that is depicted in the show, although at times they did journey to Atlantic City and did at least know Johnson. Winter stated, "I have the license then to say, 'OK, I know these guys knew the real Nucky. They did spend time there.' I can then comfortably create fictional relationships for them with people who they may or may not have known."[49] The fictionalized relationships keep the storylines unexpected, one of Winter's key goals when creating the show. And, by "staying true to the spirit" of Capone when crafting these storylines, the show continues to convey information about him. Capone's sense of humor, for example, is showcased throughout season 1, often during encounters with his invented friend Darmody.

The treatment of Capone in *Boardwalk Empire* shows that it is possible to take a familiar figure, one even as exaggerated and distorted as Capone, and present an original and engrossing representation on-screen.[50] The writers have clearly engaged with the vast and varied literature on Capone and used the information, both well-known and little-known, to craft their character. To agonize over the historical accuracy of events and details—the date of Colosimo's death, Capone's involvement in Atlantic City in the early 1920s—is reductive. Achieving historical accuracy when dealing with real 1920s gangsters is problematic for any form of history. What is important is that the writers have been successful in realizing Winter's wish to stay true to the spirit of the historical figure and to ultimately leave viewers with a historically accurate *impression* of Capone: his personality, his temperament, his career.

## Between Fact and Fiction: Nucky Thompson

At the center of *Boardwalk Empire* is Enoch "Nucky" Thompson, the crooked treasurer of Atlantic County with a penchant for flamboyant suits. Thompson is based on Nucky Johnson, one of the key figures that appears in Nelson Johnson's history of Atlantic City. Nucky Johnson was an exceptionally colorful character who lived an extravagant life and associated with a vast array of notable political and underworld figures. Indeed, Thompson's most significant historical contribution to the show is in the connections he has to a wide array of personages, an element of his character that is based directly on Johnson. Winter and his writers would have been hard-pressed to create a more distinctive and well-connected character, so it is unsurprising they decided against inventing a character from scratch for the lead. However, Winter chose to only loosely base his character on Johnson and transformed him instead into Nucky Thompson.[51] Thompson, and this character type more generally, occupies a hazy middle ground, somewhere between the real figure of Capone and the invented character of Darmody. Many of the details and circumstances of Johnson's life are mirrored in his on-screen manifestation, but there are also a number of differences and elements of his life that have been sensationalized. "I didn't want to be married to the real guy's life story," Winter explains. "I wanted to take our Nucky into places that the real Nucky Johnson might never have gone—emotionally, violently. I also didn't want to sully the real person's reputation in case he has family. That wouldn't be fair."[52] Basing the character on Johnson meant Winter and his writers could borrow heavily from the real-life figure—his personality, career, acquaintances—but could freely manipulate the character to fit within the quintessential gangster mold while also endeavoring to generate and maintain audience investment through character alignment and allegiance.

Unlike Capone, Nucky Johnson had not appeared in film and television shows prior to *Boardwalk Empire,* nor has he been the subject of many written historical works. Although a national figure in his own time, Johnson was relatively unknown in the twenty-first century, at least before the show aired. When prepping for the series, Winter would go to Atlantic City and informally ask people if they knew who Nucky Johnson was. "Almost nobody knew," Winter remembered. "We realized early on that he's sort of an obscure historical character."[53] He has of course made appearances in a number of texts, including Nelson Johnson's book, as well as others that focus on Atlantic City and 1920s and 1930s gangsters such as Paulino "Skinny" D'Amato. Since the airing of *Boardwalk Empire,* a new biography of Johnson, by his former lawyer, Frank J. Ferry, has also been published.[54] Nucky is generally represented in a consistent fashion across these histories; he is described as a smart, savvy politician whose rule in Atlantic City was absolute and who was equally influential in the underworld. Alongside his eventual downfall, there are two key events that are often referenced, both of which he played an instrumental role in organizing: the creation of the Atlantic City Convention Hall and the meeting of organized crime bosses in 1929. Ultimately, though, for a general audience Nucky Johnson does not carry expectations and the baggage of the other historical characters.

Even though Johnson may not be as well-known as Capone, his life was no less extraordinary. As Nelson Johnson explains, "For nearly 30 years, Enoch 'Nucky' Johnson lived the life of a decadent monarch, with the power to satisfy his every want." Johnson was ambitious and sought power from an early age. He was sheriff and secretary to the Republican County Committee before he became county treasurer in 1913, a position that he held for almost thirty years. While in this post Johnson reorganized and revolutionized the graft and protection system in Atlantic City and became a powerful force in New Jersey politics. He made sure to meet every job applicant who sought to get on the Atlantic City public payroll, especially police, to make sure they understood the system before they signed on to the job. Johnson had a dual identity; he "was the most powerful Republican in New Jersey, who could influence the destinies of governors and senators, and a racketeer, respected and trusted by organized crime."[55] His town was awash with liquor during Prohibition and, unlike other major cities, it was not confined to speakeasies and private clubs. It was out in the open, a fact that drew tourists and conventioneers to the resort town and inspired the admiration of established gangsters. He ruled from the ninth floor of the Ritz Hotel and was known as a man about town, throwing and attending the biggest parties, more often than not with a young showgirl on his arm. Johnson won the hearts (and votes) of Atlantic City residents, Black and white alike, by always helping out in times of need with food, coal, a job, or perhaps the loan of one of his personal automobiles when there was a funeral. His reign came to an end in 1941 when he was sentenced for tax evasion after a four-and-a-half-year investigation by federal authorities.

The incredible life of Nucky Johnson provides a substantial base or "skeleton" for Nucky Thompson that is built upon from week to week and season to season. The basics of Johnson's life—his job, connections, residence, and even dress sense—form the basis of Nucky Thompson in season 1. Johnson owned over a hundred suits in rich tones such as lavender and chocolate, and kept warm in winter in a full-length $1,200 raccoon coat.[56] His trademark was a fresh carnation pinned to his lapel, "a sartorial flourish that remained his signature til the day he died."[57] Thompson's luxurious wardrobe is clearly modeled on Johnson's. Week after week, Thompson wears elaborate three-piece suits in contrasting patterns, colors, and textures, and the carnation features prominently, even in the opening credits of the show.[58] Like Johnson,

Thompson is the treasurer of Atlantic County and has a strong presence in Republican politics. He socializes and brokers deals with Frank Hague, the mayor of Jersey City, Senator Walter Edge, and Attorney General Harry Daugherty, just as the real Nucky did. According to Jonathan Van Meter, "no political boss in America ever wielded as much power in one state as Nucky Johnson did in New Jersey," something that audiences certainly get a sense of in the show.[59]

The key benefit of basing Thompson on Johnson is Johnson's connection to high-profile underworld and political figures. Audiences are "aligned" with Thompson, as he is at the center of *Boardwalk Empire*'s character constellation. Murray Smith describes "alignment" as "the process by which spectators are placed in relation to characters in terms of access to their action, and to what they know and feel."[60] In the opening minutes the viewer follows Thompson from his speech at the Women's Temperance League meeting, where he condemns alcohol, to Babette's Supper Club, where he organizes his ward bosses for the bootlegging business. Throughout the episode main characters are generally introduced as they come into contact with Thompson. As both the episode and the season progress, it is not only Thompson that the viewer is aligned with, but it is largely through him that new characters are introduced and multiple attachments are made. He hosts a dinner meeting in the first episode between the crime bosses of New York and Chicago, which is where the viewer is first introduced to Rothstein, Luciano, Colosimo, Torrio, and Capone. From this initial meeting in Atlantic City, the scope of the show expands, incorporating storylines in New York and Chicago.

This access to an array of characters is arguably Thompson's most important historical contribution. His historical value lies not in the insight he gives into one historical figure (as does Capone's character) or into a larger group (as does Darmody's) but from the connection he provides to other characters. Nucky Johnson's extravagant career and ties to both the political system and the underworld provided a basis and inspiration for the inclusion of different elements and figures in 1920s society. Many historical topics are incorporated through the inclusion of the rich array of characters, real and invented, with which viewers become aligned, including Darmody, Capone, Rothstein, Margaret Schroeder, Esther Randolph, and Chalky White.[61] The inclusion of the invented character Margaret, for example, brings in issues surrounding immigration, women's health, and suffrage, while historical figures Harry Daugherty and Jess Smith provide insight into how machine politics operated. Viewers' knowledge of and engagement with the 1920s are

Nucky Thompson (*center*) meets with the heads of the Chicago and New York crime syndicates.

limited to what each character brings to the show and are consequently heavily centered on Prohibition, bootlegging, and the underworld. But in many subtle ways the characters are so diverse that *Boardwalk Empire* manages to be more than simply a gangster show or, when thinking in terms of history, a 1920s gangster compendium.

Nucky Johnson even serves as the starting point for more than one character on *Boardwalk Empire.* Chalky White, the leader of the African American community in Atlantic City, is an analogue to Thompson. Winter was interested in incorporating African American characters after reading about the crucial role Black individuals played in the creation and maintenance of the seaside tourist resort. Nelson Johnson touched upon their role in his book and followed up with a more focused study of the Northside and Atlantic City's Black community.[62] "There really had to be somebody in charge of that community that was probably similar to Nucky," Winter explains. "There was probably one guy who ran that town, that side of town, the way that Nucky ran his side of town, so I invented Chalky."[63] Thompson and Chalky share some characteristics as well as a strong bond on the show. While Thompson serves as benefactor to Atlantic City citizens, Chalky occupies a similar position in the African American community, and it earns him their loyalty and respect. Throughout season 2 the viewer learns that Chalky looks after his people by providing them with food and money, and when he orchestrates a strike of the city's Black hospitality workers, the workers oblige him. Even

Chalky's costume is designed to mirror Thompson's. He, too, wears luxurious suits in rich and contrasting tones and patterns, as well as fur-trimmed coats, but instead of a carnation boutonniere, his signature style is a brightly colored bow tie. "He is to the Atlantic City African American community the yang to Nucky's yin," costume designer Lisa Padovani elaborated.[64] The use of Nucky Johnson as an inspiration for more than one character on the same show opens up intriguing possibilities and highlights the potential and flexibility of this particular character type.[65]

For all of these reasons—Johnson's eccentric character, high-profile connections, and potential to serve as a starting point for more than one character—it is clear why Winter chose to base his lead character on Johnson. But it is also crucial to understand how and why Winter and his writers departed from the historical figure. Changing Nucky Johnson to Nucky Thompson allowed the writers to use what they wanted of the real figure while freeing them up to radically alter aspects of his life. Many of Thompson's relationships on the show are completely invented, including his relationships with Darmody and Margaret. Nucky Johnson did not have an Irish mistress whom he later married, and while he did know and associate with many of the historical gangsters, such as Capone and Luciano, he did not have close relationships with them in the early 1920s. Arguably, the event that really separates Thompson from his historical counterpart takes place during the season 2 finale. In this episode he shoots and kills Darmody, his former protégé. Darmody himself is of course a completely fictional character, so it is impossible for this particular event to be based on fact. But, as far as the historical record shows, Nucky Johnson never shot or killed anyone. He was undoubtedly corrupt and involved in numerous illegal endeavors, but there is no evidence he engaged in violent acts. "By making him Nucky Thompson, he's Nucky, but he's not Nucky," Winter explained. "Our Nucky can do anything and veer off into any direction. That's much more freeing creatively, for myself and my writers."[66] Many of the changes and additions to Nucky's history serve to shape him into a readily identifiable gangster figure.

It is in part because Thompson is an "inspired-by" character, rather than a historical figure, that radical changes can be made to his character without jeopardizing the wider historical integrity of the show. *Boardwalk Empire* charts Thompson's evolution from corrupt Atlantic City politician, a character element rooted in history, to fully-fledged gangster, an aspect that is almost completely invented. While Johnson has been called a racketeer and was an associate of known gangsters, he himself cannot be described as one.[67] A racketeer is "a person who engages in dishonest and fraudulent business dealings," while a gangster is "a member of a gang of violent criminals."[68] With the advent of Prohibition, Thompson and his associates recognize the possibilities for making more money, but it will essentially be business as usual, although on a bigger and more profitable scale. He is initially unwilling to "get his hands dirty" and, in the pilot episode, berates Darmody for hijacking Rothstein's carload of liquor and acting rashly. While Darmody appears unperturbed at the violence carried out during the hijacking, stating the need to make sure there were no witnesses, Thompson is clearly not happy that he "killed four fucking guys." Whether his concern is moral or simply because of the headache it is causing him is up for debate. "I could have you killed," Thompson threatens Darmody after learning of his reckless actions. "But you won't," Darmody replies. "Look, you can't be half a gangster, Nucky, not anymore."[69]

Winter and his writers take Johnson's criminal activities as a starting point but exaggerate and invent many aspects so that his character more clearly fits into the classic gangster mold. For Thompson to become a fully-fledged gangster, he must prove himself willing to engage in violent acts and thereby display one of the important signifiers of the gangster genre.[70] Thompson has skipped over the apprenticeship stage of gangsterdom, a position Capone and Darmody clearly occupy in season 1. For Thompson to become a gangster, he too must take up the gun to prove to himself and others that he deserves his position of power, not only in the fictional world he occupies but for the audience as well. Thompson must be able to hold his own against the legendary figures of Capone and Luciano if he is to remain the center of the show. The night Darmody is brought to Thompson to face his death, he looks around at Thompson's men and asks, "Who's going to do it?" Thompson surprises both Darmody and the audience by taking out a gun and shooting him twice after much hesitation. The man who had told Thompson he could not be half a gangster anymore is the one who enables him to cross that line. Promotional material for season 3 played heavily on this, with one advertisement showing Thompson, gun in hand, standing above a prostrate body, with the tagline "You can't be half a gangster." Thompson lives up to his "full gangster" status in the season, not being content to let others carry out violent acts for him. In episode 4 he shoots a young bootlegger in the back of the head at close range, in part because he stole from Thompson's outfit, but also to show his men that he is the boss, as he feels his authority waning. But for Thompson to earn his place as an equal amongst the exulted antiheroes of the postnetwork quality TV serial, he cannot simply be a one-dimensional gangster.

The addition of violence to Thompson's character facilitates the need for further changes to ensure that viewers can ally with Thompson and also to make sure he fits comfortably in HBO's pantheon of "complicated heroes." Thompson bears a striking resemblance to HBO's quintessential complicated hero and fellow televisual gangster, Tony Soprano from *The Sopranos.* Murray Smith has attempted to answer the question of why Tony Soprano is such an appealing, attractive character to audiences when they are well aware of his violent, brutish actions. Smith comes up with a variety of suggestions, but the one he favors is that viewers can sympathize with the character because he is, at least partially, a moral character. Tony displays anxieties, vulnerabilities, and frustrations that viewers can identify with, as well as a moral code, "and the idea of family is central to that moral code."[71] Thompson's character is constructed following a similar blueprint. His relationship with Margaret and her children, Teddy and Emily, balances the "business" side of Thompson and creates a more rounded character. Thompson presents himself as a father figure to Teddy and Emily after the death of their father and treats them with the kindness and respect he never received from his own father. After Emily contracts polio in season 2, Thompson spends time with her, helping and encouraging her to walk on her crutches. Of course, the truth is that the two children are fatherless thanks to Thompson, as he was the one who ordered their father dead. But, like Tony Soprano, though the means may strike the audience as immoral, his motivations are often moral. Thompson only decided to do away with Hans Schroeder and pin the season 1 hijacking and murders on him when he found out Hans had beat Margaret so badly she ended up in the hospital and lost the baby she had almost carried to term. Thompson is both criminal and righteous; his invented relationships and interactions create a rounded, partially sympathetic character.[72]

These inventions encourage the audience to become allied with Thompson. "Allegiance" is a term that Smith adopted in his scholarship on character in film. He is critical of the fact that alignment—which he defines as viewers' "spatio-temporal attachment and subjective access" to characters—is often conflated with allegiance.[73] He argues that allegiance is distinct from alignment and that the former refers to the "business of assessing a character's attitudes, traits, and actions, a process that results in a more or less sympathetic or antipathetic attitude on our part toward a character."[74] Once allegiance is established, viewers respond emotionally to the actions of characters and the situations they are placed in. Viewers' sympathies are not only determined by "external factors" or "real world attitudes" but by the "internal 'system of values' in the text."[75] While Thompson would be reprehensible to many if judging his actions by an "external standard of morality," within the text and in contrast to other characters he appears in a more sympathetic light. For example, in season 3, while viewers may have lost faith in Thompson after his actions in the season 2 finale and reassessed their opinion of him, the introduction of violent sociopath Gyp Rosetti helps place Thompson in a comparatively positive position on the spectrum. Allegiance does not have to be limited to one character; indeed, in *Boardwalk Empire,* viewers are likely to become allied with more than one of the numerous characters, and this may take the form of perverse or partial allegiance.[76] As characters are key to keeping audiences tuning in week to week, crafting characters that generate allegiance and keep viewers invested in the narrative is of central importance. The inspired-by historical character gives writers the freedom to manipulate historical figures to fulfil these requirements.

*Boardwalk Empire,* while a historically conscious drama that aims to capture the sensibility of the Prohibition period, is first and foremost a gangster show. Winter identified a fascinating historical figure in Nucky Johnson but recognized that he was not suited to fronting a gangster series. Changes would have to be made to transform Johnson from a racketeer to a fully-fledged gangster and leading man. That Nucky Johnson was changed to Nucky Thompson demonstrates that Winter was aware he could not invent freely with a historical figure and that, in crafting this transformation, he would need to make some sort of distinction between the two. The changes made to Nucky Johnson—his invented relationships, his increased gangster involvement—do not inherently impact the on-screen history negatively. Through the simple act of changing Nucky's last name, Winter gave himself the freedom to not have to worry about "staying true to the spirit" of the real Nucky and the license to invent a character that both fulfilled genre expectations and remained historically conscious.

## Inventing a Historical Character: Jimmy Darmody

Vying for the role of main character in seasons 1 and 2 is James "Jimmy" Darmody, Thompson's protégé, surrogate son, and eventual adversary. The storylines of the fictional characters account for a substantial portion of the show and are often used to connect and flesh out the stories of real historical figures and characters based on historical figures. Darmody has significant contact with both Capone and Thompson and also brings with him a cohort of other fictional characters that are directly related to him in the character constellation—Angela, his girlfriend and later his wife; his son, Tommy; his mother, Gillian; and his friend Richard Harrow. Though Darmody is fictional, a great amount of research went into crafting the character, and through him significant historical issues are addressed and presented to the audience. The defining element in Jimmy's character construction is his service in the Great War. For Winter, it was an important historical issue to include on the show, as he felt that most Americans were largely ignorant about World War One and the impact it had on those who fought. "World War One is sort of this forgotten period of American history for people of our age nowadays," he explained, especially when compared to the attention World War Two receives in popular culture.[77] The Great War makes up only one layer of Darmody's character—there are many other elements at play—but it serves as an example of how fictional characters can successfully explore historical issues. Jimmy is as much a "historical character" as Capone, and his presence in the narrative imbues the past with a sense of contingency and uncertainty.

Unlike with Capone, and even Thompson, Winter and his writers started with a blank piece of paper with the character of Darmody. To build and sustain an engaging three-dimensional fictional character, several basic components are necessary. Firstly, a character must have a well-developed backstory and history, as it is often this backstory that will provide the motivation, or the push and drive, of the character. This is the second aspect: the character must have a goal or a desire, something that motivates action. Finally, the character must experience some sort of change or transformation over the course of the story—not remain static and unchanged in the eyes of the audience.[78] The character that is created on paper is expressed in the narrative through "signs of character" crafted not only by the writers but by the actors; the art, makeup, and costume departments; and the promotional and marketing departments. As Richard Dyer explains, signs of character are "the signs that we as viewers latch onto in constructing character" and include audience foreknowledge, name, appearance, objective correlatives, speech of character, speech of others, gesture, action, and mise-en-scène.[79] It is through these signs that viewers come to know and understand characters.[80]

Darmody demonstrates that when historical events form the foundation of a character's backstory, that character has the potential to meaningfully highlight and engage with historical issues. Like a character's personality, this history is "not something given in a single shot."[81] Small pieces of information are revealed by the characters themselves and those around them. As

Roberta Pearson points out, characters develop depth and complexity as biographical details are accumulated episode by episode, resulting in "highly elaborated characters."[82] Over the first two seasons of *Boardwalk Empire,* scenes involving Darmody build up a picture not only of what life was like for American soldiers during the Great War but also of the tribulations they faced when they returned stateside. The viewer first meets Darmody when he collects Thompson from the Women's Temperance League meeting, and as he waits he listens to Thompson's story of how, as a boy, his family was so poor he was forced to kill and eat rats. "In the trenches we ate dog meat once, but rats!" Jimmy exclaims afterward. The first words out of his mouth allude not only to his service but also to the hardships he suffered, and indicate that this history is key to the character. In virtually every episode Darmody's time as a soldier is discussed or alluded to; by the time he dies, the fragments of memory have joined together to reveal the full impact the horrors of the war had on him.

Darmody is by no means the first World War One soldier turned gangster in popular culture. In fact, it is a common trope of pulp novels and gangster films of the interwar period. In the 1930s, just as revisionist histories began to appear that reconsidered America's role in the Great War and its effect on postwar society, Hollywood, too, explored similar issues. "References to the Great War, foreign conflict, and the troublesome lives of returning veterans" were not unusual in films of the 1930s, according to Smyth. Journalists, novelists, and filmmakers "emphasized the veteran-gangster connection," particularly in the 1930s.[83] There were, of course, variations in the formula from text to text. In Armitage Trail's pulp novel *Scarface* (1930), the central character is a hood before he goes to war, and he resumes his life of crime on his return. His time in the army in a machine gun company has better trained him "in the fine art of murder."[84] On the other hand, Eddie Bartlett in *The Roaring Twenties* (Walsh, 1939) enters the army as an ordinary citizen and fights admirably. Upon returning home, Eddie realizes that he has lost his job to men who did not fight, and he struggles to make ends meet. While moonlighting as a cab driver, he gets drawn into the bootlegging business and flourishes until the repeal of Prohibition. In this sense, Darmody's personal backstory is not unique, as there is already a well-established precedent. What separates Darmody from earlier filmic representations of gangster veterans is the detail and depth given to his war service.

The historical record was a crucial source when constructing Darmody's backstory; consequently, his actions in the present and his reflections on the past provide insight into American soldiers' experience during World War One. His involvement in the Battle of Saint-Mihiel and the Meuse-Argonne offensive forms the basis of his backstory. The American offensive at Saint-Mihiel took place in mid-September 1918 and was followed later in the month by the Meuse-Argonne offensive, which lasted more than six weeks. On a number of occasions Darmody tries to explain what he saw and did during the war and the effect it has had on him. Before he has one of Torrio's rivals in Chicago killed, he opens up to him about what it was like during the war. "It's almost impossible to describe the horror. It's a living, waking nightmare," Darmody confesses. He vividly recounts the story of a German soldier he shot who became entangled in barbed wire and cried out in pain and called out for his mother for days before he died. Although invented, Darmody's experiences and the ways he describes them mirror the reminiscences of frontline servicemen in the Saint-Mihiel and Meuse-Argonne offensives. One soldier from the latter campaign remembers advancing through barbed wire as part of the second wave of an assault when machine gun fire opened up. We "lay waiting to follow them, horrified by their dying screams. . . . The next few minutes were among the worst of the war for me as we lay helpless to aid, listening to our friends being torn to pieces by gunfire."[85] While Darmody's experiences are not representative of all American men who participated in the Great War, his character highlights some of the traumas faced by the 40 percent of American troops that served in combat roles.[86]

Even Darmody's body is shaped by his World War One service and becomes a vehicle for history. The physical disability displayed by Jimmy is a constant reminder to the audience of his service in the war and serves as a sign of character. The limp is part of the actor's performance, and also part of the appearance of the character. Jeremy Butler breaks down Dyer's category of appearance into three subsections—face, body, and costuming. Butler suggests that the build and physique of characters has the potential to indicate elements of their character.[87] In the case of Jimmy his build is unremarkable; he is a young, slender, fit-looking young man. His limp, however, disrupts this otherwise healthy appearance. Many men who fought suffered from a variety of disabilities and handicaps, both mental and physical. Beth Linker estimates that by mid-1919 approximately 120,000 soldiers had already passed through the US Army's rehabilitation program.[88] Darmody's limp is noticeable from the first scenes he is in, but it is not until episode 4, when he and Capone go for their suit fitting, that the web of scars on his leg is clearly visible. Due to the pain it is causing him, he visits an army hospital a few episodes later. He explains to the doctor that the first surgery was done at a field hospital outside Verdun and was followed up by three more at Walter Reed in DC. It is at this army hospital that Darmody meets Richard Harrow, a sniper from the war who, like Darmody, is physically wounded, although his injures are much more severe, with almost half of his face literally missing. The fictional characters of both Darmody and Richard, with their dual physical disabilities, inform audiences of the deadliness of the first industrial war and the lasting impact the conflict had on the lives of individual men who suffered numerous surgeries, pain, handicaps, and, in the case of the latter, public revulsion as a result of their service.

Darmody's position in society, as well as his position in Thompson's organization, is shaped by his war service. Not only does his backstory illuminate the horrors and physical consequences of the Great War, but what motivates him—and holds him back—also grows out of his wartime and postwar experiences. Darmody's goal is to reconnect with and provide financially for his family, but he finds himself with few prospects upon his return. The fact that Darmody has been away has stalled his progress in Thompson's organization and makes it difficult for him to make ends meet. Darmody is not unlike many returned servicemen who were faced with "widespread social unrest, rising unemployment, and economic hardship."[89] According to Richard Severo and Lewis Milford, soldiers struggled to survive economically when back at home and often turned to crime.[90] Darmody's lowly economic status is observed through his clothes and his surroundings, examples of what scholars call an "objective correlative," which is an object or environment that "comes to signify something about the character."[91] It may reflect the mental state of the character, the personality of the character, or, as in the case of Darmody, the social and economic status of the character. There are numerous objective correlatives for each character, Jimmy included, but in season 1 his small one-bedroom apartment signifies his financial difficulties, certainly when contrasted with the opulent (Thompson's Ritz apartment, the Commodore's mansion) and more modest (Eli Thompson's family home) dwellings of others. The war does not drive Darmody to a life of crime—he is already involved—but after returning home to Atlantic City, he does find that he has been passed over for a ward boss position. The job has gone to Paddy Ryan, a young man who, unlike Darmody, did not serve in the war. Nucky Thompson later explains that if he had stayed stateside and continued his studies, the job would have been his, but Darmody's service left him in a disadvantaged position. From the pilot episode Darmody is driven to regain what he feels is lost ground, making him into an active, goal-oriented protagonist.

While Darmody's wartime experience provides motivation, it also creates conflict for the character. Conflict is an integral part of any narrative and can be generated between characters, be sparked by environmental factors, or manifest within a character. In a sprawling long-form series like *Boardwalk Empire,* multiple conflicts are ongoing amongst the various storylines and characters. Darmody certainly engages in a number of conflicts with other characters over the course of two seasons, but the internal conflict he faces is the most significant in terms of his character development. Similar to many soldiers who served on the front lines, Jimmy appears to be suffering from shellshock. What would be termed "post-traumatic stress disorder" (PTSD) today was at that time a relatively unknown phenomenon. Nonetheless, thousands of servicemen suffered from it. It is now recognized that "PTSD is a complex and multidimensional latticework of symptoms, memories, events, responses, and beliefs" manifesting in numerous ways and causing "disruption to very primary notions of self, family and society."[92] Darmody's PTSD manifests in distrust, emotional turmoil, and reckless and self-sabotaging decision-making, which proves to be the biggest obstacle he faces in achieving his goals.

Darmody ultimately cannot overcome his past; while his character transforms on a superficial level, acquiring flashier clothes and possessions (much like Capone), he can never escape his own history. The memory of the war clearly haunts him and threatens to overwhelm him. Before going to his fateful meeting with Thompson, he says a cryptic goodbye to Richard, his mind lingering on the war.

> Darmody: "Nobody was meant to be there."
> Richard: "But that's where we were. We're still there, aren't we?"
> Darmody: "Time to come home, Richard."
> Richard: "How?"
> Darmody: "I dunno, but promise me you're going to try."

Darmody encourages Richard to move on from his wartime experiences, but he is unable to do so himself; he goes to his death knowingly, telling Thompson that he "died in a trench, years back." The staging of Darmody's death reflects the profound effect the war has had on him. He's shot in front of Atlantic's City's newly erected war memorial, and as his life slips away, he appears to gaze up at the solemn face of the statue. A haunting orchestral score begins to

In his final moments, Jimmy Darmody flashes back to his time in the trenches during World War One.

play as the scene cuts to a flashback in which men with guns, bayonets attached, huddle in the trenches, nearby trees on fire. Mortars explode in slow motion near the front lines, and the camera tracks to Darmody, who waits pensively in a prayer-like stance. The whistle sounds, and Darmody's figure is lost from sight as he heads over the top of the trench.

Darmody's war service is so integral to his character that it ends up retarding his growth; unable to move past his personal demons and evolve as a character is required to do, it is only fitting that Darmody dies at the end of season 2. Viewers are often aligned with Darmody and are witnesses to his evolving romances and friendships, his complicated family situation, and the twists and turns of his bootlegging career. Each facet of his life is shaped by the war; he is not simply reduced to a set of Great War facts and statistics. His character brings attention to an oft-ignored period in US history and, most importantly, encourages viewers to care deeply about it, because it is packaged in a multifaceted character with whom they are likely allied.

It is worth remembering that, like all characters in film or television, Darmody is constructed only in part on paper by the writers; he is also constructed through the lens of the camera and the performance of the actor. Patrick Phillips argues that "characterization is as much visual as it is verbal," and of particular importance is the actor.[93] Michael Pitt, the actor who plays Darmody, is an inseparable part of the character and is, in fact, the viewer's first contact with the character. Casting and star identification can potentially have a major impact on character and the audience's response. Dyer, in particular, attributes great importance to star identification. He suggests "the phenomenon of audience/star identification may yet be the crucial aspect of the placing of the audience in relation to a character. The 'truth' about a character's personality and the feelings which it evokes may be determined by what the reader takes to be the truth about the person of the star playing the part."[94] The question then becomes whether viewers can get past or overcome the prior roles and associations the actors bring with them. In part, this will depend on the audience's familiarity with the actor. Arguably the biggest "star" on *Boardwalk Empire* is Steve Buscemi. He is best known as a character actor, appearing in everything from Michael Bay blockbusters to Coen brothers indies.[95] Pitt, while an established actor, is undoubtedly less well-known. His filmography prior to *Boardwalk* consisted mainly of low-budget independent films, such as *The Dreamers* (Bertolucci, 2003), and his most mainstream exposure came via a stint on *Dawson's Creek* (The WB, 1998–2003). Many of the viewers coming to the HBO show may have been unfamiliar with his work, and so star identification most likely did not have a major impact on viewer response to the character.

Nonetheless, Pitt, as the actor playing Jimmy Darmody, still contributes elements to the character through his physical appearance and performance. After Darmody's demise at the end of season 2, many viewers took to online forums to express their thoughts on his death. Alan Sepinwall's weekly recap on HitFix for episode 12, season 2, for example, received over twice as many comments as episode 11 of the same season and more than ten times the amount of comments as the first episode of the season. Clearly, the death of Darmody elicited strong responses in viewers, and their feelings towards the character frequently connected back to Pitt. "At the end, as Jimmy lay dying, I found myself standing up in front of my television and yelling at the screen," viewer DC posted. "Michael Pitt brought such charisma and screen presence, the show isn't going to feel the same."[96] At the other end of the spectrum, one audience member, having "always found his performance as Jimmy Darmody extremely self-conscious," "sang the Hallelujah Chorus when he made his exit in this episode."[97] For other viewers it was Pitt's physical appearance that drew them to Darmody's character. "Jimmy was the main reason why lots of women tuned [in]. It wasn't to watch Nucky!" declared one viewer, whose sentiments were echoed by stravu9's angry post: "Jimmy was my POV character. Buscemi is too ugly to carry a show. I'm cancelling my HBO."[98] What makes a compelling character differs from individual audience member to individual audience member, but the actor behind the role can undoubtedly have a significant impact on how viewers respond to them.

What Darmody's character ultimately provides, along with the other invented characters, is a level of unpredictability and contingency. At the start of the series he occupies a similar position to the other "gangster toddlers," but unlike the trajectories of the real historical gangsters, whose careers are firmly established and mythologized, Darmody's future is always uncertain. William Guynn succinctly captures the hypothesis of philosopher of history Louis O. Mink "that the reader of history adopts a specific position in relation to historical narrative that is different from the position he adopts in relation to fictional narrative." For example, a reader reading a novel does so with a certain amount of anticipation; unsure what is going to happen next, the reader has the "impression of the contingency of events."[99] On the other hand, the reader of a nonfiction historical text will most likely already have some knowledge of the topic, and the author may lay out the approach and argument at the start of the text in the introduction, thereby partially eliminating any sense of the unknown. Mink does concede that historians will present and interpret events differently, still allowing a sense of contingency for the reader. The same rules apply to historical television series and their characters. Viewers familiar with Capone will know where his character is ultimately headed, but because *Boardwalk Empire*'s representation differs from other popular representations, there is still an element of uncertainty; he is "both contingent and determined," especially given the invented nature of many of his scenes.[100] Darmody is an even more unpredictable character because there are no landmarks to adhere to, no historical figure to consult to provide clues as to what is coming next.

This sense of contingency is valuable in a historical text, as it gives history itself an element of chance; the impression that things could have turned out differently. The evolution that Capone undergoes and the signifiers he adopts over season 1 are mirrored in Darmody, and the two are ultimately on the same career path. Within the structure of the show, Darmody is just as, if not more, important than the real figures, receiving greater screen time, and viewers likely become equally invested in his character. Winter describes Darmody as the type of figure who become "the little asterisks in the history books." "Not every bootlegger or low-level criminal made it into the history books," he explained.[101] Darmody ultimately has an interesting effect on the real historical characters around him, helping to demythologize them. The fact that Darmody dies and does not succeed helps to illustrate that the gangsters remembered today were not untouchable figures or predestined "great men" of history.

Overall, Winter and his writers achieved a great level of depth and detail relating to Darmody's war service, firmly rooting it in history. This area of historical inquiry does not die with Darmody but is carried on through Richard, who faces similar issues adjusting to life after the war. Darmody serves an interesting function on the show, both as a representative of an unsuccessful gangster that history has not remembered, and a representative of combat soldiers in the Great War. Rosenstone discusses a corresponding idea in relation to historical events portrayed on-screen that do not "accurately reproduce a specific, documentable moment of the past." For Rosenstone, "generic historical moments" created for the screen are still valuable and claim their "truth by standing in for many such moments."[102] In the case of Darmody it is not an event but a character that has a similar effect. He is a proximate figure, not based on any one person, meaning that the writers could draw upon a much larger pool of historical literature. Rather than being confined to the experiences of one man's life, an invented character can embody the experiences of a much larger group, or multiple groups, as is the case with Darmody.

## Conclusion

So did Winter succeed in his aim to make the characters and the show unpredictable by mixing the three character types together and weighting the series in favor of fictional characters? There has been a mixed response from viewers, with some greatly enjoying the depictions of the real gangsters and others feeling that the inclusion of real people destroys the sense of uncertainty. On HitFix, Ever complained that "the historical characters are not that interesting because we already know what will happen to them."[103] Likewise, Brian felt that the inclusion of real gangsters could "potentially weaken the series overall" because he knew what could and could not happen to them.[104] Such criticisms have been echoed by other viewers and critics. A solution that many have suggested is to set the show in an "alternate universe" and play with the histories of the established gangsters, or fictionalize them as the writers did with Nucky Johnson. An anonymous commenter posted: "I would actually like to see them kill a Lucky Luciano or Meyer Lansky just to show us that this is a different universe and anything goes. It would add an air of unpredictability I think the show lacks."[105] For these viewers it is clearly not enough that the writers have created new relationships and scenarios for the real-life figures.

Knowing how and when the gangsters die or fall into the hands of the law is too much of a "spoiler" to overcome. In the case of the real gangsters, viewers are also still able to do what Winter himself was guilty of when watching *Deadwood:* turn to Google to find fast answers. "This is the third week that BE has driven me to Google stuff which I like, Deadwood was the same," wrote Gridlock.[106]

For others, though, the historical figures are the most satisfying on the show. Greg Grant opined that "Al Capone, Arnold Rothstein, Lucky Luciano, and George Remus are all more compelling characters than Nucky Thompson, because . . . well, how many people heard of Nucky Thompson's character before this show? There's a reason we remember Al Capone."[107] His sentiments were echoed by Dr. Gross, who wished *Boardwalk Empire* "was the story about the rise of these gangsters, rather than the Nucky Thompson story."[108] It is also worth considering that not all audience members will be familiar with the background of the historical figures, and, for them, what happens to these gangsters remains a mystery. In part of an ongoing debate over "spoilers" and whether discussing history constitutes a spoiler, one person took issue with reviewer Sepinwall and other viewers who post comments. "It's a little presumptuous of you to assume America's criminal history is so well-known outside of the US," the commenter complained. "Hell, I'm willing to bet not every American knows who was who and who did what. Capone? Sure. Luciano? In broad strokes. But the others? Well, thanks to you, I now know that they're untouchable."[109] Not everyone's historical knowledge is the same, so viewers will be approaching the real figures, and even the invented characters and the characters based on historical figures, with a different base of understanding from which to draw upon.

It is difficult, then, to gauge whether Winter is successful, as the variety of responses illustrates that audience members read and respond to characters differently. "What the text tries to get the reader to construct," Dyer states, "may not in fact be what s/he constructs."[110] While the writers attempted to present viewers with a new interpretation of Capone, shaped Thompson's character in an effort to generate allegiance, and aimed to construct an engaging invented character in Darmody, not every viewer will have the desired response to the character. "Meaning is the product not just of a film text, but also of personal response," as each viewer privileges certain signs of character over others, resulting in varied evaluations of each character.[111] Character construction is only partially in the control of the show's creators and the actors who play the roles; the rest resides in the audience, who may also "infer what a character 'is like' beyond the definite information supplied," thereby continuing to build upon and expand the character.[112] While this issue is to a large extent a matter of personal taste, some conclusions can be drawn regarding the success and capabilities of each of the three character types in terms of presenting history on-screen.

The historical characters serve a number of functions on the show, including drawing in viewers and rooting the show in a specific place and time. As sociologist Gary Alan Fine notes, when we focus on a specific individual, one with a well-known reputation, "he or she stands for a historical period and set of events." Capone was undoubtedly a celebrity in his own time and in the following decades has appeared in countless films and television shows, not to mention written historical texts, which has maintained and strengthened his reputation. He brings with him a flood of associations—of urban America in the 1920s, ethnicity, crime, and, of course, Prohibition. A reputation such as Capone's "is a powerful metaphor for thinking about a period."[113] *Boardwalk Empire* utilizes the reputation of Capone, and to a lesser extent gangsters such as Rothstein and Luciano, as a type of shorthand for the twenties and the era of Prohibition. By including these real figures, the show's creators did not have to create a historical world from scratch because of the associations and prior knowledge the figures carry with them. These characters essentially lay the foundation upon which the show is built. Although *Boardwalk* uses Capone's reputation, it also complicates it. The complex treatment of Capone illustrates that television is a medium capable of presenting a multidimensional representation of historical figures. Even while engaging in invented dialogue and scenarios, *Boardwalk Empire*'s Capone manages to capture the real Capone's personality.

However, there are limits to what can be done with a historical figure, and there will always be some areas that leave people unhappy. Jonathan Eig, a Capone biographer, generally applauds both *Boardwalk*'s handling of Capone and Stephen Graham's performance, although he finds fault with Graham's physique. "He's way too short. I have a really hard time with that," Eig explained. "Just him standing in front of the Four Deuces was an intimidation, and I just don't get that with Stephen Graham."[114] An actor can embody a historical figure with great sensitivity and success, but there will always be "a 'real' person in this equation—the actor," an obstacle that cannot be overcome.[115] When portraying a real historical figure, there are, as Jean-Louis Comolli explains, "at least two bodies in competition, one body too much," something that is not an issue with invented characters.[116] If the creators want to stay true to the spirit of the real person, as Winter and his writers aim to, then they are also beholden to the documented facts and existing knowledge about that figure. There are limits to what Capone's character can do and the historical issues that can be explored through him. Winter felt it was important to include a significant storyline surrounding World War One and its residual effects in the 1920s, but he could not have done this through Capone. There are boundaries for historical figures that cannot be crossed without invalidating the representation of that individual.

The characters based on historical figures circumvent this issue, but carry with them their own drawbacks. This character type has a lot of potential in that it allows for the incredible and colorful histories of real people to be used either as a starting point or a general guide that the writers can then freely change and manipulate. Of the three character types it is the best example of the blurring between history and invention, which is where it also becomes problematic. Although most viewers were not familiar with Nucky Johnson at the start of the series, when *Boardwalk Empire* was released, fans did start to ask questions and investigate the central figure. This has led to some confusion over the relationship between the real and the invented Nucky, and to what extent Nucky Thompson is tied to Nucky Johnson's real-life trajectory.[117] As the seasons progress, Thompson moves further and further away from his real-life inspiration. The Thompson of season 5 bears little resemblance to Nucky Johnson; by this point he has resigned as county treasurer, remarried (both during season 2), ditched his suite at the Ritz, and abandoned his trademark carnation (start of season 4), not to mention the changes to his criminal activity and the different time and circumstances of his death. While Nucky Johnson was clearly the basis for Nucky Thompson at the start of the series, there is almost nothing to link them together by the fifth season. The fictional character evolved and developed independently of his historical inspiration over the seasons, complicating how viewers may comprehend the character and his relationship to history; it may be difficult for viewers to negotiate where the "real" ends and the fictional begins.

This confusion is potentially exacerbated by the different kinds of inspired-by characters that viewers will have encountered on TV. Even though *Deadwood*'s Seth Bullock and Al Swearengen, for example, share the name of real historical figures, they fit more comfortably into the inspired-by/based-on category. If Terence Winter did Google what happened to Al Swearengen, he would have seen that Swearengen died in Denver in 1904 under suspicious circumstances, not that he passed in 1899 in his room at the Gem (as he appears to do in *Deadwood: The Movie*).[118] While both Bullock and Swearengen generally hew closer to their historical counterparts over the course of *Deadwood*'s three seasons and a film than Thompson does in *Boardwalk Empire,* there are enough changes to the historical figures that they cannot be assigned to the real historical figure category. They do, however, fit perfectly in the inspired-by category—creators took the contours of fascinating lives but developed facets independent of the historical record. Choosing to name *Deadwood*'s characters after the real-life figures is possibly misleading, but even *Boardwalk Empire*'s attempts to change names is likely confusing for audiences, given the similarities between the names of the real figures and their fictional counterparts: Nucky Johnson / Nucky Thompson; Louis Kessel / Eddie Kessler; Mickey Duffy / Mickey Doyle; Louis "The Commodore" Kuehnle / Louis "The Commodore" Kaestner. Inspired-by characters come in many shapes and sizes across TV series, and *Boardwalk Empire*'s characters are just one example of the forms this character type can take.

The inspired-by character type on *Boardwalk Empire* has also affected viewers' understanding of other characters, namely the invented characters, prompting many to believe that all the characters in the show have some specific basis in history. Viewers have taken it upon themselves to research all the characters and try to find some basis in history, creating links between characters on the show and historical figures. There are numerous websites dedicated to such endeavors, and while some of the parallels drawn are clearly correct—Nucky Thompson being based on Nucky Johnson—many of them make incorrect connections. Jimmy Darmody has been consistently linked to Jimmy Boyd, a member of Johnson's Atlantic City operation in the 1920s and 1930s. One website ambiguously explains, "Boyd, who may or may not have been a Princeton dropout and World War I veteran, emerged as an assistant to Nucky during the bootlegging period, though not as early as the show suggests (1920)."[119] This website, and others, acknowledges that while Boyd "did do dirty work" for Johnson, he did not violently rob and kill bootleggers.[120] However, Winter has always openly discussed which characters are based on or inspired by real historical figures, and Darmody is not one of them. Apart from them sharing the same first name and both working for Nucky, there is nothing to connect the two. While Darmody is a historical character in the sense that he is part of a historical television series and, more importantly, incorporates historical discourse, he is not based upon any one person. Having three different types of historical characters means the lines sometimes become blurred for viewers, not only in the case of Darmody but also in the case of many of the other fictional characters.[121]

Completely invented characters perhaps offer the greatest possibilities for presenting history on-screen in terms of character. There are no limits to the historical issues that can be explored using any one character, an obvious benefit when dealing with history on-screen, as it is limited in terms of both time and space as to how many characters can reasonably be included. That is not to say that all invented characters are created equal in terms of historical value. This is evidenced through a brief comparison of Margaret Schroeder and Lucy Danziger, two of the invented female characters. While Lucy is not as central a character as Margaret, she still accrues a reasonable amount of screen time over seasons 1 and 2. Lucy's scenes tend to involve sex or revolve around her relationships with men. On the other hand, through Margaret, numerous historical topics, including suffrage, immigration, and women's health, are incorporated into the show. There is great potential for completely invented characters to bring both well-known and little-known historical issues to the attention of viewers, but that does not mean that this capacity will (or even should) be utilized for every single invented character.

Historical TV series can mix and match these character types in an infinite number of ways depending on the historical story the creators want to tell. *Band of Brothers,* for example, based on a nonfiction book and dealing with a specific US Army company, employs real historical figures for its central cast. *Treme,* on the other hand, features an invented cast of main characters to capture the wider experiences of a city in the wake of trauma. For audiences, depending on their knowledge of the period/event depicted, some research may be required in order to identify the character types employed on the show they are watching. A viewer unfamiliar with gangster history could have no idea that Lucky Luciano is a real historical figure and that Jimmy Darmody is not. While some audience members will seek out further information beyond the series itself, it is, ultimately, what's up on-screen that matters—the narrative, driven by the characters, should engage the discourse of history regardless of whether the characters are real, invented, or inspired by historical figures (or a mixture of all three). It is, perhaps, for creators and writers of historical TV series that these categorizations are most useful. Knowing the strengths and limitations of each character type can potentially aid in the process of constructing historical characters and deciding which are best to populate the narrative with.

What is striking about *Boardwalk Empire,* and, indeed, all of the shows under examination, is the number of complex historical characters that the show is able to incorporate. *Treme,* for example, has on average a regular main cast of twelve and avoids placing any one character in a clear "lead" position. A potential concern in putting history on-screen is that the actions and significance of individuals may be overstated when not sufficiently placed within a larger context—a concern that the discipline has also expressed in regard to biography, microhistory, and narrative history more generally.[122] History on-screen, with its limited time frame, must necessarily concentrate on a limited number of characters, and the camera, by its very nature, records the actions of individual figures, rather than abstract groups. While no kind of filmed history will ever be able to escape these confines, history on TV's ability to incorporate multiple nuanced characters who bring with them a variety of historical storylines is surely an advantage of the medium. The number of characters in serials and the time viewers get to spend with each, potentially generating allegiances, have significant ramifications for the history being presented, as the next chapter suggests.

3

# Crafting Complex Historical Narratives in Serial Television

## *Treme*

*Treme* begins three months after Hurricane Katrina devastated the Gulf Coast in 2005 and the failure of the levees caused 80 percent of the city of New Orleans, Louisiana, to be underwater. Series showrunners David Simon and Eric Overmyer had long discussed making a television show about New Orleans, and Katrina provided them with a way to frame the show.[1] The series follows a range of characters from mixed social, economic, and cultural backgrounds as they try, and often fail, to rebuild their lives in the Crescent City. Multiple narratives involving these characters are woven together, providing the potential to understand the momentous impact of Hurricane Katrina on a variety of individuals while also exploring the various cultures and traditions of the city.

Television's ability to incorporate multiple storylines like this has long made it an ideal medium for exploring historical stories. Glen Creeber argues that while film is limited in the scope of the story it can tell, TV can combine multiple narrative levels and produce more complex histories that incorporate the personal and the political, the micro and the macro. The structure of television serials—the longer running time and multiple narrative strands—is a hallmark of the medium and not unique to postnetwork quality dramas.[2] However, developments within the television industry during the postnetwork era, often pioneered by HBO, have further enhanced the potential of TV serials to tell rich historical stories. This examination of *Treme* starts to uncover some of the ways complex and nuanced histories are crafted on-screen in contemporary television serials.

The link between character and narrative in television serials is central, and so this chapter and the previous one (on *Boardwalk Empire*) are intimately tied together. Television narratives depend on "strong chains of action—causes and effects generated by characters and motivated by those characters' traits and goals."[3] The characters in *Treme,* like those in *Boardwalk Empire,* fit into a variety of categories. Most notably different in *Treme* is the array of people who play themselves—chefs, musicians, politicians, and ordinary New Orleans residents—and engage with the fictional characters. All of the ten to fourteen central characters of each season are invented, although they do take inspiration from numerous individuals. Janette Desautel and Albert "Big Chief" Lambreaux, for example, are completely invented, but situations and moments in their on-screen lives come out of the consultants working on the show, informed by their own experiences or of others they know. A few of the central characters, including Davis McAlary and Creighton Bernette, come close to the "inspired-by" characters from the last chapter, but the connection to any one real person is too tenuous to be categorized as such.[4] Catherine Dessinges, Dominique Gendrin, and Wendy Hajjar argue that Simon and Overmyer "have gone to extraordinary lengths to create believable characters and plot scenarios representative of lived lives and shared experiences, often nuanced with great detail."[5] The broad range of invented characters, all with their own narrative threads (which may or may not be connected to others in the show), results in a complicated narrative capable of presenting complex historical interpretations.

*Treme,* like both *Deadwood* and *Boardwalk Empire,* is structured as a serial with character arcs and storylines developing over multiple episodes, rather than an episodic series. As Jeremy G. Butler explains, "Unlike the *series,* the *serial* expects us to make specific and substantial narrative connections between one episode and the next. In the series, the link between each week's programmes is rather vague. In the serial, the connection is fundamental to its narrative pleasures."[6] The nature of a *series* is episodic, focusing on a new storyline each week that is generally resolved within the thirty-minute or hour-long time frame.[7] In a *serial,* storylines run across more than one episode and may develop over a number of episodes, or even an entire season. Though serials were predominant mainly in daytime soap opera during television's formative decades, they have since emerged in prime-time television; many scholars, including Jason Mittell, Jeffrey Sconce, Thomas Schatz, and Sarah Kozloff, have explored this emergence.[8] Kozloff points out that the distinction between the two types of television programming has never been clear-cut, with episodic series as old as *I Love Lucy* (CBS, 1951–57) including some serial elements.[9] All agree that the 1980s was a pivotal decade in the development of serial television with the creation of prime-time shows such as *Dallas* (CBS, 1978–91), *Hill Street Blues,* and *St. Elsewhere,* which focused less exclusively on the mystery/crime/patient-of-the-week story and more on the ongoing development of the central characters and their relationships. This trend continued through the 1990s, and now purely episodic series are a rarity on TV, while serial narratives have become increasingly experimental and complex.[10]

History, too, is a "species of narrative," but while serial television narratives like *Treme* have become increasingly popular and critically acclaimed, in the historical profession narrative has been a hotly contested issue since the mid-twentieth century.[11] History is more than just a simple chronicle or list of events. A chronicle makes no attempt to join the dots between listed events and explain how one event leads to the other. What is missing in chronicle is a narrative voice that provides explanation and gives meaning to the events, thereby transforming it into a (hi)story.[12] Historians distinguish their work from fictional narratives, emphasizing that although the two share a similar form, historical narratives represent real events and are beholden to the sources. While the writer of fiction has infinite freedoms, historians are bound by facts. Traditional historians often took their method of delivery—written narrative—for granted, assuming that the sources would allow them to re-create and reproduce the "true story" of what happened in the form of a written narrative. These firm epistemological beliefs were debated and reevaluated with the advent of the linguistic turn and with the rise of new schools of thought such as the Annalistes, who turned away from linear, event-based history, and of popular new approaches like quantitative history.[13]

Philosophers of history and theorists from a spectrum of disciplines, including Hayden White, Roland Barthes, W. B. Gallie, Louis Mink, Arthur Danto, and Paul Ricoeur, weighed in on the place of narrative in history precisely at the time when practicing historians moved away from the grand narratives of the Romantic historians.[14] Shaped by their interdisciplinary approach and heavily influenced by the social sciences, historians began to favor analytical, thematic, and structural histories. Indeed, White noted in 1996 that "in modern, 'scientific' historiography, the tendency has been to suppress storytelling" in favor of "impersonal" approaches. "Storytelling in historiography," White concludes, "has for quite a while been deprived of its traditional function of explaining historical events and consigned to the more modest roles of explication and illustration."[15] This trend does not mean, however, that narrative is no longer a crucial element in history; a number of theorists argue that there still exists a narrative element to structural, concept-led, and thematic histories and readers' understanding of them.[16] Nor have narrative histories died out, with not only traditional historians continuing to work in this form but also those influenced by new approaches to history.[17]

The central issue for theorists and philosophers such as White and Barthes is that "narrative is not a neutral form into which content is stuffed, but is ideologically freighted." "Narrative," Elizabeth A. Clark summarizes, "serves to impose coherence, continuity, and closure on the messiness of life and of the historian's sources; the historian then smoothes over the gaps and absences to create an 'effect of the real.'"[18] For Alun Munslow, it is imperative that historians recognize the artifice of narrative and the role that they themselves play in the creation of historical narratives. While the story—that is, the events of the past documented in the sources—can be said to have existed, historians narrate the events of the past, providing meaning and explanation through emplotment. They make narrative choices, choosing how the narrative is structured and plotted, how events are prioritized, and ultimately what is included and what is excluded in order to maintain the momentum and focus of the narrative. "Because the process of 'telling' or narrating the past constitutes a complex system of representation," Munslow argues, "*how* a history is told is just as important as *what* is told."[19] Since narration is crucial to the construction of historical texts, it is important to explore how history is narrated on the screen, as well as on the written page.

That history on-screen tends to follow a linear, chronological path, similar to traditional narrative histories, has been a point of contention among a number of historians skeptical of the medium's capacity to engage with history. Written history has remained the primary form of delivery for professional historians because of its "apparent ability to fulfil the 'meaning function' through the mechanism of the numbered references" and the ability to directly enter into debate and challenge the findings of other scholars.[20] Robert Rosenstone has addressed such issues head-on. He admits that the narrative strategy of film, to tell a closed linear story "with, essentially, a single interpretation" is a troubling aspect, as this strategy denies historical alternatives and "does away with many of the complexities of motivation or causation." Rosenstone, though, points to the many celebrated narrative histories and biographies that fail to enter into direct debate or reference the larger field of study while he also emphasizes the need to connect with a wider audience. Historians have made a number of methodological breakthroughs since the middle of the twentieth century enriching the history they produce, but if they cannot connect their work with the wider public and tell "stories that matter" both inside and outside of the discipline, he questions the extent to which the profession will remain relevant.[21] Film and television are mediums that have the potential to reach a wide audience because of their narrative thrust while still meaningfully engaging with the past. In fact, *Treme* demonstrates that a dramatic television series can present multiple interpretations and express the complexities of motivation and causation, although how it achieves this is, of course, different from written history.

Developments in programming have aided television's ability to create rich and nuanced histories. *Treme* is an example of what Mittell has dubbed "narratively complex TV," and, indeed, he sees HBO as having "built its reputation upon narratively complex shows."[22] Narrative complexity is a catch-all phrase used to denote more elaborate storytelling techniques employed on television shows. There are no set characteristics, and shows that appear vastly different in terms of style, subject, and structure can be cited as examples of narrative complexity.[23] "Temporal play, shifting perspectives and focalization, repetition, and overt experimentation with genre and narrative forms" are just some of the elements of narrative complexity, according to Mittell.[24] While devices such as flashback and flash-forward may not be new to the form, how they are employed is; a key difference is that they "are constructed without fear of temporary confusion for viewers."[25] This type of TV can be challenging for viewers, demanding their full attention and a level of mental engagement to follow the narrative.[26] However, it is also a satisfying experience for audiences as they "build up their comprehension skills" and come to appreciate "the aesthetic sophistication that can bring its own rewards."[27] *Treme* can be classified as narratively complex due to the expansive storyworld it creates on-screen. Temporal devices are rare and the show follows a linear narrative. The complexity here comes from the vast array of characters, relationships, and narrative threads interwoven on the show. What is also notable on *Treme* is the lack of explicit explanation. Viewers are, effectively, thrown into the deep end of New Orleans culture and tradition, and context and explanation are provided slowly, paying off for dedicated viewers.

Numerous factors, including demographics, technology, and changes within the industry, have coincided with the rise of narrative complexity. With the numbers of channels increasing and the size of audiences shrinking for each show, expectations within the industry have changed. A small but cult following can be enough to sustain a show, allowing for niche series that do not have to try to appeal to the widest audience possible. The advent of new technologies (VCRs, DVD and Blu-ray players, the internet, streaming) has been important because viewers can rewatch entire episodes or replay specific scenes to dissect complicated plot twists and revelations, and also watch an entire season in the space of a few days. The internet has also allowed viewers and fans to be in constant contact, share knowledge and theories, and create a community.[28]

As a subscriber service driven to remain at the cutting-edge of programming, HBO has either spearheaded or embraced many of these changes. Anthony N. Smith points out that HBO's business model "places a low priority on servicing the needs of casual viewers."[29] Instead, the focus is on crafting complex narratives that will draw viewers in week after week, building a loyal base willing to pay the subscription fee in part for that show. HBO helps viewers build this loyalty by making the episodes readily available to subscribers—replaying them multiple times on the cable channel and, more recently, by making them available on HBO Go, HBO Now, and HBO Max. HBO "does not care *how* subscribers watch its content, just as long as they watch it."[30] In contrast, broadcast networks driven by advertising dollars want audiences to tune in for the premiere.

The significance of these changes within the industry and HBO's approach to serial dramas can be observed in the production and reception of *Treme*. From its first season the show had a small audience that fluctuated but averaged around five hundred thousand in live and same-day viewings, a small number compared to other HBO serials.[31] Despite the low ratings, HBO continued to green-light subsequent seasons. "We're as proud of 'Treme' as we are of anything on the network," stated HBO chairman and CEO Richard Plepler when the show was renewed for a third season. "Do we wish more people watch it? Of course we wish more people watched it. But it's hard, a story of human beings in distress."[32] Online forums have also been important for this particular series, providing viewers with a space to share thoughts, frustrations, and theories and a place to seek out an appendix to the show. Dave Walker's weekly posts on the *Times-Picayune* website provided a guide to the often obscure New Orleans references on the show and were regularly recommended by TV critics and praised by viewers seeking out greater explanation.[33] While it is impossible to state definitively, it seems safe to assume that a show like *Treme* would not have appeared on television screens during the TVI or TVII era (see introduction) or, if it had, that it would not have lasted three and a half seasons. The TVIII period, however, has been particularly conducive to producing historical dramas with depth and complexity.

Because *Treme* is a show populated with invented characters, the question becomes how free the show's creators were to invent in terms of the historical narrative being told. Both Simon and Overmyer stated in interviews that their wish was to capture the realities of life in post-Katrina New Orleans. Though the central characters are invented, this does not mean they were writing a fictional narrative with the freedom to change the historical record. It is useful here to employ the terms "satellites" and "kernels," created by narrative theorist Seymour Chatman. As David Herman explains, these names "refer to the core and peripheral elements of story-content respectively. Delete or add to the kernel events of a story and you no longer have the same story; delete or add to the satellites and you have the same story told in a different way."[34] In *Treme* we can think about the documented historical events as being the kernels. Like any historian writing a scholarly monograph, storytellers should refrain from significantly altering these kernel events, as to do so would mean it would no longer be classified as history. "Some things, you just don't make up," Simon explained, although as noted in the previous chapter, changes to date and location in historical film can be accommodated without impacting the overall veracity of the history being presented.[35] The characters and their storylines, then, are the satellites; conceivably Simon and Overmyer could have created ten different central characters in season 1, which would have resulted in the same history documenting New Orleans in the aftermath of Hurricane Katrina, but told in a different way, through the experiences of ten new characters.

The inclusion of so many main characters requires an elaborate structure able to accommodate numerous ongoing storylines. Several metaphors have been employed by TV critics and scholars to capture the complex structure of television serials. In a piece published by the *New York Times* in 1995, Charles McGrath declared "The Triumph of the Prime-Time Novel," referring to those TV series that developed storylines across episodes and became the nineties' "equivalent of the serial novel, unfolding epic stories instalment by instalment."[36] This analogy has remained popular, with Greg Metcalf updating the terminology to fit with changes in technology, arriving at the term "DVD Novel."[37] For both McGrath and Metcalf, episodes equate to chapters in a book, developing ongoing characters and plot. Not everyone is content with this comparison though; Sean O'Sullivan finds that TV serial narrative is in fact more closely related to poetic structures, particularly the sonnet, which he compares to a TV season. For O'Sullivan, "the multiplot spectrum of characters, events, and thematic context in a single serialised episode far exceeds the ambit of a traditional novel chapter."[38] Brett Martin dispenses with literary metaphor in favor of an architectural one, describing each episode in a TV serial as a "brick with its own satisfying shape, but also part of a season-long arc."[39] However, Mittell argues that despite influence from literature, film, comic books, and videogames, TV narrative structure is, in fact, unique, with its own strengths and weaknesses.[40] "An understanding of the medium-specific potentials of moving-image storytelling," he asserts, "allows us to appreciate what they offer on their own terms."[41] Mittell is correct that it is counterproductive and impractical to judge television narrative by the standards and capabilities of literature, whether novelistic or poetic. Still, such comparisons can provide a useful frame of analysis.

The full series of *Treme* can be compared to a complete book, while a season is analogous to a chapter, and an episode to a series of paragraphs in that chapter. Exploring a serial in this way does not entail the expectation that television should mimic a written history text, nor does it elevate one form above the other. Instead, such juxtaposition provides a starting point by which to understand how history is constructed across a series, a season, and an episode. Each of the following sections focuses on one of these storytelling units. The first looks at how an episode operates in isolation and explores the nuts and bolts of how narrative is constructed on-screen. Just as written history is more than a chronicle of events, history on-screen must also imbue events with meaning. As White argues, film has a different language and discursive mode than that used in traditional history. A close reading and analysis of the episode "Shame, Shame, Shame" allows for an examination of how a dramatic television series constructs and presents historical facts, themes, and ideas.[42] The second section focuses on season 3 and one of its major storylines. The issue of rebuilding New Orleans—both at the individual level, in terms of private housing, and at the public level, in terms of city infrastructure—is a central theme of this season involving a number of the main characters. Linking back to ideas from the previous chapter on alignment and allegiance, this chapter demonstrates that a television show has the potential to present more than just a single, straightforward historical interpretation. The final section on the series as a whole considers *Treme*'s overarching argument: that the city of New Orleans is rich in unique traditions and culture and it is vital that it continues to thrive in the aftermath of the storm. *Treme* is not unlike new narrative histories, especially microhistories, which use a traditional narrative form to bring to light the stories of ordinary people and, in doing so, illuminate wider issues. It is also necessary to consider paratexts, the extra material packaged within the DVD and Blu-ray sets, as they expand on the central text, effectively functioning as the show's footnotes.

## History in Beats: Episodes

David Simon has often been vocal in interviews that *Treme* is not a show that can be judged or evaluated on an episode-by-episode basis, stating in one interview that the measure that he cares about "is not the episodic." Instead, Simon, Overmyer, and the creative team wrote for "people who have a complete DVD set in front of them, or who are watching the show via HBO On Demand, or who can otherwise absorb it all as a piece and watch [the episodes] all in a row."[43] Storylines do evolve slowly on the show, and it often takes an entire season for what could be considered mundane narrative threads (such as LaDonna Batiste-William's roof woes in season 1) to find any sort of closure or resolution. Evaluating the season as a whole, especially a TV series such as *Treme* that is character driven and eschews the "standard tropes of a standard television drama," is, of course, imperative.[44] But TV, by its very nature, is episodic, and episodes need to function to a certain degree on their own in order to keep viewers tuning in from week to week during its initial airing. It is live viewing, plus the number of additional viewers tuning in for repeats and watching DVR recordings within the first seven days, that have a strong bearing on whether or not a cable or network show will be picked up for subsequent seasons.[45] Though HBO's primary concern may not be casual viewers, individual episodes need to first reel viewers in and then keep them engaged to build loyalty.

Although the writers of *Treme* clearly favor long-running arcs over self-contained episodic storylines, it is crucial still to examine individual episode structure in order to understand how complex narratives are presented on-screen and how events are assigned meaning. "Shame, Shame, Shame," episode 5 of season 1, provides a standard example, following the same general structure as most of *Treme*'s episodes, weaving together numerous storylines that branch out beyond this one episode. "Shame, Shame, Shame" charts the lead-up to the largest second line parade since the storm while also developing a number of longer-running narrative threads relating to the central characters. Annie and Sonny's relationship continues to slowly crumble, exacerbated by the presence of house-guest Arnie; Davis recruits local musicians to play on his CD as a part of his effort to run for city council; Albert pursues his inquiry into the housing projects; Antoine Batiste attempts to salvage his livelihood with the help of a Japanese jazz fan willing to buy him a new trombone; and LaDonna and her lawyer, Toni Bernette, continue their fight to learn the fate of LaDonna's brother Daymo, missing since the storm. The episode climaxes with the second line parade and closes on a somber note, with many characters recognizing problematic elements in their own lives and/or in the community.

This section on "Shame, Shame, Shame" looks not only at the story but also at the discourse, the two central elements of narrative theory. As Chatman simply puts it, "The story is the *what* in a narrative that is depicted, discourse the *how*."[46] Russian formalists utilize the terms *fabula*, "the complete story," and *syuzhet*, "the selection and ordering of the action explicitly presented on screen."[47] David Bordwell prefers the latter terms for discussion of narrative in film, taking narration to be "the process by which film prompts the viewer to construct the ongoing *fabula* on the basis of *syuzhet* organization and stylistic patterning." It is not enough to consider the story, or *fabula*, alone; the *syuzhet* arrangement is equally important, as "it is the very force that conjures the *fabula* into being."[48] Breaking down the individual narrative threads and understanding the patterning employed helps make clear the key facts and themes conveyed to viewers in this one episode alone. While "Shame, Shame, Shame" is just one small part of a much larger and complex whole, it serves to illustrate how narrative is crafted on-screen and how historical facts and ideas are generated.

The structure, or architecture, of *Treme*'s episodes follows the basic patterns employed by most cable and network ensemble drama series. While cable shows, and especially HBO series (with their tagline "It's not TV. It's HBO"), are often considered to be very different to their network counterparts, they are essentially constructed the same way. Anthony N. Smith argues that the episode architecture of the seminal HBO series *The Sopranos*, which was lauded by critics and scholars for breaking the television mold, basically still follows many of the same formulas, although it was certainly more creative and subtly edited together.[49] "Situation comedies, episodics, and serial dramas all organise their stories into rather short segments," Michael Z. Newman explains. These "beats," or what viewers might think of as scenes, are "television's most basic storytelling unit" and are rapidly cut together with each one generally lasting no longer than two minutes.[50] The beats alternate among multiple plots contained within that episode, a structure that "both permits contrast and resonance between distinct storylines."[51] Television episodes also often follow a three- or four-act structure. Even though premium cable series do not have the commercial interruptions of network TV, which necessitates a clearly defined and evenly timed four-act structure, acts are still employed because they allow for rising and falling action and turning points that complicate the action.[52]

Given the multiplicity of characters and both the isolated and interconnected relations to one another, there are multiple storylines at play in episodes of *Treme*, with different numbers of beats dedicated to each.[53] The inclusion of a myriad of storylines is certainly a common feature of narratively complex television. In a brief study of TV narratives, Steven Johnson compares four series—*Dragnet* (NBC, 1967–70), *Starsky and Hutch* (ABC, 1975–79), *Hill Street Blues*, and *The Sopranos*—and plots the narrative threads in order to demonstrate the stark difference between the former two episodic series, which focus predominately on a single narrative, and the latter two serials, which contain multiple threads.[54] *Treme* fits into the second category, with upwards of ten narrative strands per episode, some of which may only briefly appear in one or two beats. Generally, individual episodes can often be analyzed and separated out into A, B, C, and D stories, with the greatest number of beats divided between the A and B threads, and declining numbers of beats for the minor storylines, however many there may be.[55] In *Treme*'s episodes it is difficult to identify such a clear structure due to the number of narratives included and the scattered number of beats given over to each (see graph on opposite page). In "Shame, Shame, Shame" the trombone and Daymo storylines could be considered the A and B storylines, respectively.[56] It is not a clear distinction, though, as two other storylines have only one fewer beat than the Daymo thread. The story of Antoine's trombone also has two main lines of action, each with a very different focus: Antoine's journey to replace his instrument is bookended with conversations between Toni and Lieutenant Terry Colson that are initiated by Toni's quest to find his original missing trombone. With the number of beats per episode (approximately forty for a fifty-five-minute *Treme* episode) and the number of storylines per episode, there is potential for each individual show to raise a number of historical issues.

Beats, and the storylines they contain, are edited together to form a cohesive narrative that viewers can engage with and follow. Robin Nelson describes this as a "flexi-narrative," a "fast-cut, segmented, multi-narrative structure."[57] This structuring serves a number of purposes: omitting what is considered unimportant, telescoping time, and keeping up audience interest by not allowing one storyline or group of characters to dominate airtime.[58] The beats do not conform to a rigid pattern, nor are the storylines evenly

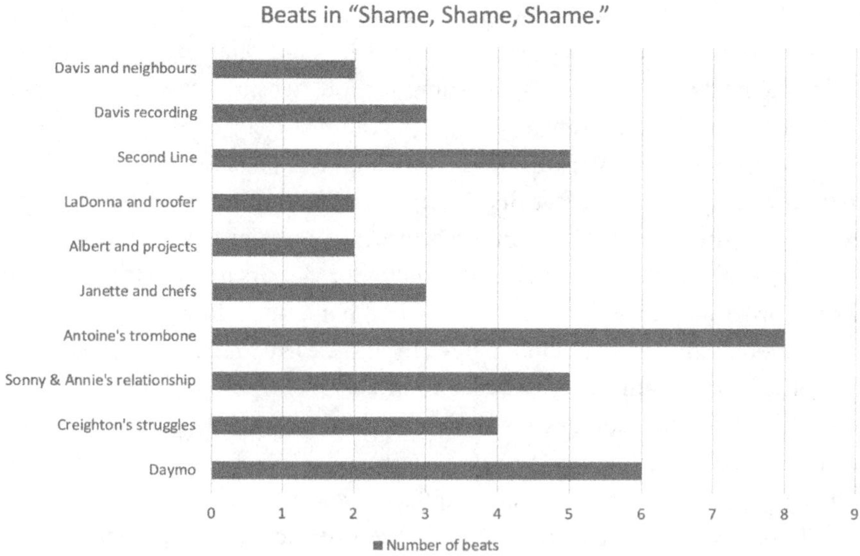


Number of beats assigned to each storyline in "Shame, Shame, Shame."

spaced throughout the episode, demonstrated by an analysis of "Shame, Shame, Shame." The trombone story is first introduced in the fourth beat after the opening credits, as Toni meets with police officer Colson to discuss Antoine's missing trombone. In the following beat, LaDonna stakes out her roofer, waiting to serve him papers, before the next beat returns to the trombone story, and is again succeeded by a continuation of LaDonna's roofer storyline. After this beat, LaDonna's roof thread does not reappear in this episode, and the trombone story does not reemerge until the nineteenth beat. The same patterning is more substantially replayed here with Antoine's interactions with the Japanese jazz fan, Koichi Toyama, documented in four beats, alternating with two other storylines: one beat on Albert's housing project thread and the three remaining beats on Janette's restaurant vignette.[59] Some storylines, such as the Sonny/Annie/Arnie arc explored in this episode, have beats more randomly plotted throughout the episode. However, double beats or longer groupings of beats alternating with other storylines are more usual.

The alternating rhythm of beats often found in *Treme*'s episodes allows for fairly rapid development of plot within the featured storylines while also keeping viewers engaged with the flexi-narrative structure. It also helps audiences follow some of the more complex storylines. Midway through "Shame, Shame, Shame," Toni searches through water-damaged papers in an effort to find any clues that will aid her search for Daymo. Sofia Bernette manages to read the word "Webster," and Toni wonders aloud if it could refer to Webster Street. After the next scene of Davis's recording session, the show cuts to an exterior shot of Desautel's restaurant, a street sign reading "Webster St" clearly visible, before jumping to an interior shot of Toni talking to Janette and Jacques about the previously unknown fact that Daymo was an employee. With too long a gap between the two beats, Toni's discovery of the word "Webster" and the visual cue of the street sign could be difficult for viewers to piece together. Just as the order and structure of sentences and paragraphs in a written text are fundamental for conveying ideas logically and clearly to the reader, so too are the order and organization of beats in an episode. Operating within a flexi-narrative structure that viewers have become accustomed to, beats are carefully ordered and structured to help viewers follow complex narrative threads and signal important focal points at different stages of the episode.

Many of *Treme*'s narrative threads are historical in nature and require explanation and evidence. On the surface, individual storylines in "Shame, Shame, Shame" are clearly delineated, but many revolve around similar concerns, revealing the central themes of the episode. Due to the number of characters and narrative threads, these themes are given substance through repetition and layering ideas, often subtly, across storylines. Two main topics are evident in this episode. The first is that many New Orleanians felt abandoned by those in power at local, state, and federal levels, and disillusioned with efforts to get the city back on its feet. The second is that, in 2006, crime began to return to the unprepared city. Presenting such historical facts and ideas in a written text can be straightforward—dates, statistics, and contextualizing evidence can be listed in a forthright manner. However, conveying historical facts and ideas in a dramatic series is more difficult, as they must be naturally and convincingly integrated into the narrative while still being fully explained and supported. In "Shame, Shame, Shame," song, YouTube monologues, character conversations, and action are used to illustrate historical issues and provide meaning and context. While these ideas are not unique to this episode alone and are, in fact, expanded on throughout subsequent episodes and seasons, they are both sufficiently documented and explained in this one episode alone that they can function independently.

The most easily readable issue included in this episode is that crime began to return to the city several months after the storm. The main supporting evidence for this comes from the second line sequence during which shots ring out amid the celebrations and several people are injured. This is a restaging of the All-Star Second Line Parade on January 15, 2006, organized by thirty-two social aid and pleasure clubs, shortly after which three people were injured by gunshots. New Orleans crime rates prior to the storm were among the highest in the country, but in the aftermath "the bullets and drugs and the fear" disappeared, according to the *New York Times*, "swept away by Hurricane Katrina."[60] Crime data for Orleans Parish in the immediate months after the storm is unreliable, but as Michael Leitner et al. contend, "There is some support to suggest that crime rates fell drastically after the storm," in part due to the number of National Guard troops in the area, the amount of government aid being given out, and the reduced population.[61] This lull in criminal activity did not last long, and the second line shooting included in "Shame, Shame, Shame" is used to signal the returning presence of violent crime. Crime rates for larceny, burglary, and robbery began to return to pre-storm levels during 2006, but murder and aggravated assault rates rose well beyond figures for previous years.[62] Taking into account reduced population numbers, Mark J. VanLandingham's study of 2006 murder rates shows the "murder rate in New Orleans increased substantially over both 2004 and 2005."[63] *Treme*'s characters eagerly anticipate the second line, but the mood of optimism and hope created by the parade is dampened by the sudden appearance of violence.

Alongside the return of violent crime was the return of drugs to the city, and this element is also addressed in "Shame, Shame, Shame." During the second line, LaDonna spots Marcus, an old friend of Daymo's, and it becomes clear during the course of their conversation that Marcus is a drug dealer. He explains to LaDonna that he was in Atlanta until the start of 2006 and then came back to New Orleans to see what was happening. LaDonna's signature arched eyebrows in response to Marcus's dubious and vague comments indicate that she knows he returned to the city for less than lawful reasons. Like Marcus, many dealers and drug users did in fact evacuate the city during and immediately after the storm, along with the hundreds of thousands of law-abiding residents. While New Orleans was never completely drug free after Katrina hit, availability was scarce and prices skyrocketed, resulting in reduced visibility of drug culture and crime.[64] "The dope men, like, they're out of town," one local resident commented in November 2005.[65] As this scene indicates, it did not take long for the drug market to reestablish itself once evacuees began returning home.

The second line shooting and LaDonna's interaction with Marcus are single instances provided on-screen that are representative of what is happening on a larger scale. These basic facts are discussed in an exchange between Toni and Colson that explicitly provides both context and meaning for what has occurred earlier. "Crime is coming back and we ain't ready," Colson asserts. He lists the problems standing in the way of maintaining law and order in New Orleans: criminals may be coming back to the city, but the police force is not functioning at full capacity, those police working are themselves homeless and struggling with the personal aftereffects of the storm, and the district attorney's office and judicial system are in a shambles. Not all these problems were new, but they were exacerbated by the storm.[66] The *syuzhet* organization and construction of these scenes encourages the viewer to grasp the larger story (*fabula*) of the problem regarding crime in New Orleans. Toni and Colson's conversation, coming towards the end of the episode, functions as a conclusion, drawing together key pieces of evidence and evaluating the broader significance of what is happening. These three scenes consisting of action, inference, and straightforward character discussion across a range of storylines clearly articulate the issue of returning crime.

Perhaps more difficult to convey than a relatively straightforward fact is the mood or emotion of a community. Abandonment and disillusionment come through most strongly in Creighton Bernette's personal struggles. After the opening credits, the show opens with Creighton recording a YouTube video (as his character has become accustomed to doing), this one addressed directly to President George Bush. Bordwell argues that the ordering of events is key because the "order of events governs how we understand them, and the first item has greater saliency."[67] On *Treme* it is often the first scene after the opening credits that sets the tone for the episode and highlights important storylines and themes, rather than the cold open.[68] Creighton lays out the problems still facing the city: half the population still not home, hospitals closed, people dying for lack of medical care, and the next hurricane season just five months away. In the second half of the monologue he references Bush's September 2005 Jackson Square speech in order to highlight the failure of the government, and of Bush personally, to follow through on promises made.

> What I mean to say, Mr. President, is that I continue to believe in the better angel of your nature. The one who, a few days after the storm, stood in front of a flood-lit Jackson Square and promised to rebuild the Gulf Coast. So let me banish from my mind the image of you lightly joking about the high times you spent here in our city as a

> youth while bodies floated in our streets. Far be it from me, with all my excesses and impulses, to judge you for a few untethered, unfocused words. All will be forgiven, Mr. President, if you just simply take a moment, as I often do, and watch yourself at Jackson Square, and listen to those stirring words. And then keep your fucking promise.[69]

Using a similar technique, Davis's recording scene midepisode clearly gives voice to civic problems and discontent with authority figures, again singling out Bush during his parody of the Smiley Lewis song "Shame, Shame, Shame."

> Look up in the sky
> It's a bird, it's a plane
> It's, "Oh hell yeah I'm with ya, New Orleans
> "Bring this bird down 8,000 feet
> "Let's have a look see
> "Oh no, oh no, that's not good at all
> "Your city is wet, really wet
> "It must be twice as bad on the ground"
> Twice as bad, twice as bad, ya think?
>
> Shame, shame, shame on you now, W
> Shame, shame, shame on you now, W
> Shame, shame, shame what you done
>
> We was on the ropes, we were down and out
> You flew on over, never did come down

The feelings of disappointment, frustration, and neglect espoused by both Creighton and Davis reflect the reality of the slow and often mishandled recovery of New Orleans. Looking back a year after the hurricane, independent reports and news outlets expressed concerns over the slow rate of progress and inefficient plans for rebuilding the city.[70] The transmission of Creighton's concerns via his YouTube clip and Davis's critique via song are clever delivery techniques that allow for one-sided dialogue capable of conveying a straightforward summation of the feelings of some New Orleans residents that do not have to be more subtly embedded into intercharacter dialogue.

However, unlike the evidence presented on the return of crime, this particular message requires more careful reading on the part of the audience. Viewers' understanding of Creighton's YouTube argument, and the argument developed as a whole across the different storylines of the episode, will be affected by their prior knowledge of the show. Taken out of context from the rest of the series, Creighton's presentation of the facts may be taken by the audience at face value, though his belligerent attitude may not endear him to them. If they have witnessed Creighton's prior actions and remarks, they will take his criticisms with a grain of salt and approach this episode with the knowledge that Creighton is quick to anger and prone to hyperbole (as is Davis).[71] Although Creighton is known to be an unreliable narrator, the fact that his discontent is mirrored by Davis and by Albert, who voices frustrations at the authorities over the issue of public housing, does support his grievances.[72] That they interact with other characters who are sympathetic to their troubles (most notably the praise Creighton receives for his YouTube posts later in the episode) signals they are not expressing a radical point of view. A *New York Times*/CBS poll conducted in August 2006 found "Americans critical about the pace of recovery and lacking in full confidence of the government," with 39 percent surveyed "dissatisfied with progress in the region" and an additional 11 percent angry.[73] In a poll of those impacted by Katrina in the Gulf Coast region, 69 percent of those surveyed rated the federal government's response as "only fair" (36 percent) or "poor" (33 percent), leaving only 30 percent rating the response as "excellent" (5 percent) or "good" (25 percent). The ratings for state governments, mayors, and local officials were higher overall, but followed the same general trend.[74]

In "Shame, Shame, Shame" it is largely the characters who assign meaning through conversation and commentary. This is not the only way history onscreen can provide meaning; editing, for example, is another effective means of crafting ideas. Unlike the author of a historical monograph, though, the characters are a physical presence known to the audience and cannot make claims to objectivity. As Munslow points out, historians often write in the third person to give the effect of objectivity, even though this ideal has long been debunked in the historical profession.[75] Indeed, Peter Burke argues that "historical narrators need to find a way of making themselves visible . . . as a warning to the reader that they are not omnipresent or impartial and that other interpretations besides theirs are possible."[76] This is precisely what happens in a television series like *Treme,* as the illusion of objectivity is more difficult to maintain in a dramatic televisual representation. Ideas are necessarily filtered through characters, and their presentation of the facts is inherently subjective. Even with characters largely unknown to audiences, such as Colson (as this is the first episode he appears in), the characters' positioning and status in the narrative, as well as their delivery of the message, affect how viewers will understand them.[77] What could be termed a "side effect" of the medium is one of its most interesting aspects. TV (and film) takes what could be termed a postmodern approach to history, acknowledging the bias of those shaping the interpretation presented.

## Rebuilding New Orleans: The Season

"Shame, Shame, Shame," while illuminating some key issues, is, of course, simply a snapshot, a small piece of a much larger whole. The season, as a storytelling unit, is much better able to elaborate and develop historical storylines. By focusing on a season and one of its central storylines, *Treme* demonstrates that history on television has the potential to overcome a number of the perceived pitfalls of the medium. Through the inclusion of a wide spectrum of characters who occupy various positions in the narrative, multiple perspectives can be supplied on any one topic, creating complex and multidimensional representations. Simon has explained that there are central ideas to each of the seasons: season 1 focuses on people returning to the city and what it meant to come back to New Orleans; season 2, starting approximately fourteen months after the storm, introduces major problems plaguing the city, particularly the rise in violent crime; and the third and final full-length season, beginning twenty-five months after, revolves around money coming into the city and how that money was often misappropriated.[78] These themes identified by Simon do in fact run through each and every season, but the structure of the season—the finite length with a clear beginning and end—provides shape and coherence, allowing certain themes to come to the fore. Not only does HBO's preference for short seasons of approximately ten to sixteen episodes allow for bigger budgets per episode, but shorter seasons, free of hiatus, are likely to achieve a "greater degree of narrative coherence" that audiences can follow.[79] *Treme*'s seasons each work like a chapter in many ways, advancing the overall argument of the series but also working on its own as an isolated unit.

Or perhaps it is more accurate to say that within each season of *Treme* there are multiple chapters in play given the number of storylines and characters in the show. As Rosenstone points out, film brings together many elements that are often separated in history texts. "This characteristic of film," he argues, "throws into relief a certain convention—one might call it a fiction—of written history: the strategy that fractures the past into distinct topics, categories and chapters; that treats gender in one chapter, race in another, economy in a third."[80] Within the flexi-narrative structure of *Treme*, different topics are developed alongside one another over the course of not only an episode but also the season and series. And as is the case with "Shame, Shame, Shame," important ideas and themes are built up through layering. Within season 3, for example, there are two major themes or chapters. Incompetence, corruption, and wrongdoing by the New Orleans Police Department (NOPD) are investigated by Toni, visiting journalist L. P. Everett, and Colson, working within the police department itself. Each of the characters pursues his or her own line of investigation, although the individual threads often connect. The other major theme of season 3 deals with the rebuilding of New Orleans and again includes a number of separate storylines: Delmond and Albert become involved in the planning phase for a proposed national jazz center, and Desiree and Nelson both become embroiled in the New Orleans Affordable Homeownership program, with Desiree falling victim to it and Nelson endeavoring to cash in on the scheme.

As noted in the chapter on *Boardwalk Empire*, viewers are aligned with characters and may develop allegiance to them, a crucial factor in the creation of historical representations on-screen. "Structures of alignment are produced by two, interlocking character functions, cognate with narrational range and depth," Murray Smith explains, "*spatio-temporal attachment* and *subjective access*." In season three of *Treme* the narrative follows the spatio-temporal path of around fourteen characters, dividing its attention roughly equally among them. In terms of subjective access, the audience is privy to characters' motivations and emotional states; they are transparent to the viewers. This places all the characters on a level playing field, so to speak, giving the audience equal access to each of them and not privileging one character over others. Allegiance, on the other hand, refers to how spectators respond emotionally to characters. According to Smith, "to become allied with a character, the spectator must evaluate the character as representing a morally desirable (or at least preferable) set of traits, in relation to other characters within the fiction."[81] In the case of *Treme* each of the central characters is developed enough, especially by season 3, that both positive and negative traits have been established. The idea of partial allegiance is perhaps the most apt for describing viewers' attachment to characters on *Treme*, as partial allegiance is when "we find ourselves sympathetic to some attitudes and actions of a character, but antipathetic to others."[82] The multitude of alignments and allegiances generated on a show like *Treme* can have significant historical ramifications, demonstrated in the storyline surrounding the development of a new jazz center.

Varied and conflicting viewpoints on the jazz center are provided through the characters, an example of what literary critic Mikhail Bakhtin termed "heteroglossia," a mixture of voices within a text coming from differing classes and groups. There are two main lines of debate: one side of the argument is supplied by central characters Albert Lambreaux and his son Delmond, Black working-to-middle-class New Orleans residents, and the other by two white developers: Will Branson, a new minor character, and C. J. Liguori, a recurring character from season 2, who recruit Nelson Hidalgo, a central character who also first appeared in the second season. Delmond and his father are both brought on as local consultants, with the developers stressing that they want the project to be done correctly, with insight from both the old and the new, making the father and son an ideal team.[83] While the plan on *Treme* is largely fictional, it works to illuminate some of the larger debates surrounding the rebuilding of the city, including corruption, preservation, and commodification. In the days, months, and years after Hurricane Katrina, politicians, ordinary citizens, journalists, commentators, and scholars debated how New Orleans should be rebuilt and what the priorities should be. Racial issues were at the fore, with many holding responsible those in power for trying to remake the city with a diminished African American presence.[84]

Nelson, Liguori, and Branson view the creation of a national jazz center as a positive move for the city, stating the need to "monetize the city's culture" in a smart and effective way. Their argument, advocating the conversion of New Orleans culture into an asset generating money for the city and aiding its recovery, is one with a long history. As the local economy began to decline in the latter half of the twentieth century, the "city pursued a strategy to generate urban revitalisation and bolster the tax base," building new attractions and hosting "mega-events" to draw in both national and international visitors.[85] These endeavors yielded results; in 2003, 8.2 million people visited New Orleans, and one in six of those working in the city relied on the tourism industry for a job.[86] Tourism was central to the New Orleans economy before the storm, and getting tourists and conventions to return would be fundamental to getting the city back on its feet.[87] The tourist sector experienced the greatest job loss (approximately 22,900 jobs) after the storm, a loss in wages of about $382.7 million.[88] The argument presented by Branson, Liguori, and Nelson is in line with a number of objectives of the Bring New Orleans Back Cultural Committee's January 2006 report. This report, created by sixteen prominent New Orleanians, including the jazz musicians Wynton Marsalis and Irvin Mayfield, stressed the link between New Orleans culture and the economic revival of the city, stating at one point that "culture is business in New Orleans."[89] This in itself though is a contentious issue for many locals—the commodification of their culture, their traditions, and their music.

There is a certain irony to the developers' argument for building a national jazz center to celebrate the city's musical heritage when *Treme* shows important heritage sites being left to deteriorate. Although seemingly unrelated to the jazz center storyline, Davis's Musical Heritage Tour, which he starts in season 3, raises questions about the preservation of cultural areas outside the tourist hubs and provides audiences with the necessary history and context to assess the proposed jazz center plan. The tour starts in a laundromat, formerly the home of J&M Recording Studio, before moving on to the dilapidated Eagle Saloon and later Perdido Street, where he points out where Louis Armstrong's house once stood before being demolished in the 1960s. Davis is constantly fielding questions about the neglected state of the buildings, and one guest asks whether "you people actually ever preserve anything of note." The sites that Davis shows the tourists, mostly significant sites in jazz history, lie outside of the Central Business District and French Quarter and are instead located in Black neighborhoods. Anna Hartnell and Lynell L. Thomas both point to the fact that historically the city has relied on Black culture to draw visitors to the city and in the process has commodified and exploited Black culture to suit the expectations of visitors.[90] New Orleans opens up "the experiences of the largely underprivileged for corruption by the privileged," allowing tourists to do so in the "safe" confines of the French Quarter, without having to venture into actual Black neighborhoods where the performers themselves reside and the traditions originated.[91] Jonathan Mark Souther suggests that over the course of the twentieth century, as tourism became ever more important, city leaders gave their blessing to "projects that destroyed neighborhoods whites viewed as blighted, even as they more or less oiled the preservation machine in the French Quarter."[92] While there has been a concerted effort on the behalf of preservation societies to save and recognize Black heritage sites since the 1990s, they have struggled to secure government support and funding. There is clearly a discord between what the developers are proposing—even though their logic is sound—and what Davis's tour scenes reveal about tourism and cultural heritage in the city.

The question the developers ultimately raise with their jazz center plan is, Who are they rebuilding for? Are they rebuilding to better the lives of New Orleans residents, many of whom are poor and Black, or are they rebuilding for tourists to bring back this much-needed economic base? Both are important considerations for the survival and future of the Crescent City, and the show acknowledges that. As the season progresses, though, it becomes increasingly clear that it is only the latter they are concerned with. Albert and Delmond, as native New Orleanians, present an opposing point of view and voice the concerns of local residents. Delmond is initially more optimistic than his father and opines that a jazz center "would be a fine thing if it could happen." He shares a number of ideas with the developers, the most important being that they remove the fence from around Armstrong Park that keeps "all the little Louis Armstrongs out." This one issue is chosen to highlight the opposing points of view of the two sides. Delmond's recommendation to remove the fence echoes views expressed by individual Tremé residents and neighborhood organizations during planning meetings on the future of the park conducted after Hurricane Katrina. Tremé residents charge that the fence was constructed to keep them out of the park, even though much of the Tremé neighborhood was destroyed to create the space. "There are no entrances from three sides of that Park," stated Joyce Williams, a local resident in 2009. "To me it speaks volumes about what you think about the community. The community has no place in that park."[93] People United for Armstrong Park, a local group that has aimed to revitalize the park, conducted surveys of neighboring residents and found a divide between the wishes of those of the French Quarter side of the park and those on the Tremé side regarding the fence.[94] This divide is revealed when Delmond restates his concerns and Nelson and Liguori cite the cost of pulling it down and city issues over "public safety." Albert elaborates that these concerns over safety are really about "Black kids from the neighborhood using the park, which is right on their front steps."

Albert remains skeptical across the season, reflecting a general distrust of the intentions and motivations behind much of the rebuilding of New Orleans. His wariness is augmented by the outcome of the long struggle against the proposed demolition of the "Big Four" public housing complexes, which he has been involved in since season 1. With the council decision to tear down the projects and with the closure of Charity Hospital (both real events), he concludes: "They are trying to wash us away . . . what the storm and them broken levees didn't finish. This is their golden opportunity." Like Albert, during the long proposal and planning phases for rebuilding, many, including professor and community leader Mtangulizi Sanyika, charged white elites with trying to produce "a smaller, leaner, whiter, and richer New Orleans."[95] Alongside such concerns, it was also widely recognized that the process of awarding post-Katrina work contracts was greatly flawed and produced less than exemplary results.[96] Albert boils it down for Delmond and for the audience: "A lot of talk in the press, a lot of money changing hands, few people get rich, but nothing gets done." It is a valid argument given revelations of corruption, favoritism, and profiteering at the local, state, and federal levels. Indeed, the real 2009 proposal for the Municipal Auditorium in Armstrong Park failed to progress, as shortly after its announcement the inspector general urged the city council to reject the plan on the grounds that bid-rigging and favoritism could have been involved in the choice of developer for the project.[97] Delmond eventually comes around to his father's way of thinking, conceding in the season finale: "If it gets built or doesn't get built, ain't never taking that fence down."

Having spent the greatest amount of time developing Delmond and Albert's point of view that the rebuilding of New Orleans is not always in the best interest of the majority, the show ultimately comes down on their side of the argument. However, it is crucial that alternative perspectives are acknowledged and considered. That both arguments are coming from characters that viewers are aligned and allied with gives both sides of the argument weight. It would have been easy to paint the developers as one-dimensional "bad guys" working to exploit the city and line their own pockets. That motivation is certainly acknowledged, but so too is their appreciation of New Orleans's musical heritage and their love for the city. By including Nelson as one of the developers involved in the project, the show makes an attempt to balance the argument of Albert and Delmond. Even though Nelson is constantly hustling to make money off the disaster, he embraces the food, the music, and the people, developing friendly acquaintances with the rest of the main cast of characters. While allegiance is, of course, subjective and not something that can be guaranteed, it is fair to conclude that viewers may share partial allegiance with Nelson's character. Consequently, that side of the debate is fairly represented, more so than if it were given by just Liguori and Branson, minor characters whom viewers may be more likely to dismiss. The debate over the rebuilding of New Orleans as presented in *Treme* demonstrates one of the possible ways history on television can engage with multiple arguments over the course of a serial narrative—by aligning different characters with differing sides of an argument.

Not only can television series present more than one interpretation or viewpoint, but they can also convey the complexities of history, as demonstrated through the New Orleans Affordable Homeownership Program (NOAH) storyline. Again, it is both time and access to a variety of characters that facilitate the construction of a detailed historical representation. There are numerous areas relating to housing that could have been documented on *Treme,* given that housing stock was severely damaged and consequently would be one of the most difficult and costly areas to rehabilitate after flood levels had dropped. As Karl F. Seidman notes, conservative estimates of the damage had "over 134,000 houses and apartments destroyed or damaged by the hurricanes and flooding—71 percent of the city's occupied housing units." Some districts, such as the Lower Ninth Ward, New Orleans East, and Village de L'Est, had even greater percentages of occupied housing units damaged, with 84 percent, 90 percent, and 91 percent, respectively, reported as being in need of repair after the hurricane.[98] Most of *Treme*'s main characters have experienced damage to their homes (and businesses) and have struggled with insurance payouts, rental housing, the Road Home Program, and the desire to rebuild.[99] The Road Home Program, as the "primary grant for rebuilding permanent housing for uninsured or underinsured homeowners," is the most widely known rebuilding program, and much has been published in news reports and scholarly articles on the myriad problems it experienced since its inception.[100] While the Road Home does crop up in a number of storylines, season 3 of *Treme* is focused on exploring a much smaller and less well-known housing scheme. In fact, in scholarship on Hurricane Katrina and the rebuilding of New Orleans, NOAH has thus far garnered little to no attention, making *Treme* one of the first secondary texts to document this sequence of events.

The NOAH program, and the many controversies associated with it, is a tangled and elaborate sequence of events to convey on-screen. NOAH was supposed to help elderly homeowners gut their damaged properties and was promoted in 2006 by Mayor Ray Nagin. The program first hit mainstream news headlines in New Orleans in July 2008 with a news report from 4WWL journalist Lee Zurik. Zurik had been in contact with Karen Gadbois, a concerned private citizen who was one of the first to notice NOAH discrepancies, posting information on her blog *Squandered Heritage.* Gadbois's first post on NOAH, "What Is up with This?" posted June 28, 2008, included photographs

The camera lingers on the New Orleans Affordable Homeownership Program (NOAH) sign outside Desiree's mother's house.

of a property gutted by NOAH that Gadbois also found to be on the imminent health threat list.[101] More posts followed showing houses where NOAH had claimed to have done remediation work but clearly had not, and others revealing houses ineligible to be on NOAH lists. Further reporting by Zurik and the *Times-Picayune* exposed the full extent of the backroom dealing, misappropriation of funds, and general disorganization of city departments, leading to investigations by the FBI and the US Department of Housing and Urban Development. The program was immediately suspended, and corruption charges against a number of contractors were eventually made.

*Treme* details the lead-up to the NOAH scandal through Nelson and Desiree, who encounter the scheme from very different positions. Nelson's side of the story predominantly focuses on the perpetrators, demonstrating how the network of corruption operated. At the start of the season he aggressively pursues his goal of becoming a NOAH contractor, in the process doing his own investigation into another fictional contractor. What Nelson discovers in the course of the investigation mirrors what journalistic probes into NOAH found. Working through a list of the contractor's NOAH properties, he finds one address to be an empty lot, another where the remediation work was actually done by a Milwaukee church group, and another where substandard work was being performed. His investigation is ultimately about getting the "local connect" that he needs to become a contractor for the scheme.

Stacey Jackson, the executive director of NOAH who is referenced in episode 2, awarded the majority of work to a small number of contractors that she had close ties to. Jackson would overpay these contractors using federal funds, and they would send kickbacks to her, securing them more work in the future. Nelson's character is not tarnished by his involvement in the NOAH scheme because, unlike the other contractors, he and his business partner actually do the work they are paid for. This is important for keeping viewers allied, or partly allied, with his character, a central consideration in the jazz center storyline, as previously shown.

Through Desiree an equally important side of the story is explained, that of a victim and the grassroots activism that leads to NOAH's exposure. Desiree sets out to find answers after her mother's house is first assigned as a NOAH property without her permission and then is subsequently demolished without warning. She expresses frustration at the lack of answers when she queries what happened and expresses the emotional toll the demolition had on her family. Through local meetings Desiree connects with Pam, a fictional character, and Gadbois, who explains how and why she is documenting what is happening with the housing stock. Desiree comes to serve as one of Gadbois's volunteers, trawling the streets to check up on the status and condition of empty properties. What is also worth noting is that Desiree is not the hero of this storyline; it is Gadbois and Zurik who are given credit for bringing this issue to the attention of the public. As Simon has stated, in making the show, he and his staff were "actually interested in what happened in New Orleans," making this goal a priority over entertainment, which, in this case, probably would have seen Desiree, a character viewers are allied and aligned with, be the hero of this narrative thread.[102] The NOAH storyline draws to a close in the season finale with the airing of Zurik's first exposé on 4WWL and the press conference Nagin held in response a few days later. The charges, trials, and sentencing of those involved in NOAH stayed in the news until 2014, but given the length of time it took for the legal process to happen, far beyond the time span of the show, it is unsurprising that Simon and Overmyer chose to conclude the NOAH narrative here.

The NOAH storyline appears in nine out of ten season 3 episodes, cropping up in just one beat in episode 8, but seven beats in episode 2. When detailing an issue of relative complexity such as this over an entire season, it can be difficult, especially if viewing during the initial airing with weekly gaps, to completely grasp and understand the intricacies being played out on-screen, even with a shorter season. Likewise, it can be equally difficult to detect the often subtle alternative viewpoints and issues at play in the jazz center storyline upon first viewing. Simon and Overmyer note on the audio commentary that *Treme* is the type of show viewers need to focus on; if they are eating, texting, or doing the laundry, they are going to miss both important plot developments and little nuances.[103] The need for viewers to concentrate is true of many narratively complex shows, whether they are historical in nature or not, and rewatching scenes, episodes, and entire seasons is something dedicated audience members do to make sure they catch each and every nuance.[104] Just as historical monographs may need to be read more than once to fully understand and absorb the intricacies being described and to capture the author's argument, so, too, are multiple viewings of television series often necessary to fully comprehend the history displayed on-screen. Thankfully, rewatching individual episodes and entire seasons is much easier with the advent of streaming, downloading, and DVD and Blu-ray box sets.

## New Orleans Matters: The Series

A work of history, be it written or filmed, should seek to answer historical questions and present a clear and persuasive argument. Narrative histories, such as *Treme,* must fulfil this function too, "even if their arguments, slippery as eels, are difficult to fish out of the oceans of story."[105] Looking at *Treme* as a whole, one can start to identify questions driving the narrative: Why does New Orleans matter? Is it a unique American city? Why should it be rebuilt? Simon and Overmyer pose these questions across the seasons using the techniques discussed previously—conversation, commentary, action, and editing, among others. They also offer an argument in response to these questions: that the culture and traditions of New Orleans are worth saving and that it is "a great city that lives in the imagination of the world."[106] This argument is crafted not only through the characters and their actions but through the detailed exploration and documentation of New Orleans culture. Brass bands, modern and traditional jazz, Mardi Gras, second line parades, and New Orleans cuisine are incorporated throughout the series, while bounce music, jazz funerals, and other elements of New Orleans culture are covered to a lesser extent. Arguably the most prominent and compelling aspect of local culture incorporated by the show is the Mardi Gras Indians.

In keeping with *Treme*'s particular brand of narrative complexity, little context or explanation is initially provided on the Mardi Gras Indians and their traditions, but over the course of three and a half seasons a comprehensive

Albert Lambreaux cuts a striking figure as he emerges out of the dark in *Treme*'s pilot episode.

study emerges. Towards the end of the pilot episode, Albert Lambreaux emerges out of the dark attired in a fantastical full-length orange feathered and beaded costume. He sings that he is the "Big Chief" and dances in the center of the road for an audience of one. No explanation is given for the suit or for what Albert is doing, but it is a visually arresting scene that works to pique the interest of the audience. During the rest of season 1, as Albert attempts to reorganize his tribe, the Guardians of the Flame, the groundwork for understanding the Mardi Gras Indian tradition is laid and subsequent seasons continue to develop and flesh out their cultural practices. In a sense, what is produced is not unlike an example of what anthropologist Clifford Geertz termed "thick description," reworked to fit within the format of a television drama. Thick description is a "technique which interprets an alien culture through the precise and concrete description of particular practices or events," allowing someone outside of the culture the chance to fully understand its function and meaning within a particular society.[107]

Many of the day-to-day practices of Mardi Gras Indians, as well as their rituals, are documented on *Treme*. The show pays particular attention to the creation of Mardi Gras suits, which are made from scratch every year, requiring hundreds upon hundreds of hours of work. In the first season alone there are at least fifteen beats that show Mardi Gras Indians working on or discussing their suits. This trend is continued across every season, with characters often conversing as they sew, stitch, and tack. Most Mardi Gras Indians rely on family and friends to help sew sequins and the many beaded patches that adorn the crown, chest piece, and apron. They frown upon taking shortcuts such as using glue guns rather than needle and thread, reusing patches from old suits, "renting" parts worn previously by other Indians, or paying a third party to create an entire suit.[108] *Treme* conveys each of these points, along with many others, resulting by the end of season 4 in a comprehensive and intricate description of the Mardi Gras suit-making process. Viewers potentially come away from the series with an appreciation and understanding of a cultural tradition, little-known even within the city itself.[109]

However, *Treme* does more than demonstrate *how* New Orleans residents mask Indian; it suggests *why* they do it. The show supplies viewers with some of the meaning behind the tradition so that they will see it as more than just a tourist spectacle of African American men dressing up in extravagant costumes and parading through the streets. Although only a few scholars research Mardi Gras Indians, often disagreeing with one another over the origins of the Mardi Gras Indian tradition, most agree that masking Indian served as a form of resistance during a period when Blacks were being increasingly marginalized.[110] "Masking Indian was a form of protest in a Jim Crow New Orleans," Mitchell Reid explains, "a symbolic rebellion against white institutions."[111] The city has undergone many changes since the 1880s, when Mardi Gras Indians are first said to have appeared, but masking Indian still serves a similar function, allowing working-class African Americans to take control of the streets, assert their power and pride, and galvanize the African American community, which continues to be marginalized and entrenched in poverty. Many of *Treme*'s storylines provide the context needed to understand the meaning behind these rituals. Albert, for example, rails against the New Orleans Housing Authority, which, by keeping the Big Four housing complexes closed, is keeping many poor Blacks from returning to the city. During this conflict he comes into contact with NOPD officers, who not only unlawfully beat him but disrespect his Indian tradition. In response, when released from prison, Albert works furiously on his suit and challenges police emissaries when they come to discuss the continual conflict between police and Mardi Gras Indians: "I understand pride, officers, but it seems that your gang don't think anyone other than themselves is entitled to any." He steps out that St. Joseph's Night, and when surrounded by police, Albert and his tribe stand their ground until the police back down. Through the inclusion of Darius in season 1, a Black youth who starts to work for Albert, viewers also learn how and why this tradition continues to attract new members. Mardi Gras Indians are "viewed as community heroes," and elders pass on their knowledge and moral codes to youths, explains Cherice Harrison-Nelson, who grew up in the tradition.[112] Darius finds himself at a loose end, with little to keep him occupied or out of trouble, until he and his aunt become involved in the Indian tradition. Darius is clearly intrigued, first watching the Indian practices, then learning the moves from Albert and accompanying the tribe out on St. Joseph's Night. Albert is a positive role model for Darius, teaching him the importance of hard work, discipline, and self-respect and instilling in him a desire to mask Indian.

*Treme* captures and conveys the culture of New Orleans, including Mardi Gras Indians, in drawn-out beats that serve no other purpose in the narrative *except* to do just this. Smith identifies this "unhurried plotting" as a hallmark of HBO and other premium subscriber services; inaction is allowed to play out and linger on-screen in order to provide insights into the characters and their environs. Given the flexibility of episode structures (both in terms of length and lack of ad breaks), an alternative to the fast-paced network episode structures has emerged.[113] *Treme* takes particular advantage of this, integrating long scenes involving cooking and music, that highlight the culture of New Orleans and work towards supporting the series' overarching argument. As Martha M. Nochimson argues, "local colour" could have been provided in shorter and fewer scenes. The point is that these long scenes are "not just background; they are foreground. They are as much a part of the spectator's experience as the problems and complications of the numerous plots that crisscross as the season progresses."[114] New Orleans culture is central to the show, a fact that is explicitly elucidated by the characters and their storylines but also more subtly through the long, unanchored beats that document New Orleans culture.

Over the course of four seasons *Treme* reveals itself to be, perhaps, closest to a microhistory in its approach. Microhistory came to the fore in the 1970s with a number of celebrated works published by European scholars, including Emmanuel Le Roy Ladurie's *Montaillou,* a probe into peasant life in the fourteenth century, and Carlo Ginzburg's *The Cheese and the Worms,* a study of a sixteenth-century cheese miller. It is difficult to pinpoint just what microhistory is, as it "eludes formal definition. It is less a method than an orientation, sensibility and aesthetic" that has become popular across the humanities and social sciences.[115] Microhistories can be about places (Montaillou), people (Martin Guerre), or events (the Great Cat Massacre), although they do typically share some traits.[116] What *Treme* shares first and foremost with microhistory is its narrative form. When Lawrence Stone identified a revival of narrative in the late 1970s, many of the authors he cited were pioneers in microhistory or were soon to make their mark in that area. Although "asking new questions, trying out new methods, and searching for new sources," these authors turned away from analytical approaches to history and instead returned to narrative.[117] Such narratives were different to the grand historical narratives of the past in that they engaged in analysis as well as description, were concerned with the thoughts, feelings, and actions of ordinary individuals, and sought to illuminate wider currents in culture and society. Microhistory did not abandon poststructuralist concerns; rather it used narrative as a tool to better address certain areas in history. For Stone and other advocates of microhistory, like István Szijártó, an additional advantage is its appeal to a wider audience.[118] New methods, ideas, and approaches to history can be shared with readers outside the profession who are drawn to an engaging narrative but who would otherwise be put off by analytic and structural histories. This, of course, relates back to Rosenstone's call for historians to connect their work with the wider public. As microhistory demonstrates, narrative does not mean having to sacrifice the key principles of history, but it can popularize it, and the same potential holds true for television serials.

Beyond its basic narrative structure, *Treme* shares a number of features with microhistory, including its focus on ordinary individuals. As Richard D. Brown points out, the goal of microhistories is to access "the experiences and *mentalités* of peasants, giving voice to people who had hitherto been silent."[119] *Treme*'s characters, though invented, are representative of a range of working- and middle-class New Orleans residents, Black and white, and their post-Katrina stories. Although these stories are increasingly being documented in scholarly texts, they have been less visible in mainstream media.[120] Structural histories can often overlook the role of human agency, whereas narrative histories, including microhistory, place individuals and the actions and decisions they make front and center, demonstrating that "people as well as abstract forces shape events."[121] To borrow an example from Peter Burke illustrating the difference between the two approaches, a narrative historian may explain, "The window broke because Brown threw a stone at it," while a structural historian may suggest, "The window broke because the glass was brittle."[122] The characters on *Treme* are not pawns, pushed and pulled by structural forces, their fates determined. Instead, they make conscious decisions and instigate chains of action and reaction. *Treme,* of course, is not unique in this respect, as all histories on-screen necessarily focus on individuals, as established in the previous chapter. What *Treme* also starts to do, though, is explore structures as well as the actions of individuals.

Microhistory is separated from more traditional forms of narrative history by its attempt to link the micro with the macro. For instance, unlike in biography, which emphasizes the extraordinary nature of the subject's life, in microhistory the value of examining a life "lies not in its uniqueness, but in its exemplariness, in how that individual's life serves as an allegory for broader issues affecting the culture as a whole."[123] Microhistories, although focused on a particular person(s), place, or event, aim to illuminate wider issues and structures in society, functioning as a peephole to the past "that reveals a wide expanse of culture and society, not a tiny chamber."[124] *Treme* is a microhistory of New Orleans, or rather, a section of it. The show's characters are "weighted to culture bearers" and "those who supported, patronized or contended with culture bearers," as this was the group Simon and Overmyer were particularly interested in.[125] While *Treme* certainly manages to produce an informative narrative about the varied and colorful cultures of New Orleans, it also evokes the mentalité of post-Katrina New Orleans as a whole (see the disillusionment of residents with authorities in the "episodes" section) and issues plaguing not only the Crescent City but American cities in general.

While New Orleans is viewed as a city of excess, in terms of both positive and negative attributes, many of the issues explored in *Treme* have relevance far beyond the city itself. Colson, for example, struggles to function within the NOPD, coming up against corruption, incompetence, prejudice, excessive violence, and a culture of protectionism. These are not problems unique to the NOPD, as viewers of Simon's other long-running serial *The Wire,* and those who regularly read or watch the news, will know already. Albert's prolonged fight to stop the demolition of the Big Four highlights many of the problems faced by predominantly poor Black inner-city residents and the realities of structural racism in the United States. These storylines, along with many others, "fill out in small-scale and human detail some of the social and cultural features that are otherwise known as generalizations."[126] However, the link between the micro and the macro is not overt in *Treme;* the show relies on viewers' existing knowledge to make these connections. *Treme* is not alone in this, as a common critique of microhistory is the failure to adequately bring the micro and macro together, alongside the potentially distracting intensity of the central narrative that may obscure the larger issues.[127] There are layers to *Treme* that the viewer may or may not comprehend. On one level, it is a story about a group of loosely associated individuals; on another, the stories of those individuals illuminate the history and cultural traditions of the city, both new and old; and on another level, the stories of those individuals also reveal broader issues affecting the United States as a whole. Even if some viewers do miss these broader implications, *Treme* undoubtedly functions as an effective microhistory of the city of New Orleans.

When considering *Treme* as a whole, we must not only look at each of the episodes and all of the seasons, but we must also consider the entire work contained on the DVD or Blu-ray set. If we continue with the analogy between a history book and a historical television series, the DVD or Blu-ray box set is the equivalent of a published book that comes complete with a cover, contents page, footnotes, bibliography, and index. When judging and evaluating history on-screen, scholars and critics should consider the paratexts included on the DVD—making-ofs, featurettes, and audio commentaries—alongside the primary text, just as a complete book is put under review, not only selected sections of it. It is in the paratexts that a number of answers to historians' criticisms of film can be found. Gérard Genette used the term "paratexts" to describe productions like the title page and illustrations that function as a "threshold" or "fringe," packaging the central text and preparing the reader for its consumption. He identified two spatial categories: peritexts, paratexts located within the book; and epitexts, paratexts "located outside the book, generally with the help of the media (interviews, conversations)."[128] These ideas and terms have been adopted by media scholars and applied to different forms of media, including film and television. Jonathan Gray, for example, distinguishes between "entryway paratexts," those that reach individuals before they view the central text, and "in medias res paratexts," those that are consumed during or after the central text. For Gray, the television program itself, while central, is only part of the complete text: paratexts are also intrinsically part of the text too.[129] This is a salient point to consider for history on-screen, with paratexts packaged within the DVD set, most likely consumed in media res, being of particular significance.

Technological innovations have facilitated the proliferation of paratexts and, in turn, their potential in conjunction with history on-screen. From the mid-1970s, VHS allowed viewers to own their own movies and TV shows and watch and rewatch them within the comfort and convenience of their homes. However, VHS was problematic on a number of fronts, with its low picture quality and the limited running time available on each individual VHS, obviously a major obstacle for long-running TV series. The transition to DVD, which began in the mid-1990s, overcame these particular obstacles and enabled the inclusion of multiple supplements and special features far beyond the scope of VHS. The format of DVDs derives from the Criterion Collection laser discs of the mid-1980s. Commentaries with directors and scholars, multiple language options, original aspect ratios, and additional materials such as documentaries appeared on laser discs that were marketed to cinema aficionados.[130] "Most of Criterion's innovations have become adopted, popularized, and extended by mainstream studios," Craig Hight explains, with supplementary material created not only for big-budget, special-effects-driven films but for dramatic and independent films, and now television as well. Hight also points out that digital video, which is much cheaper than traditional film stock, allows for greater documentation of the production process. When digital video is paired with the much greater storage capacity of DVDs, there is "opportunity to develop these materials as a normal part of film production," even for films and shows with a relatively small budget.[131] As noted in the *Deadwood* chapter, HBO invests in such paratexts to promote the showrunner as auteur, but often its series box sets also contain information from a variety of departments and on a spectrum of topics. The fact that special features are cost-effective to create and easily packaged alongside the central work is advantageous for historical productions, as they can potentially serve important functions.

The commentaries and featurettes included on the *Treme* DVDs effectively act as the show's references and footnotes. "The adage that 'you can't footnote a film,' often cited as an objection to the medium by historians who favor written accounts, is challenged through extra features," contends Debra Ramsay. Using the special editions of Clint Eastwood's *Flags of Our Fathers* (2006) and *Letters from Iwo Jima* (2006) as examples, Ramsay argues that the bonus features serve to "contextualize the events within the bigger framework of World War II" while also pointing to "alternative interpretations." She concludes that "some of the old objections to representing the past on screen are diluted by the paratextual material available in extra features."[132] Unlike the footnotes used in scholarly texts, which are (ideally) orderly, precise, and complete, the DVD versions of footnotes are admittedly haphazard, anecdotal, and incomplete. Nonetheless, they still do similar work, informing the viewer as to where some of the information was sourced, pointing towards other avenues for study, explaining why particular interpretive or narrative choices were made and how conclusions were reached, and providing further context to help the audience better understand the central text. As Ramsay further points out, the special features for historical film and television shows often foreground the constructed nature of the work through what she calls "acts of showing." Behind-the-scenes features create "an intense awareness of the processes through which the past is recreated in this medium," meaning that the audience is made aware that what they are watching is not the past as it actually happened but a *representation* of it created by a group of filmmakers.[133]

While many of *Treme*'s bonus features also double as promotional materials, they do still provide useful insights into the creation of the show and the history presented on-screen. The longest special feature included in the season 1 DVD, "Beyond Bourbon Street," contains sections that mix information on the history and culture of New Orleans with discussion on production of the show. It is an "act of showing," one that describes, for example, how the scenes of devastation were re-created five years after the storm, alerting viewers to the constructed nature of what they are seeing on-screen. The section on Mardi Gras Indians employs a number of talking heads, including cast and crew members, a museum historian, and an author. It runs for just under two minutes but manages to touch on the history of the Mardi Gras Indians, cast affiliations with tribes, and the ritual of suit making and Mardi Gras Day. It is helpful in that it fills in potential gaps in viewers' knowledge and also confirms the facts that have been implied across season 1. In this brief segment alone, two related but differing reasons behind the origins of the Mardi Gras Indian masking tradition are provided by two of the commentators. While extremely short, this snippet demonstrates that behind-the-scenes features are a place where debates can be voiced and alternative views expressed, most likely through the employment of several commentators. A ten-minute featurette on the season 2 DVD, as well as repeated references throughout the audio commentaries, provides further information on the Mardi Gras Indians and how they are represented on the show.

Audio commentaries are often the most useful and informative paratexts. There are commentaries for five episodes of season 1, and they are performed by a range of individuals, including creators Simon and Overmyer, actors Khandi Alexander, John Goodman, and Wendell Pierce, episode director Anthony Hemingway, episode writer George Pelecanos, producer Nancy Noble, and TV critic Alan Sepinwall. If we judge these commentaries as historical footnotes, the value varies greatly. The commentary by

Alexander, Pierce, and Sepinwall is often entertaining but yields fewer insights into the reasoning behind choices made in the narrative. It is those by Simon, Overmyer, and Pelecanos that hold the most valuable information, although even these are not exhaustive.[134] The audio commentaries are an excellent forum where the showrunners and writers can provide extra context, offering insights into the people, places, and music being played. This is crucial for a show like *Treme,* which includes many local musicians and public figures generally unknown outside of the city, as well as "insider references" and local vernacular. The audio commentary allows those speaking to alert viewers to creative liberties taken and instances when historical facts have been altered for the sake of the show. The erroneous inclusion of a Hubig's pie in the pilot episode and the change in time frame for the closing of the New Orleans branch of Tower Records are just two examples that are discussed in season 1 commentaries. It is not a perfect science, as some lines of discussion can run so long that what the commentators are discussing has long since passed on-screen, with the consequence that other scenes may be passed over. In theory there is no limit to the number of commentaries that can be included for each episode (some of *Treme*'s episodes include both a commentary by cast and crew and a commentary specially focused on music) meaning that a television show can actually incorporate "footnotes" from many individuals, covering a variety of different topics and issues. Furthermore, when viewers watch an episode with an audio commentary, they have, most likely, watched the episode already and are returning to it to glean additional insights. Watching a second time gives viewers not only extra information from the commentators but a second chance to view the episode with a more critical eye, without being focused on following the narrative.

The fact is, however, that paratexts such as making-ofs, audio commentaries, and behind-the-scenes featurettes are becoming increasingly rare—or aren't conveniently packaged together with the show itself. Watching a television series on DVD or Blu-ray is, perhaps, the ideal way to engage with history on television, as the box set comes complete with the supplementary material that complements and expands on the primary text. All the materials are packaged together, making it easy for interested viewers to segue from the episodes to the special features that build upon and expand the central narrative (although many viewers will choose to watch only the show itself). The reality is, though, that DVD and Blu-ray are already almost redundant, with streaming currently the most popular way to watch TV. Certain streaming platforms, such as Netflix, rarely produce special features for films and TV shows, which means that this element of the history-on-screen experience is missing for some historical TV narratives.[135] While this does not negate a historical series that comes without paratexts, it is surely sad to see such potential go unfulfilled. HBO is currently continuing to release DVD and Blu-ray sets complete with special features (although the number of special features included does appear to be dwindling), and it is also releasing other supplementary materials, such as podcasts, online.[136] Like audio commentaries, podcasts give showrunners, cast, and crew the opportunity to supplement the on-screen narrative, albeit in a purely aural form (which brings its own advantages and disadvantages). Apple TV Plus and Amazon Prime are streaming services that are producing special features and bonus content, although the quality and quantity vary greatly from show to show (and even season to season). Paratexts are yet another aspect of the TV industry that is in flux, and it remains to be seen what approach will be embraced by audiences and streaming services in the long run.[137] *Treme* is not the HBO show with the most extensive supplementary material created and included on the DVD sets, but even its modest extras demonstrate the potential of special features.[138] What is vital is that paratexts remain accessible for those who are inclined to pursue the topic further and who want to question the central text and need a starting point to do so.

## Conclusion

Simon explained in an editorial for the *Times-Picayune* that the show used "the post-Katrina experience to create a narrative about some people" and that although it was set in a real time and place, it was a fiction—a television drama.[139] I believe this undersells what *Treme* and other historical television dramas are able to achieve.[140] Although dealing with predominantly invented characters, *Treme* can be classified as a narrative history—or, more precisely, a microhistory—that brings to light both the cultural practices of New Orleans and difficulties facing residents in the wake of Katrina. As Burke argues, authors of fictional works, particularly historical novels, have long managed to produce written works fulfilling the goal of new narrative historians to "juxtapose the structures of ordinary life to extraordinary events." Burke suggests that historians would do well to learn from novelists such as Shimazaki Tōson and Leo Tolstoy, but acknowledges that historians have a handicap that fiction writers do not: they are not as free to invent and thus "they are unlikely to be able to condense the problem of an epoch into a story about a family, as novelists have often done."[141] However, based on the findings of the previous chapter—that invented characters have the greatest potential in history on-screen—it is acceptable and indeed advantageous to create and employ invented characters in a microhistory on-screen. Likewise, using invented characters potentially makes it easier to present alternative sides to an argument by utilizing alignment and allegiance as demonstrated in the "Rebuilding New Orleans: The Season" subsection. This is not to advocate abandoning the use of real figures in history in favor of invented ones; rather, I would like to suggest that this level of invention, given the constraints of the medium, is a useful tool for crafting complex historical narratives that does not necessarily detract from these narratives' integrity. Simon is correct in stating that *Treme* cannot and should not "supplant the journalism, the documentarianism or, ultimately, the historical scholarship that has been generated and continues to be generated about post-Katrina New Orleans," but it should be recognized that it is a valuable part of the discourse and has equal historical value.[142]

This analysis of how a historical narrative is constructed in serial television only starts to scratch the surface of what is possible. While the basic units of beats, episodes, seasons, series, and box sets are fairly standard, how a story is developed across each can differ dramatically. *Treme* offers an example of a sprawling ensemble series that generally follows a linear chronological path, but one only has to look at a selection of other narratively complex shows to see how narrative is being experimented with. *Damages* (FX, 2007–10; Audience Network, 2011–12) uses flash-forwards in each of its seasons to create mystery and suspense, while, in its final season, *Boardwalk Empire* employs substantial flashbacks to Nucky Thompson's childhood and the start of his career in order to bring the series to a satisfying conclusion. *Hannibal* (NBC, 2013–15) blurs the lines between the real world and dream world of the narrative, and Fox's action series *24* (2001–10) uses a "real-time" structure. Showtime drama *The Affair* (2014–19) often splits its episodes into two, telling the story from one protagonist's point of view, then switching and replaying the same set of events from the other protagonist's point of view, complete with inconsistencies and variations. A similar setup used for historical series could explore issues relating to the role of memory in history, the unreliability of sources and bias. Not all these narrative structures, or the many others that currently exist on television, will result in useful history on-screen, but it does show that there are exciting new avenues to be tested and pursued.

As well as changes to the industry that have opened up the possibilities of constructing historical narratives on-screen, one other aspect must be considered—how changing viewing practices may affect audiences' engagement with them. Does the shift from appointment viewing (one episode per week, as per a traditional linear TV schedule) to binge-watching (multiple episodes in a single sitting) have an effect on how historical narratives are processed and understood? Scholars are now starting to examine the phenomenon of binge-watching and its implications. Thomas J. Billard's experimental study, for example, found that the prosocial effects of appointment viewing a TV show were longer lasting than the prosocial effects of binge-watching.[143] Similarly, a study by Jared C. Horvath et al. concluded that those who watched a TV series weekly had better memory of what they had watched when tested months later than those who had binge-watched the series.[144] While this is a very new field and there have not been any studies that focus particularly on the differences between binge-watching and appointment viewing historical TV series, we can tentatively conjecture that watching via appointment viewing results in the historical message remaining with the audience member for longer. For a show like *Treme,* weekly breaks also give the audience time to sit and stew over the complex plot points and research any elements of New Orleans culture or politics that may have piqued their interest. This is not to say that there is a *right* and *wrong* way to consume historical series, but it is an evolving aspect of the televisual experience that deserves consideration. HBO continues to release new shows in weekly installments, meaning that audiences can engage via appointment viewing or may binge-watch at a later date on a streaming service or with a box set.

There still exists, of course, a number of potential problems with rendering history in serial form, even when produced by premium subscription services such as HBO. One key concern is unpredictable length and the possibility that a narrative may be cut short. Films, miniseries, and the increasingly popular anthology series (such as FX's *American Crime Story,* 2016–) do not share this problem, as they are generally conceived and produced as an individual unit. Serial television, though, can be canceled at any moment, leaving the story without a satisfactory conclusion and without the show's creators fully achieving what they set out to do. Although HBO co-president Plepler stood behind *Treme* and its very modest ratings when season 3 was announced, HBO was only willing to continue the show for so long. The fourth and final season of *Treme* was "half a loaf," as Simon put it, five episodes rather than the usual ten or eleven. Simon was grateful that HBO executives fought to provide a budget for a shortened season 4, but he admits that "every character suffered a little bit" by the writers' need to speed up and condense each of the character arcs.[145] "It's not an ideal solution," concluded Sepinwall, "but given the ratings for *Treme* relative to HBO's other original series, the existence of any kind of fourth season is something to be celebrated."[146] Simon and Overmyer were lucky that they were able to produce this "half loaf" and wrap up a number of loose ends and bring the series to its conclusion. Other shows, such as *Deadwood*, were not so lucky, and the narrative was left open for thirteen years, like a book abruptly ending after one of the body chapters. On the other hand, some series, including *Boardwalk Empire*, run long enough that the creators are able to choose when and how to end the series without having to rush or force a conclusion.

Every medium has its drawbacks, but in the case of television serials the positives far outweigh the negatives. Serials offer a unique form for engaging with history on-screen, and the advent of narratively complex television has opened up even greater possibilities. As Mittell points out, writers and showrunners "embrace the broader challenges and possibilities for creativity in long-form series, as extended character depth, ongoing plotting, and episodic variations are simply unavailable options within a two-hour film."[147] It is for similar reasons that historians should also embrace the long-form serial. Not only does the longer running time set it apart and provide greater opportunities, but changes in audience expectation and developments in style and aesthetics open up new avenues for presenting history on-screen. Ambiguity, subtlety, unresolved endings, and often a move away from clichés and standard TV tropes are hallmarks of narratively complex television. There does not have to be a single hero, a tidy (happy) ending, and answers provided to every question in serial television. While it is impossible to make accurate generalizations about the reactions of the viewing public or sweeping generalizations about the different kinds of narrative complexity employed in post-network quality TV dramas, it is fair to say that narratively complex serials allow for a more multifaceted rendering of history on-screen.

4

# Listening to History

## *Band of Brothers*

Television (and film) is generally thought of as a visual medium, and, indeed, up until now this book has in many respects focused on the image on-screen: the mise-en-scène in *Deadwood,* visual signifiers of character in *Boardwalk Empire,* and visual icons of New Orleans culture in *Treme.* Many of the names and phrases assigned to the two media—television, motion pictures, moving pictures, video, film, silver screen—include reference to the visual without acknowledging the aural aspect of the television or motion picture experience.[1] "This neglect," Herbert Zettl fears, "may have caused some people to believe that sound is either a less important or nonessential adjunct of the visual fields of video and film. Far from it. Sound is indispensable to video and film communication."[2] Although Zettl, like many others, singles out the importance of sound in film, it is equally important to TV. Television, too, is an audiovisual medium, and viewers' understanding and enjoyment of a narrative involve both visual and aural senses.[3]

Sound is undoubtedly an integral part of the ten-episode World War Two miniseries *Band of Brothers.* This is not to say that sound has not been crucial in all the series under discussion, but war, much like science fiction, is a genre in which the soundtrack often stands out. Sound is integral to all film and TV experiences but can escape the notice of viewers, who tend to be drawn to visual spectacle. It can take a resounding soundtrack to make audiences pay attention, and the often unrelenting and inescapable soundtrack of *Band of Brothers* does just that. Produced by Tom Hanks and Steven Spielberg, the series was an unofficial follow-up to *Saving Private Ryan* (1998), starring the former and directed by the latter. *Ryan* clearly served as a blueprint for the series; not only does it utilize the same "filmmaking language," but it shares the film's interpretation of the American experience during World War Two and focus on ordinary American men.[4] The sound for *Ryan,* designed by Gary

Rydstrom, as well as the music, composed by John Williams, also clearly influenced the sound team working on *Band of Brothers.* Based on the book by Stephen Ambrose, the series follows the men of Easy Company, 506th Regiment, 101st Airborne, from their training in the United States through D-Day, Operation Market Garden, and the Battle of the Bulge, to the capture of the Eagle's Nest at Berchtesgaden. Most memorable are the intense combat scenes like that at Brécourt Manor in "Part Two: Day of Days," when the soundtrack positions viewers right in the center of the action. Sequences such as these are balanced with quieter moments, when Michael Kamen's musical score is subtly employed to underline often complicated feelings of victory and defeat experienced by an individual soldier or by the company at large.

An analysis of the sonic elements in *Band of Brothers* demonstrates that the soundtrack is an incredibly intricate construct that is crucial to the history-on-screen experience. The music, sound effects, and human voices all create meaning and contribute to building and shaping the series' historical interpretation. As with the visual elements discussed in the previous chapters, aural history benefits from the longer running time and flexi-narrative structure of TV. More speaking roles (almost five hundred in this series), more battles involving various weaponry, and more opportunity to experiment with how sound is employed across individual episodes result in an incredibly dense and complex sonic narrative. Furthermore, what sound contributes to the historical narrative has been strengthened by recent developments in audio and home-theater technology that allow for crisp, clear, multilayered, and immersive sounds.

Once again, HBO has been at the forefront of these new technologies and has not shied away from spending a premium to both acquire the content it desires and to maintain its "cinematic" production values. *Band of Brothers* was a $125 million production, a sum almost unheard of in 2001 for a ten-part series. "I'm not saying they didn't bat an eye," Hanks stated when discussing the budget. "Oh, they did bat an eye. But the reality is this was expensive. You have to have deep pockets. And HBO has deep pockets."[5] Jeff Bewkes, then chairman of HBO, insisted publicly that HBO took on the project because they "could treat this story in a way no other medium could treat it" and because "no one else could have given it this level of authenticity."[6] The large budget and the desire for authenticity shaped not only the mise-en-scène but the sound design as well. Mike Dowson, an experienced rerecording mixer at Shepperton Studios, explained that "TV productions don't have the same kind of money as feature films do." "However, on this particular project," he continued, "HBO has spent a lot of money and time, and as far as I can tell, they're very keen to promote 5.1 and high-definition in the home."[7] On this point HBO was in agreement with Hanks and Spielberg, who insisted from the get-go that the series be mixed in surround sound.[8] While 5.1 surround sound mixing has since become standard for both cable and broadcast networks, in 2001 only a limited number of shows were mixed this way. HBO began mixing and broadcasting many of its drama series—*The Sopranos, The Wire, Six Feet Under* (2001–5), *Carnivàle* (2003–5), and, of course, *Band of Brothers*—in 5.1 Dolby Digital surround sound before it became standard practice.[9]

Film and television sound is often considered to be a technical aspect of production, but it is an area with incredible scope for creativity. As Vincent LoBrutto points out, there is a certain illusion when watching film and television that the sound "has been captured by a single, magical microphone which records the dialogue, sound effects, and music on-set in perfect balance." In reality, though, "just as every visual component in a film is designed and executed by the writer, director, cinematographer and design team, each single sound in a film is carefully conceived, chosen, recorded, edited, and mixed by an array of sound artists and technicians."[10] Those in charge of sound must not only gather or create all of the sounds—capturing them live on set, recording out in the field, utilizing sound libraries, producing Foley effects, and manipulating sound electronically—they must also mix all the sounds together so they work in harmony and add to, rather than detract from, the central narrative.[11] Rydstrom explains that sound is about more than adding the "obvious" and matching up what the audience members hear with what they see on-screen; he chooses sounds based on whether or not they "are appropriate to the drama of that scene."[12] "You've got to be very selective," states fellow sound designer Ben Burtt, "because you can't hear everything that's on the screen."[13] Trying to incorporate every sound that might be heard in a given environment would create a cluttered soundscape in which the sounds become muddied, so chosen sounds should serve a purpose in helping to tell the story and enhance the drama.

Sound, or aurality, has been a relatively obscure area in historical studies until recently. George H. Roeder Jr. proclaimed in the mid-1990s that "ours is a nearly sense-less profession," and outlined how smells, tastes, tactile sensations, and sounds were generally missing from the work of historians.[14] One of the potential difficulties of studying sound is the "lack of hard evidence," especially before the late nineteenth century when sounds started to be recorded. Historians must largely rely upon written sources to get both a sense of the sounds of the past and to understand the significance of those sounds to the people experiencing them. Even when sounds have been recorded, they remain elusive to an extent; "sound recording allows for the temporal dislocation of a sound from its time and place or origin, but does not facilitate the ability to do the auditory equivalent of sustaining the gaze on an image for as long or as short as one desires."[15] There is, however, currently an emerging interdisciplinary field that takes "the culture, consumption, and politics of sound seriously" and places sound firmly at the center of its scholarship.[16] Historians are very much a part of this movement, with key works authored by Alain Corbin, Richard Cullen Rath, and Mark M. Smith, and the appearance of collections like *Hearing History, The Auditory Culture Reader,* and a special issue of *American Quarterly* on "Listening to American Studies."[17] It is not only historians, though, who have been slow to recognize the importance of sound.

While history on-screen has become an increasingly popular area of scholarship, it is only recently that the specific role and function of sound in historical film and television series started to garner significant attention. Many works simply overlook sound, giving it an occasional mention, particularly the music tracks, without analyzing in-depth what each of the different elements of the soundtrack has to offer. Robert Rosenstone is one scholar who does regularly acknowledge the importance and centrality of sound in the creation of history on-screen. He states that dialogue in the sound film is a "crucial element that allows us to understand characters and their motivations, situations, particular events and their course, outcomes and impact."[18] More importantly, he often identifies the soundtrack as part of what makes history on-screen a unique way of experiencing the past. In Rosenstone's most recent edited collection, J. E. Smyth and Guy Westwell both delve into more detailed analysis of elements of the soundtrack—sound bridges in the case of the former and sound montage and design in the case of the latter—and look at how the sounds affect or shape the history being presented on-screen.[19] Alison Landsberg is, perhaps, the scholar who has paid greatest attention to sound and the part that it plays in "soliciting complicated forms of engagement" in historical films and television shows. In *Engaging the Past,* Landsberg focuses her analysis of *Deadwood* on the soundscape, particularly the human voice and human sounds, and the way these sounds encourage empathetic engagement with the past.[20] Winfried Pauleit's, Rasmus Greiner's, and Mattias Frey's articles from 2018 delve deeply into the construction and role of historical film sound and signal a promising new level of attention in this area.[21]

That history-on-screen scholars have been slow to focus their attention on sound is unsurprising given that it has also long been a subject on the periphery of film and television studies. Gianluca Sergi identifies a clear "bias towards the image" and argues that "the majority of scholars and critics have by and large remained impervious to all things sound for nearly a century."[22] Although film sound does not receive the same level of attention as other areas of film studies, there has always been a small group dedicated to exploring this topic, including John Belton, Elizabeth Weis, Rick Altman, and Michel Chion, whose work in particular has been central to the development of film sound studies. Similar sentiments to Sergi's can be found in nearly all works on film sound, although many of the most recent acknowledge an increased interest in the subject and a steady appearance of new works (mirroring and overlapping with increased interest from other disciplines in the social sciences and humanities). New collections such as *Lowering the Boom* and *Sound and Music in Film and Visual Media,* as well as individual works by Sergi, Mark Kerins, K. J. Donnelly, and William J. Whittington, explore the full scope of the soundtrack, not only music and dialogue, the two areas that have received the most attention. Alongside these sound histories, theoretical approaches, and case studies are a range of practical guides to film and television sound that cover the entire process, from preproduction through to final rerecording mixes.[23]

Except for these more technical guides, the majority of scholarship focuses on sound in theatrical films, not on television programs.[24] As briefly discussed, in many fields sound has "arrived," yet, as Michele Hilmes points out, TV sound remains "neglected in academic study."[25] Synchronized recorded sound was introduced in the cinema, and the first experimentations with on-screen sound and sound technology took place in movies and movie theaters. Correspondingly, most of the literature is centered on feature film and its exhibition in public spaces. Major milestones in the history of sync sound have been fairly well documented and analyzed, including the 1927 release of the first ever talkie, *The Jazz Singer* (Crosland); Disney's *Fantasia* (Algar et al., 1940), which, with its specially created "Fantasound," was the first real attempt at cinema surround sound; *Star Wars* (Lucas, 1977), a film with a highly innovative soundtrack that showcased the potential of Dolby Stereo; and the rise of digital surround sound in the 1990s with blockbusters like *Jurassic Park* (Spielberg, 1993). Theatrical films are just that—they are produced knowing that they are going to be screened in theaters equipped with surround sound, allowing the audience to experience the full impact of the soundtrack.[26] Feature films have traditionally been "mixed down" for release on home video, simplifying the soundtrack so it functions more effectively for the standard two-channel TV set.

Sound in the home, however, is now in a state of flux. The changes brought about by DVD and Blu-ray technology, discussed in the previous chapter, also extend to sound. DVDs, with their greater data capacity, allow "higher fidelity sound with more audio channels and a richer set of mixes, so that it has become standard for films to be released encoded in 5.1 sound whenever appropriate."[27] More and more households are also investing in home theater systems that allow them to experience sound through a number of discrete channels, similar to how sound would be heard in a cinema. A 5.1 home theater package includes a center speaker, left and right front speakers, left and right surround speakers, and a subwoofer to be arranged at various points around the viewing room. This conversion to surround sound in the home is by no means total. Mark Kerins notes that although high definition television takes 5.1 surround sound as its audio standard, many people still "hear those mixes downconverted to two-channel stereo for playback over their television speakers, making it difficult" for TV networks "to incorporate sound design as an integral part of their shows' aesthetics."[28] That television shows have previously been "conservative" in their use of sound, in part due to this discrepancy in technology and in part due to smaller budgets, partially accounts for the focus on sound in feature film.[29] *Band of Brothers,* though, shaped by HBO's generous budget and the network's commitment to cutting-edge technology, demonstrates that sound produced for television can be just as complex and integral to TV as sound is for feature film. Dowson explains that he did not make concessions for the reductive qualities of TV sound when producing the final sound mix for *Band of Brothers.* "I want it to sound as good as I can make it," he stated, even though he was well aware of the fact that not everyone watching would be able to hear it as it was intended to be heard.[30]

Screen sound can be broadly separated into three main categories: music, sound effects, and speech. The following sections address each of these areas in order to better understand what sound contributes to the narrative and history on-screen. The first section on music establishes the historical interpretation of World War Two that *Band of Brothers* puts forward. Music plays a central role in fashioning the series' historical interpretation, which is further developed by other aspects of the soundtrack. Focusing particularly on the "Main Titles" theme and the music from "Part 9: Why We Fight," this section examines how music is used to help audiences capture the preferred meaning of a text. Different melodies and musical themes are employed to convey the feelings experienced by the men of Easy Company and to elicit similar emotions in the audience. Indeed, sound contributes just as much to the various elements that make up the "feel of the past" as the image track does, with music playing a significant role in influencing and heightening emotions. Sound effects, probably the most overlooked aspect of the soundtrack, or at least the most taken for granted in history-on-screen scholarship, create sonic textures that affect viewers in a bodily way, especially in a home theater environment. Building on the ideas in chapter 1, this section considers the process behind the creation of the sound effects track and the historical work that goes into it. Sound effects (as well as the voice) again raise interesting questions about the role of invention in history on-screen, with many of the sounds of the past recreated and invented using sources of sound far removed from the original. The final section on speech looks less at what is said than at how things are said. How lines of dialogue are articulated by actors and how the speech is recorded and mixed on the soundtrack help to shape viewers' understanding of the characters and are yet more elements that affect the development of allegiance. Rather than analyzing only one element of the soundtrack, or addressing different sound elements haphazardly, this chapter methodically, although not exhaustively, explores the role that sound plays in the creation of history on-screen. It is difficult to analyze a TV series soundtrack, as they are mixed in numerous ways—there is often a 5.1 master, a Lt/Rt master, and a mono master—and so not all viewers will hear the show the same way, depending on how and where they are watching it. This particular study of sound in *Band of Brothers* has been based on its original 5.1 mix.

## Anchoring the Image in Meaning: Music

Music has always been a part of the film and television experience. Whether this is because music and drama have always gone hand in hand dating back to Greek theater, or because of more practical reasons (such as covering the sound of noisy projectors and audiences during the silent era), music, in its various forms, plays a significant role in how on-screen narratives are shaped and understood. As film sound scholar Claudia Gorbman notes in her seminal text, music occupies a unique position because it "takes many more liberties with the diegesis than does the image track" and has a certain flexibility within the "realist" televisual narrative.[31] The image track is often composed and edited so as not to alert viewers to the constructed nature of what they are watching, and even within the soundtrack itself dialogue and sound effects are generally designed to maintain the illusion of reality. The nondiegetic voiceovers provided by Richard "Dick" Winters, Carwood Lipton, and David Kenyon Webster in *Band of Brothers* are considered "narrative intrusions," while the nondiegetic music that accompanies many scenes is not.[32] Music is a "subliminal signal for most audience members" and "is not apprehended with the same semantic precision as dialogue or even sound effects."[33]

The music in *Band of Brothers* helps to tell the story by enhancing the emotional tone of individual scenes while also establishing and fortifying the series' historical interpretation of World War Two as the "Good War." The majority of the music is nondiegetic, with only very rare instances of diegetic music. Diegetic music (just like all diegetic sounds) emanates from within the storyworld, while nondiegetic music comes from outside the storyworld and is unheard by the characters. All of the nondiegetic music for *Band of Brothers* was scored for the series by Michael Kamen, who worked extensively on film and television scores throughout his career.[34] Each episode opens with the "Main Titles" theme and closes with a different arrangement of the same music. Within the episodes a variety of music is employed; some themes, such as "Winters on Subway," only appear in one episode ("Part 5: Crossroads"), whereas other pieces of music are used at numerous points throughout the series.[35] How music is employed in each of the episodes also differs greatly: there is only one instance of nondiegetic music in "Part 6: Bastogne," perhaps because of the exceptionally bleak and stark tone of the episode, while in "Part 10: Points," there are ten instances of music in order to help unify what is otherwise a less focused and more sprawling narrative.

To fully understand and appreciate the role that music plays in *Band of Brothers,* we need to briefly explore the historical interpretation the show presents and how the series fits into wider popular representations of the war. The Second World War occupies a special place in American public memory; it is remembered as the Good War, fought by the "greatest generation." Amongst other things, these myths stress the unity, sacrifice, and heroism of the American people, both on the home front and the battlefront.[36] They are based in truth, but are problematic largely because of what they omit. According to Michael C. C. Adams, Americans looking back on World War Two "have come to see the war years as a golden age, an idyllic period when everything was simpler and a can-do generation of Americans solved the world's problems."[37] Film, and later television, played a significant role in shaping the Good War and greatest generation myths, which are constantly changing and adapting with the passage of time. Many modern representations choose not to stress the grand ideals of God, freedom, and the American way, as many 1940s films did, instead focusing on the courage and bravery of the average American soldier.

World War Two, and particularly the World War Two combat film, has remained a staple of Hollywood, although there have been ebbs in their production and popularity at times. The most recent cycle of World War Two films was in large part sparked by the popularity of *Saving Private Ryan.* Historian John Bodnar argues that despite the graphic depiction of war, the film is ultimately a "retelling of how the Americans won with daring and ingenuity" that supports the Good War narrative of "victory and virtue."[38] "The fact that combat was so frightening," he states, "serves mainly to reinforce our admiration for these soldiers and their gallantry."[39] Similarly, Tanine Allison has identified how Hollywood's digital revolution has contributed to the evolution of the Good War myth. Films like *Ryan* self-consciously re-create the look of World War Two documentary footage to generate nostalgia and employ visual effects to enhance the violence. The focus in these recent war films is on the extreme pain and suffering experienced by American victim-heroes; the camera lingers on spilled intestines, missing limbs, and spurting blood.[40]

Many of the films that followed *Ryan,* including *U-571* (Mostow, 2000) and *Pearl Harbor* (Bay, 2001), present similar interpretations of the American war experience, although others, such as *The Thin Red Line* (Malick, 1998) and *Flags of Our Fathers* (Eastwood, 2006), complicate and challenge the Good War and greatest generation myths. *Band of Brothers* fits into the former group and closely parallels the interpretation of the war presented in *Ryan.* Anne Mork concludes that the series "clearly confirms the myth of 'the Greatest Generation' by its overwhelming positive portrayal of Easy Company and the special bond the soldiers shared."[41] While this is potentially a problematic and simplistic historical interpretation, the intent of this chapter is not to critique the historical argument of *Band of Brothers;* rather, it is to examine the role that sound plays in shaping this particular interpretation.

Even before the episode proper begins, it is evident that *Band of Brothers* will adhere to the Good War and greatest generation myths. Following the first montage of veteran interviews, the two-minute-and-fourteen-second opening title sequence starts, effectively setting the tone for the entire series. The opening credit sequence, which for most television shows almost always involves both a set of edited images and theme music, serves both phatic and connotative functions. In terms of the former, the theme music signals the start of a program and draws viewers to the TV and, along with the closing credit music (which may or may not be the same every week, depending on the show), acts "as a sort of sonic frame or curtain by demarcating and separating the diegetic text from the extradiegetic televisual flow."[42] This is arguably less important these days, when viewers do not have to settle in to watch a show when it first airs on television but can instead choose to stream, download, DVR, or watch on DVD or Blu-ray at their own convenience, outside of the televisual flow. The theme music, however, through its repetition at the beginning of each episode, still forms a "phatic semiotic bond with the program" so that the theme music and the television program are intrinsically bound together in the audience's mind.[43]

Perhaps most crucially, the theme music serves a connotative function, helping the viewers to interpret the images they are seeing on-screen and guiding them towards the preferred meaning of the text. Music for film and television cannot be analyzed in isolation but instead must be considered in conjunction with the other sensory channels: written language, spoken dialogue, sound effects, and the image track, which ideally work together to create a message or meaning that is comprehensible to the audience.[44] "Music," Ronald Rodman asserts, "functions by combining or *correlating* with the other sensory channels to produce a preferred meaning."[45] How audiences interpret and understand a television text is not something that can be guaranteed with any certainty: education, personal experience, and varying cultural, ethnic, and social backgrounds can result in differing readings of the same text.[46] Music, though, is a tool that can be used to promote the intended meaning of a text. Borrowing from Roland Barthes, Gorbman uses the term "ancrage" to describe how music anchors the image in meaning, supplying "information to complement the potentially ambiguous diegetic images and sounds."[47] This ancrage applies to music employed during the episodes, as well as the theme music that plays over the opening credits. Of course, music interpretation is subjective too, and it is impossible to definitively state how people will respond to and perceive individual pieces of music. However, as Anahid Kassabian notes, in analyzing film and TV music, "we can at least begin by considering the usual or dominant meanings."[48]

Music for film and television draws upon common musical tropes or codes that viewers will be familiar with. For music to be able to communicate with a wide range of viewers and reinforce the desired meaning, "it must express a musical language that is understood by and accessible to the recipients of that text."[49] Gorbman argues that the institutionalization of musical meaning occurred well before the coming of sound in film. Meanings were "inherited from a long European tradition whose most recent forebears included theatrical, operatic, and popular music of the latter-nineteenth century."[50] These were solidified and reinforced during the silent era with the publication of popular lexicons such as Erno Rapee's *Encyclopedia of Music for Pictures* (1925), which included categories such as "Sinister," "Oriental," and "Wedding."[51] Audiences have a competence in decoding musical codes that is learned through experience. "As with language and visual image," Kassabian states, "we learn through exposure what a given tempo, series of notes, key, time signature, rhythm, volume, and orchestration are meant to signify."[52] Drawing upon a study undertaken by Philip Tagg and Bob Clarida, Kassabian concludes that in "mass-market narrative film music, correspondence between producer's intention and consumer's reading, between transmission and reception, between encoding and decoding, and among decodings, is high."[53] Music, then, is used in film and television to encourage audiences to interpret and understand the text in a specific way, and it achieves this through employing established and familiar musical codes.

The theme music and opening credit sequence in *Band of Brothers* signal not only a show that fits within the war genre but one which will focus on the heroic actions of the soldiers and the hardships they faced while fighting for the greater good. The image track is made up of numerous short clips and still images from the series, often arranged to give a time-lapse-like effect. These scenes and images have been manipulated for color, mirroring the look of the episodes proper, but intensified here to an even greater degree.[54] Some images are washed in an icy-blue hue, while others are saturated in olive or ochre tones. Unlike the main narrative, which has sharp, clear visuals, many of the images in the opening sequence have been given a soft-focus or gritty look. The impression is of looking at old photographs or camera footage, enhanced by the creases, lines, scratches, and textures that have been imposed over the image. The music itself is performed by a choir and orchestral strings, with the choir adding a human expressive element and the strings recalling late Romantic classical music. The piece centers mostly around the F-major chord for the bass movement, with the choir and orchestral strings adding and weaving melodies on top to create additional upper chord extensions. The shift from F-major to a D-minor chord towards the end of the piece results in a melancholy conclusion to the "Main Titles" theme.

This type of music for a Good War and greatest generation interpretation may, at first, appear surprising. Combat films of the World War Two period, and many subsequent war films that presented US actions in a positive light, often contained heavy drum beats, marchlike meters, and lots of brass instrumentation. But, as Wesley J. O'Brien demonstrates in his study of combat film soundtracks, scoring practices are not static; they change and evolve. Focusing on recent World War Two films like *Saving Private Ryan* and *Flags of Our Fathers,* O'Brien contends, much like Bodnar, that common-man heroism and bravery are the focus of these films. *Band of Brothers* also fits into this new category that expresses a very particular, and very narrow, understanding of World War Two. Gone from these films are the big brassy scores featured in early World War Two combat films, replaced "with a smaller score to signify smaller (though not less significant) ideals."[55] There are "representations of soldiers ideologically motivated" in films like *Ryan,* states O'Brien; "however, those ideals are personal—even selfish—not uniformly patriotic."[56] The men in *Band of Brothers* do not fight for the "grand ideals" of freedom and democracy, as many of the soldiers in 1940s combat films were likely to proclaim. Instead, they fight for their family, for the chance to simply go home again and be with loved ones, and, of course, for the men next to them. The show's "Main Titles," as well as much of the rest of the score, manages to capture this pathos.

Replacing Kamen's main theme music with another piece of music could create an entirely different (and inaccurate) impression of the series. In *Unheard Melodies,* Gorbman explores how playing different music to the same scene from the film *Jules and Jim* (Truffaut, 1962) has an enormous impact on how viewers may read and understand the scene.[57] A similar experiment can be undertaken with the opening credit sequence of *Band of Brothers.* A traditional bombastic military score with lots of brass instrumentation would suggest a more overtly patriotic series, in which the protagonists regularly espouse the moral righteousness of their crusade and the inhumanity of their opponent. Or, set to Samuel Barber's beautiful yet somber "Adagio for Strings" (used in the Vietnam War film *Platoon* [Stone, 1986]), the series would take on a much more despairing and tragic tone, with no signs of hope or salvation. Elements of patriotism, righteousness, despair, and tragedy are evident in the series, but these themes do not adequately capture its main message. In many ways Kamen's title score, and the new breed of combat film scoring more generally, blends components from both, bringing together full orchestral minor-key music that evokes lament with familiar military musical codes. The theme music, alongside the images that appear in the opening sequence, form a microcosm of what *Band of Brothers* is about. Even without watching any of the actual series, it is possible to get a sense of the historical interpretation it is presenting—that war is a terrible thing but that those American men who fought in World War Two rose to the challenge, conducted themselves admirably, and became heroes.

That audiences have been able to accurately "read" the music and extract the desired meaning can be evidenced by the myriad reviews of the music available on Amazon. These reviews, often detailed and comprehensive (some run over five hundred words), demonstrate that audiences have understood the intended meaning, both of the series as a whole and of Kamen's music. It is clear from the majority of the longer reviews that these people have not only purchased and listened to the soundtrack but done so after watching the miniseries. One reviewer opines that "Main Titles" "reflects the series perfectly. The theme reflects the solemn honor, duty, courage of soldiers facing war. It is difficult to describe otherwise."[58] "Kamen has composed and arranged a work of music that testifies to the heroism and great sacrifice made by those who served in the war,"[59] states an early reviewer from 2001. Another comments on the fluctuating "sensations of melancholy and dreariness, where the typical military march influences sound like pounding Roman galley drums rather than proud propaganda."[60] Even reviewers who were obviously not fans of the music still understood its message: "The main theme sounds like an uneven mixture of heroism and schmaltz."[61] The music in *Band of Brothers* fulfills its role as a storytelling agent by supporting and enhancing the series' central message. Of course, it is not only the "Main Titles" music that does this; music is used to great effect throughout the body of the episodes.

The use of music in "Part 9: Why We Fight" particularly stands out because of notable uses of both diegetic and nondiegetic music. Lewis Nixon is the focus of this episode, which opens on April 11, 1945, in Thalem, Germany. Members of Easy Company watch as the German people work to clear the rubble from the town square before the episode flashes back to what the intertitles tell us is one month earlier. Nixon is almost at a breaking point after narrowly escaping death during a combat drop with the Seventeenth Airborne Division. Tasked with notifying the parents of the soldiers who died, Nixon is at a loss as to what to tell them. "You tell them what you always tell them," Winters advises, "that their sons died as heroes." "You really still believe that?" Nixon asks, and while Winters answers in the affirmative, it is clear that Nixon is experiencing a crisis of faith. By the end of the episode, though, his question about why American soldiers are fighting and dying in Europe is answered when they come across the Kaufering IV concentration camp filled with men dying of starvation and with stacked bodies of the dead. The episode concludes by returning to the scene in Thalem, where Nixon tells the Easy Company soldiers that Hitler is dead. "Why We Fight" is notable in that it is the only episode in the series that really attempts to provide "viewers with the moral justification for WWII."[62]

The nondiegetic music that plays during the discovery of the camp serves an important role in this sequence by highlighting the emotions felt by Easy Company soldiers and by transcending the scene depicted—it is not just about this one camp but about all the work camps and death camps across Europe. The scene and accompanying music help answer Nixon's question about why they fight and, in fact, draws upon a diary entry from the real Dick Winters, who wrote after the encounter, "Now I know why I am here!"[63] The music begins very quietly, playing under the sound effects of the jeep as Winters, Frank Perconte, Ronald Speirs, and Nixon pull up to the camp with a truck full of men behind them. It slowly rises in volume as Winters approaches the camp fence. Underneath the sweeping violins, a threatening and menacing chord is repeated, giving viewers advance warning of the horror that is to follow. As Easy Company unlocks the gates and moves into the camp, the music becomes increasingly complex, adding layers to express how the men of Easy are feeling. It is their experience that the music enhances, not the emotions of the camp prisoners. Immense sadness, grief, and the incomprehensibility of what they are seeing are all emotions that are underscored by the music. It plays continuously during the ten-minute sequence, lowering in volume as Winters and Joseph Liebgott interview one of the prisoners and rising as the soldiers survey various areas of the camp and are confounded and sickened by what they see. This particular piece of music, used for this extended scene, triggers a response of what Gorbman describes as "epic feeling." "In tandem with the visual film narrative," she explains, "it elevates the individuality of the represented characters to universal significance, makes them bigger than life, suggests transcendence, destiny."[64] Most audience members will realize that this is only one work camp in a much larger system, that the horrors witnessed here by Easy are evident throughout Nazi-occupied Europe.

The music helps to transform the scene, making this particular sequence not only about just one company of American soldiers but about the reasons why America as a whole is fighting the war.

The diegetic music featured in the Thalem bookend scenes adds another layer of complexity to Nixon's (and the audience's) struggle to come to terms with the evil that is presented in the course of the episode. The episode starts after the opening credits with an extended close-up of a violin. The camera pulls back to reveal a quartet of men playing music as the German townspeople clear rubble and a handful of Easy men watch from an elevated vantage point. This close-up and slow reveal ensures that viewers pay attention to the music, which Nixon informs the men is not Mozart, as Liebgott suggested, but Beethoven. Over the course of the series the audience has come to learn that Nixon is one of the more affluent and better-educated men of Easy, so it is unsurprising that he recognizes the music and, indeed, the central conundrum of the episode. The men continue to play the same piece, Beethoven's String Quartet in C-sharp Minor from Opus 131, during the second bookend, and the episode closes by reestablishing the focus on the quartet and the violin. This is immediately followed by the end intertitles, which provide some basic information on the Holocaust, including the number of Jews and ethnic minorities murdered. John Orloff, the writer of "Why We Fight," chose to use that piece of music in this episode because it prompts a specific question: "The Germans gave [us] Beethoven AND the holocaust. How can that be?"[65] How could a people so rich in culture and so industrious (as demonstrated by their efficient clean-up) be responsible for the Holocaust? Even viewers with only the most basic musical knowledge—that Beethoven was German—can piece together the significance of the music and marvel at the incongruity, along with Nixon, of something so beautiful alongside something so evil.[66]

Music can enhance a televisual narrative in many ways, and *Band of Brothers* provides only one example. Certainly, music plays a central role in *Treme,* with diegetic music often the focal point of numerous beats in each episode. But in fact, the use of music in *Band of Brothers* and *Treme* could not be more different—David Simon is notoriously wary of using nondiegetic music and avoids it as much as possible in most of his series. *Boardwalk Empire* provides yet another completely different case, mixing contemporary music for the opening title sequence with period music throughout the episode and for the end credits. In each show, though, the music serves a narrative function. Whether it is a classically composed score or a pop hit, the right

"Part 9: Why We Fight" opens and closes with a close-up of a violin, highlighting the importance of music to this episode.

music deployed at the right point can help viewers better understand either the message of a particular scene or the approach of an entire series. The classically composed scores in *Band of Brothers* generally fly under the radar and are "invisible" to audiences but are still an important ingredient in the history-on-screen experience, in this case working to shape the Good War and greatest generation interpretation of World War Two.

## A Sonic Interpretation of the Past: Sound Effects

Stephen Ambrose writes in *Band of Brothers* that, in the early hours of June 6, 1945, as the C-47s carrying the men of Easy Company passed over the coast of France, they began to get hit with light antiaircraft fire. "When it hit the planes it made a sound like rocks being shaken in a tin can," Ambrose informs the reader. Later on he describes the sounds of mortars in the distance as a "*waump, waump, waump, waump.*"[67] It is admirable that in these instances, as well as others in the book, Ambrose attempts to convey the sounds of war as the men of Easy Company experienced them. It is incredibly difficult, however, to accurately and vividly convert sounds into words. When watching "Part 2: Day of Days," it is hard to compare Ambrose's description of the C-47s being under fire with what can be heard on the series soundtrack. A very talented writer could, perhaps, do a reasonably good job of evoking the many individual sounds and the cumulative effect when all layered together, but even if all historians possessed this artistic flair, it is unlikely they would have the space to devote long passages to sound. Even so, sounds can never really be words on a page, and physically being able to hear the sounds of the past is undoubtedly an element that makes the history-on-screen experience completely unique.

Although sound effects are often overlooked in film sound studies and history-on-film studies, they are an integral component of the soundtrack. Sound effects, Stanley Alten explains, "can be classified as anything sonic that is not speech or music. They are essential to the storytelling, bringing realism and added dimension to a production; they shape what you see."[68] As noted earlier, there is not a single microphone, or even multiple microphones, on set that captures all the sounds we hear when we watch a television show. The jingling of the men's packs as they walk, the rustling of their uniforms, their footsteps, the sounds of the guns, tanks, jeeps, planes, and everything else we hear are pieced together by the sound team. Sound effects can be gathered and created many different ways: they can be sourced from prerecorded sound libraries, they can be created by Foley artists in studio producing the sound effects in sync with the picture, they can come from live field recordings carried out by the sound crew, and they can be electronically generated. Once recorded, these sounds can be infinitely altered and manipulated—sped up, slowed down, played backwards, given reverb, layered with other sounds—to create a completely new sound. Quite often the sound effects that are synced with the picture on-screen are completely unrelated; the sound of a depth charge, for example, can be achieved with a toilet flush slowed down with reverb added.[69] This raises interesting questions about the authenticity of sound effects in historical television shows like *Band of Brothers.* Developments in sound technology, particularly digital sound and surround sound, mean the audience can be immersed in the sounds of the past, but do the invented and manipulated sounds have any historical value? This section explores what could be termed "historical film sound," how it is created and exhibited and its validity as a form of history.

"Historical sound" and "historical film sound" are two admittedly broad terms that require some definition before moving on further. Here, historical sound refers to sounds unfamiliar to contemporary ears that are related to a specific time and place/event. The sounds of an M1A1 rocket launcher firing and a Tiger tank rolling through a village, for example, could be classified as historical sounds, as could all the weaponry and vehicles featured in *Band of*

*Brothers*. "Historical film sound" refers to these historical sounds produced for film or television. However, "historical film sound" is a more inclusive term that applies not only to these specific sounds but to more general ambiences. While there is nothing inherently historical about the sound of wind whipping through trees and snow crunching underfoot, they are essential components for re-creating a specific moment in history, in this case Easy Company's winter in the Bois Jacques. I also refer to the sound team that created the sound effects for *Band of Brothers* collectively, because on a production this large, it is impossible to know exactly who did what on each of the episodes, and it is ultimately, like production design and costume design, a collaborative effort.

Can historical film sounds be considered a legitimate form of history? It is useful here to employ Alun Munslow's definition of the terms "past" and "history" to explore this question as well as the differences between historical film sound and historical sounds that have been recorded. "The past," he explains, "is what once was, is no more and is gone for good."[70] Film sound theorists Alan Williams, Tom Levin, and Rick Altman make related claims about the nature of sound and the relationship between original sound and sound recordings. "Every sound is spatio-temporally *specific*," James Lastra explains, summarizing their argument. "Given that a sound is inseparable from the time and space of its production, each sound becomes an essentially unrepeatable *event*—an event distinguishable from all others."[71] We can never truly hear the sounds of the past—they are gone for good. What we are left with are representations of the historical sounds that can be used as sources by historians. Like all primary sources, a sound recording will provide only a partial picture. In a World War Two combat setting, a microphone attached to a soldier or placed in a stationary position on the battlefield would only provide one point of audition, capturing a narrow slice of the sonic event as a whole. In reality, even this much information for a World War Two battle would be rare, as "heavy and unwieldy sound recording equipment made it virtually impossible to record sound on the front lines."[72] If it exists, an original sound recording is undoubtedly a useful source as an artifact of the past, but it is not history.

History is distinct from the past, although the two terms are often used interchangeably. Munslow describes history as "a corpus of narrative discourses about the once reality of the past produced and fashioned by historians."[73] If we use this definition, it is valid to suggest that historical film sound is a form of history. Rather than writing about the past and creating a narrative of people/places/events with words, as traditional historians and the writers of historical television series do, sound teams create a narrative using a completely different "language" that nonetheless adds to this corpus. In many respects the way the sound team crafts the sound effects, and the soundtrack more broadly, mirrors the processes and objectives of historians. Research forms the bedrock of the project for the sound team, just as it does for the historian. For *Band of Brothers* this research included finding out what weapons and vehicles were used by each army during World War Two, sourcing each of them and recording all of the sounds they produce. This is no easy feat for a ten-hour-long series that covers months of combat and is set in more than six countries. In the Brécourt Manor battle alone, the American soldiers use the M1 Garand, M1A1 Thompson submachine gun, M1A1 carbine, and a Browning .30 caliber machine gun, amongst others. According to sound effects supervisor Jimmy Boyle, every weapon and vehicle featured in the series was sourced and recorded, "even down to the last running Tiger tank in Europe," found with an original engine at the Tank Museum in Bovington. As well as speaking to military advisors, they had access to multiple armorers and recorded all aspects of a weapon's sounds: loading, reloading, bullet ejections, and firing.[74] These individual recordings of vehicles and weapons and their various actions function as the primary sources used to fashion the aural representation of the past.[75]

Rather than being tied to one point of audition, the soundtrack is edited to match the images, allowing the audience to encounter a variety of sounds from different vantage points. Consequently, the *Band of Brothers* soundtrack contains more sonic information than any one historical recording could. While Lipton is up a tree during part of the Brécourt Manor battle, the soundtrack matches his point of audition, situated as he is above the battle. This contrasts sharply with scenes of Winters on the ground in the thick of combat, where the sounds are appropriately more intense. The sounds of each of the American weapons being discharged are heard at close range when the camera is fixed on the men in a close-up or medium close-up, and at one point (29:47) the camera does three rapid cuts of different men firing, giving the viewer the opportunity to hear the slightly different popping sounds and the different rhythms of how each gun fires. When the camera pulls back to a long shot, the audience hears what these weapons sound like at a greater distance. Historical film sound actually provides a more complete picture of the sounds of war than would be possible from an original historical recording. Like any work of history, historical film sound cannot claim to definitively reproduce the past—in this case, the sounds of the past—rather it is an interpretation. Based upon the research, the sound team connects the dots and fills in the blanks to create a coherent sound narrative that they believe captures the sounds of war and fits in with the series' overarching Good War and greatest generation interpretation. Much like a historian writing a historical monograph, the sound team decides what to include, what to exclude, and how to structure all the individual pieces of information in order to best shape their narrative.

As with history on-screen more generally, invention is employed in the creation of historical film sound, and *Band of Brothers* is no exception. In part, this is due to film and television sound practices that have developed over decades and affected audience expectations. As David Sonnenschein points out, very often a single realistic sound will not have the full effect required to accompany the image on screen; the sound may need to be manipulated or have other sounds added.[76] This manipulation seeks a "balance between realism and entertainment," and audiences have become so conditioned to these heightened sounds that the real sounds on their own would sound incomplete or "wrong."[77] Audiences' familiarity with war sounds and their expectations will come primarily from other films and television programs. As stated earlier, sync sound was not usually recorded with combat footage, and the sounds of war that accompanied World War Two newsreels were added in postproduction from sound libraries, blended together with music and the newsreel commentary.[78] Masha Shpolberg argues that Great War films of the 1930s were responsible for priming "audiences for what war was supposed to sound like, and the newsreels modelled their own soundtracks to satisfy those expectations."[79] These sound conventions continued on and were solidified in subsequent World War Two films. Ultimately, there is a tension between "intelligibility and fidelity when aiming at a 'realistic' sound."[80] The sound needs to be recognizable and intelligible to the audience, who draw upon a wealth of past experience with film sound, while also retaining a fidelity to the real-world sound. In this sense, the task of the sound team is not unlike that of production and costume teams, who have to balance their own historical research with the visual signifiers of a genre familiar to audiences.

Boyle explains that in *Band of Brothers* manipulation of sounds was employed for dramatic effect or proximity, often by layering Foley sounds to enhance the original sound. For the Normandy drop sequence featuring C-47s, they "added a lot of detail to basic reality." "On the interiors we hear the C-47 droning and faint turbulence shakes and the fuselage rattles," Boyle states. "In reality the interiors didn't have rattles in them because they were so loud the noise drown[ed] out any subtlety. So we used a track we recorded in one of the vehicles; a Deuce and a half truck I think, or maybe a 6×6 free-wheeling over bumps and the back bed and covering rattling."[81] Even though sounds were added to the interiors, veterans applauded the sound team for their work. They raved "about the sound inside the planes, and the sound of the flak took them back there; they thought it was very authentic."[82] Overall, the inventions in *Band of Brothers* are relatively minor; more substantial inventions are employed in *Saving Private Ryan*. At one point in the film, tanks can be heard closing in on the American troops. The noise of the engines and their squeaks and rattles echoing off surrounding buildings was created by scraping different objects against concrete and manipulating motor noises from other vehicles.[83] Inventions such as these, large or small, do not jeopardize the overall legitimacy of historical film sound and should be classed as instances of Rosenstone's true invention. Whether created from disparate sources or heightening sounds for impact, these inventions still capture the spirit of the historical sounds but make them work better within this dramatic form. They add detail and depth to the sound narrative and enhance the drama of the series overall while also satisfying audience expectations so that the soundtrack does not become distracting.

Developments in technology, particularly surround sound and digital sound, have aided sound teams in the creation of complex and rich historical film sound. One needs to first look to the movie theater and then to the home theater to understand current sound practices. Multichannel sound (sound with two or more loudspeaker channels) has a long history in the cinema dating back to the 1930s. There have been numerous cycles in which multichannel has come to the forefront only to fade once again—that is, however, until the advent of Dolby Stereo.[84] Dolby Stereo placed three audio "channels behind the screen (left, right and centre) with a fourth channel (surround) employing an array of speakers emanating non-directional sound from around the auditorium."[85] Films with innovative soundtracks, such as *Star Wars* and *Close Encounters of the Third Kind* (Spielberg, 1977), were mixed using this four-channel system and sold both audiences and exhibitors on Dolby Stereo, which was quickly adopted in thousands of movie theaters across the United States.[86] The next major step was the shift from analog to digital sound in the early 1990s. Dolby Surround Sound (DSS) and Digital Theater Systems (DTS), the two most popular and widespread digital sound systems, both use a 5.1 channel system, with three channels once again behind the screen, but with two separate rear surround channels and a low frequency channel (the .1). Digital surround sound not only offers an increased number of discrete audio channels but cancels out virtually any background "hiss" and allows for greater frequency and dynamic ranges.[87]

Developments in movie theater sound are adapted to work within home theater environments and on mobile devices. The number of American households with multichannel audiovisual systems is on the rise.[88] Not only are there an array of home theater in a box systems that offer basic 5.1 surround sound setups and top-of-the-line systems with over thirty speakers, but soundbars are an increasingly popular budget-friendly and compact alternative. As Dolby advertises, "Every DVD worldwide and all HD broadcasts in the United States use Dolby Digital," and viewers can also experience surround sound when they stream content through certain providers on an enabled device.[89] This means that millions can experience digital surround sound in the home and while watching on mobile devices. Of course, sound in the home (and on the go) still differs from sound in the cinema. Take a standard 5.1 home theater setup as an example: rather than the right and left front speakers being positioned behind the screen, as they are in a movie theater, in the majority of home theaters right and left front speakers are positioned beyond the frame of the television screen. Furthermore, in the standard 5.1 home setup there are only two rear speakers, while there are walls of speakers in the movie theater.[90] Sound in the cinema and sound in the home are not identical, but it is fair to say that sound in the home no longer has to be inferior. *Band of Brothers* is proof of this.

In at least three major ways, digital surround sound has greatly affected soundtrack aesthetics and the level of complexity sound teams are able to achieve. First, digital surround sound can be used to design and create moments of contrast. Contrasting volumes, frequencies, and use of the surrounds can greatly influence the visuals and help shape the narrative. "The more tools we have to shift a sound track, the more dramatic we can be," states Rydstrom.[91] Sound-reproduction systems, whether analog or digital, all produce unwanted background noise, but there is decidedly less hiss or background noise with digital surround systems.[92] This means that silences can be that much more complete and profound, which can have a disconcerting effect. The start of "Part Five: Crossroads" provides one such example. The main narrative opens as Winters runs through a field, his breathing, pounding footsteps, and clicking equipment audible. He stops suddenly, and the camera steadies as a young German man in uniform rises up out of the long grass. This scene is silent; there is no wind in the grass, no rustling of either man's uniform. The complete silence lasts over three seconds before an ear-piercing shot rings out. Pairing a loud sound and a soft sound together is not a new concept. However, because the dynamic range of digital sound is that much greater—loud sounds can be louder, soft sounds can be softer—the contrast between loud and soft is so much more striking.[93] Another effective contrast is employed in "Part Three: Carentan" when the use of the surrounds is abruptly altered. Edward Tipper is making his way through a pharmacy when a bomb blasts through the shop's front windows. As the loud explosion fades away, it is replaced by an enveloping underwater-like tinnitus that issues from all speakers. Liebgott can be heard calling Tipper through the center speaker, but his voice is very quiet and unclear. What dominates in the left and right front speakers and the left and right rear speakers is Tipper's breathing and his own voice as he asks, "Joe, is that you?" Liebgott's voice in the center speaker slowly gains volume and clarity as the soundtrack returns to its normal balance. Rarely are voices heard in the rear speakers, so the unconventional use of the surrounds stands in stark contrast to the usual deployment of the voice in the center speaker. These sound contrasts serve a narrative function: in the first case alerting the viewer to the significance of this shot for Winters's character and, in the latter, providing the audience with a subjective point of audition.

Second, as Rydstrom points out, digital surround sound's discrete channels can be used to overcome the masking effect. "As frequencies compete when sounds are added together," Rydstrom explains, "the characters of the sounds change, sometimes disappearing into each other."[94] If trying to incorporate a number of sounds at the same time, especially sounds of a similar frequency, adding too many in the same channel could result in individual sounds becoming distorted or muddied. Digital surround sound allows sound mixers to "orchestrate" the sounds, placing individual pieces of the soundtrack in each of the distinct channels so that they work together rather than against one another. This means that in a full-scale battle scene, such as the one on the outskirts of Carentan in part 3, sound effects can be layered without losing clarity. Roughly halfway through the scene, a German tank rolls in towards Easy Company, and Easy soldiers Harry Welsh and John McGrath enter an open field to take aim at the tank with a rocket launcher. In the course of this short sequence, we can hear Welsh and McGrath talking, the low rumble of the tank, its squeaking tracks, the bullets ricocheting off the metal hull, the tank gun fire, the debris flying, and the machine gun fire from the Germans and Americans. In one shot alone, as a dazed soldier looks up after a near miss, flying debris can be heard as well as the continued rumble of the tank, a call for a medic, and machine gun fire coming from multiple directions. The more flexible mixing environment that discrete channels offer means that more sounds can play at the same time, providing the audience with more information and greater detail.[95]

Third, digital surround sound can be used to create an enveloping environment that builds upon the on-screen image. It achieves this partly through moving sounds through space. Dowson notes that, given the subject matter in *Band of Brothers,* he and his staff were often able to use the surrounds to pan various things around: "Bombs fly over you, planes fly over you, debris flies over you when there's a big explosion on the screen; so it's a myriad of things rather than one particular thing."[96] "Part 7: The Breaking Point" features a German artillery attack on Easy Company while in the Bois Jacques. An accelerated whirring noise originates in the rear speakers, and the explosion and flying debris is picked up in the center, front right, or front left speakers to match up approximately with where the explosion lands on-screen. This creates the impression that the German shells are being fired behind the viewer and making their way across the room and exploding on-screen. Later in the episode when Easy attacks the village of Foy, the same technique is used with the sound of individual bullets, which zip back and forth between the rear and front speakers. "Surround sound," William Whittington states, "offers a kind of peripheral vision not provided by the screen directly ahead. . . . Sound and sound in the surrounds offer access into areas the image is not willing or is unable to go."[97] Even when experienced without surround sound technology, sound provides a third dimension. "Seeing is always directional," explain Thomas Elsaesser and Malte Hagener, "because we see only in one direction, whereas hearing is always a three dimensional, spatial perception, that is, it creates an acoustic space, because we hear in all directions." The body of the viewer becomes "enmeshed acoustically, spatially, and affectively in the filmic texture."[98]

Indeed, the "tactility of sound" plays a significant role in generating the "feel of the past."[99] In both "The Breaking Point" and the preceding episode, Easy Company fights not only against the Germans but against the elements, as they are woefully underdressed and underequipped to spend winter in foxholes on the outskirts of Bastogne. Sound works in tandem with the image track to create an ice-cold atmosphere. During "The Breaking Point" when Easy is not directly engaged in battle, the sound of wind whipping through the trees issues from the rear speakers.[100] Like the rich fabrics, diseased skin, and thick mud of the *Deadwood* image track, this sound connects with viewers and has a haptic quality; the sound of whistling wind is so evocative we can almost feel it on our own skin. This frigid environment is accentuated by the rough, crunching footsteps of the men as they traipse through what looks and sounds like deep, fresh snow. Along with the huddled figures of the soldiers, their red noses, and the white horizon, the wind and crunching snow add to the icy feel of the images on-screen, so much so that the viewer can almost feel the cold.

Just like the music, the sound effects in *Band of Brothers* contribute to the Good War interpretation, with its focus on the heroism and bravery of the ordinary American soldier. "The essential ordinariness of the soldiers who served in Easy Company and the extraordinariness of their achievements" is the central message of the series.[101] By immersing the audience in the sounds of the past—allowing them to be sonic witnesses—the show allows them to more fully appreciate what these men went through. Viewers are placed in the midst of the horrors of modern warfare, as well as the more day-to-day discomforts experienced by Easy Company. "New technologies have made it increasingly possible to *experience* an event or a past without having actually lived through it," Alison Landsberg points out, and surround sound is certainly one such technology that is remarkably effective in this sense.[102] It "offers a total sonic environment, which masks the real environment of the theatre space to create a sonic space with no entry and no exit."[103] The graphic depictions of war, which are made up not only of visuals but of the soundtrack as well, serve to focus the audience's attention on the remarkable actions of the soldiers in the face of such dangers. The sound effects in *Band of Brothers,* benefitting from technological improvements, help the audience understand what these men experienced and, in doing so, marvel at what they endured.

It is incorrect to think of sound effects, and sound more generally, as a purely technical endeavor, as it often is.[104] Creating the sound effects for *Band of Brothers* required creativity and ingenuity on the part of the sound team, not only to source and record all the sounds but to choose how exactly to craft them into a compelling representation of the past that worked in perfect harmony with the image on-screen and the series' overarching interpretation of World War Two. It is not only a technological feat but a creative and historical one. The historical film sound in *Band of Brothers,* taken as a whole, does contribute to the discourse surrounding the Second World War, particularly the frontline experiences of the soldiers, by presenting a sonic interpretation of the past.

## Articulating History: The Voice

The human voice is arguably the most important element of the soundtrack and the one viewers pay the greatest attention to. The voice is to the soundtrack what the face is to the image, the focal point that viewers are drawn to. Arnt Maasø explains that the voice is the most important sound in human communication and that "research on perception and cognitive processing indicates that recognition and processing of faces and voices appear more specialised than processing of other visual objects and sounds."[105] Film scholar Michel Chion suggests that "human listening is naturally vococentrist," that is, that human listening privileges the voice over all other sonic elements. "*There are voices,*" he states, "*and then everything else.*"[106] Not only does the human ear pick out the voice and center its attention on it when watching film and television, but the soundtrack is also manipulated so that voice is at the forefront. Just as the image on the screen is arranged so that the central action takes place in the foreground, the human voice is placed in the sonic foreground, while music and sound effects are usually relegated to the background.[107] In *Band of Brothers* voice is employed in a number of different forms. As they do in most current films and television series, characters speak within the diegesis and it is largely through their dialogue that the viewer is able to follow the narrative. There are also two types of voice that operate outside the diegesis: voice-over narration that accompanies a few of the episodes and voices of the veterans themselves as they tell their own stories, either at the beginning or end of each of the episodes. Most of the discussion of television speech and dialogue in this study thus far has been concerned with *what* was said and the role it played in shaping and constructing the history on-screen. This is still a consideration here, particularly with regard to voice-over narration, but this section focuses on *how* things are said—how lines written on a page are verbalized by an actor or how a veteran articulates memories carry their own set of meanings, often as powerful as the words themselves.

*Band of Brothers* is a fairly unique dramatic series in that, through the inclusion of interviews with the veterans, the audience gets to hear directly from the historical figures being portrayed. In the first nine episodes, either before or after the opening credit sequence, snippets of interviews with individual men of Easy Company are edited together, usually into segments of no longer than one minute and ten seconds. They are organized and edited thematically, either discussing what will be an important theme or event in the upcoming episode and/or commenting on the events of the previous episode. *Band of Brothers* is not the only dramatic representation to incorporate interview footage of real people being portrayed in the dramatic narrative; the German film *Downfall* (Hirschbiegel, 2004) opened and closed with the real Traudl Junge, a central character in the film, and *The Pacific*, another ten-part World War Two series created by Tom Hanks and Steven Spielberg for HBO, follows the same interview format as its predecessor. In these segments the audience gets to hear the voices of the real men—the real accents (although they likely sound quite different from how they spoke over fifty years earlier), and the real emotion behind the words. Indeed, this is what proponents of oral history cite as one of its main contributions. "We collect passion, detachment, enthusiasm, hesitancy, accent, cadence, sarcasm, sincerity, shyness, bombast, and a dozen other nuances that rarely make it into even the most scrupulously accurate transcript," argue Charles Hardy III and Pamela Dean.[108] The *Band of Brothers* interviews are audiovisual, adding yet another layer to the information provided. It is not just the words we hear and how they are spoken; we can also see "physical gestures and facial expressions" that expand on the meaning of what is being said.[109] When one of the veterans explains how he struggled after the war with the death of many of his friends and never forgot them, the power of his words and the real evidence of the impact the war had on his life comes from the slow, halting way he starts to speak, how his voice cracks right at the end, and from the nervous blinking and licking of his lips.

The inclusion of the veterans and the act of them voicing their own stories once again encourage the audience to venerate these members of the greatest generation. They provide an "emotional connection for the viewer and a legitimate sense of authenticity."[110] The interviews also have an intriguing effect, giving viewers the opportunity to see and hear the real people almost side by side with their dramatic counterparts. The actors are essentially impersonating these men, and while there is little they can do to alter their appearance, they can significantly manipulate their voices. It is not until the end of the final episode that the talking heads are actually named, so up until that point it is a guessing game as to which character in the narrative represents each veteran.[111] One of the veterans it is relatively easy to identify is William "Wild Bill" Guarnere due to actor Frank John Hughes's spot-on impersonation of Guarnere's accent, rhythm of speaking, and tone and pitch of voice.

Vocal performances are central when specifically considering what actors contribute to the history being crafted on-screen. Actors manipulate their voice in order to build and shape character and to imbue the words in the script with meaning. As Jeremy G. Butler points out, in television the viewer often does not have direct access to a character's emotions, state of mind, or personality. A written text can represent these pieces of information "simply by describing them verbally," but a TV show must do this through performance signs, one of which is the voice.[112] The human voice is incredibly expressive and can "combine a range of vocal features," all of which "are capable of fine gradation."[113] Loudness, pitch, timbre, breathiness, roughness, nasality, and rhythm are just some of the vocal features that can be manipulated to create the desired effect. How words are spoken directly affects how a listener processes and understands those words, and some studies suggest that adults place more weight on tone than on what is actually said. If the delivery and tone do not match up with the content of what is being said, it can result in confusion or misunderstanding on the part of the listener.[114]

Comparing the vocal performances of two of the characters in *Band of Brothers* illustrates just how integral the voice is to constructing character. The two central figures in "Part 1: Currahee" are Herbert Sobel (David Schwimmer) and Dick Winters (Damian Lewis). Sobel's voice, more often than not, is loud, high, and tense. When he first appears on-screen, he yells to the men lined up around him: "You *p*eople are at the *p*osition of a*tt*ention." He stresses the plosives and enunciates the words crisply and curtly in a high, harsh tone of voice.[115] As he is the company commander, this is the baseline for how he will address the men under him, whether speaking to them as a group or berating an individual soldier for infractions. He adopts a more moderate tone when addressing other officers in the company, both below and above him in rank. Winters's voice, on the other hand, is low, even, and calm in the first episode, whether speaking to his friend Nixon, addressing his platoon during a night-time march, or challenging his unwarranted court-martial. The differences in their vocal performances and how they address others encapsulate their contrasting personalities and leadership styles. Stephen Ambrose remarks that every man interviewed for his book "said Winters was the best combat commander he ever saw."[116] In his memoirs, Donald Malarkey described Winters as "cool as a cucumber when the pressure was on," "fair to all," and "absolutely willing to go through whatever [his men] went through."[117] The men of Easy remember Sobel in a very different light, as being cruel, petty, and brutal.[118] "All he did was scream," remembers Bill

The vocal performances of Damian Lewis (*left*) and David Schwimmer (*right*) help to emphasize the contrasting leadership styles of their characters.

Guarnere. "He was high-strung, ranted and raved, criticized everything, a mean son of a bitch."[119]

Accents are another consideration in the evaluation of the actor's vocal performance and construction of character. In "phonetic terms, an accent is a set of habits that make up someone's pronunciation of a language or language variety."[120] Sociolinguist Peter Trudgill states that when humans speak, "we cannot avoid giving our listeners clues about our origins and the sort of person we are. Our accent and our speech generally show where we come from, and what sort of background we have."[121] Accents provide information about the countries and regions a person has spent considerable time in, as well as social factors such as class and education. Accents are often used in American films and television series as a type of shorthand to signal the status of a character in the narrative (lead or secondary, good guy or bad guy).[122] In the American war genre the range of accents amongst the soldiers serves to signify the diversity of the combat platoon. Jeanine Basinger identifies the mixed combat group, with men from various parts of the United States, of differing ages, ethnicities, and backgrounds, as one of the core elements of the combat genre.[123] This element also aligns with the Good War and greatest generation myths, with their focus on all Americans banding together to defeat a common foe. *Band of Brothers* certainly adheres to this theme, especially since it focuses on the much larger unit of the company instead of a single platoon.

There is little time to develop many of the minor characters' backstories, many of whom appear in most or all of the episodes but do not feature prominently in any one. Their varied accents, though—Darrell "Shifty" Powers's Virginian accent and Eugene "Babe" Heffron's South Philly accent—add to the rich and varied tapestry of the Easy combat unit.

The accuracy of the accents in *Band of Brothers* received much attention from reviewers and audience members, illustrating that this is a topical issue for many. Because the series was filmed in England, many of the five hundred speaking parts went to British actors, including the central roles of Winters, Eugene "Doc" Roe, Johnny Martin, and Albert Blithe. Damian Lewis was one of the few actors to receive near-universal praise for his "perfect American accent."[124] Other British actors, including Shane Taylor, who played the company medic, generated more mixed reviews.[125] Emily Todd VanDerWerff of the AV Club opined that Taylor's Louisiana accent was, as "typical for Brits, a little shaky."[126] Various commenters agreed with VanDerWerff's appraisal, while some applauded Taylor for doing an admirable job with the difficult Cajun-inflected Louisiana accent. Others pointed out that it was not only the British actors who struggled with the regional American accents but the American actors themselves, some of whom, like Donnie Wahlberg, chose to use their natural accents rather than adopting the accent of the person they were portraying (Bostonian in the case of Wahlberg, when his character, Lipton, was from West Virginia). The actor who faced the harshest criticism was Marc Warren, who played Philadelphian Albert Blithe, a central figure in "Part Three: Carentan," with a southern accent.[127]

Accents can provide a wealth of information and add nuance to characters, but they can also prove to be distracting to audiences and thus should be carefully considered by those bringing history to the screen. Many of those commenting online appear to have done extra reading or research on Easy Company, as it is not always explicitly stated in the series where each of the characters originates. When viewers are armed with that knowledge and it conflicts with what they hear from the character, it seems to become distracting, almost taking them out of the story and potentially jeopardizing the validity of the larger history being presented on-screen. For many others, though, particularly non-Americans (myself included), the accuracy of regional accents will not even register. What matters most, perhaps, is consistency and clarity. If one actor is going to strive for authenticity (whether portraying real people, as in the case of *Band of Brothers,* or invented characters, such as Jimmy Darmody in *Boardwalk Empire,* who was meant to have been born and raised in Atlantic City), then all the actors should be required to do so. There should be a systematic methodology employed, just as there (ideally) is in written history. It is also important that the accent is understandable to a wide audience who may be unfamiliar with it. Taylor explains that when crafting his accent, he made the decision, in consultation with producer Tom Hanks, to moderate the accent and make it sound more modern and less like the tapes he had of Cajun accents from the historical period.[128] This, of course, is an issue that written histories do not have to contend with; the words are flat on the page and rarely explore what a historical voice may have sounded like. An accent can be a problematic element and detract from the history on-screen, as with Warren's performance, but when done right, as with Lewis, it can add yet another layer to the character. It can provide audiences with a sense of what historical figures may have sounded like when they lived and breathed, even if there is no interview footage included, as there is in *Band of Brothers*.[129]

Voice-over narrators provide yet another manifestation of the human voice. Three different characters provide narration in four of the episodes: Winters very briefly in "Part 2: Day of Days," and then more substantially in "Part 10: Points"; Lipton in "Part 7: The Breaking Point"; and Webster in "Part 8: The Last Patrol." They are all homodiegetic narrators, meaning they are participants in the story they are relating. Voice-over narration is, of course, an element of discourse, or how the story is told. In this sense voice-over is also relevant to the previous chapter on narrative and could have been discussed there if *Treme* had used voice-over in any of its episodes. As a purely aural storytelling technique, however, voice-over narration is equally relevant to this chapter on sound. Many television series (as well as countless films) use voice-over, although its function and frequency can vary greatly depending on the show; *Magnum P.I.* (CBS, 1980–88), *The Wonder Years* (ABC, 1988–93), and HBO's own *Sex and the City* (1998–2004) used voice-over every week, while other long-running series employ it in one-off episodes.[130] As Sarah Kozloff points out, the use of a voice-over narrator gives the audience the impression that it is the narrator controlling what the viewer sees, that he or she is in charge of the *syuzhet* organization, the way the events of the film or TV show are ordered and plotted.[131] This adds a "subjective note" to what is shown on-screen, as the voice-over privileges the perspective of the narrator, who is, in all the examples cited here, one of the characters.[132]

Voice-over has great potential in that it offers the possibility for adding another layer to the narrative, but it also has the drawback that it can be overused and become redundant, both of which can be seen in the narrated episodes of *Band of Brothers*. Lipton's narration in "The Breaking Point" generated much discussion in online reviews and comments on blogs, perhaps because seven episodes into the series, it was the first to include considerable voice-over narration. Alan Sepinwall criticized Graham Yost's script for "moments where the voice-over feels unnecessary" and for not trusting the audience to grasp certain things "without spelling it out for them."[133] There are numerous instances when Lipton's narration does indeed mirror what is being shown on-screen. Midway through the episode, as the camera rises to a high-angle long shot, we see splintered tree tops clearly visible in the foreground while the men of Easy move across ground littered with tree branches. Lipton's narration at this very point that "the Germans had been shelling our old position—there were signs of tree bursts everywhere" is superfluous given the images on-screen and dialogue provided by the characters in the diegesis. Both "The Last Patrol" and "Points," albeit to a lesser degree, feature similar instances of empty voice-over that seem to function as little more than filler to keep up the regularity of the narration.

Equally, though, there are instances when the voice-over conveys information that cannot be included in the diegesis, particularly the thoughts and emotions that a character would not express out loud. "The Last Patrol," for example, is narrated by Webster, who, after being wounded in Holland, missed the Battle of the Bulge and is rejoining Easy as it moves into Haguenau. Episode co-writer Erik Bork explained that he wanted to explore Webster's "unique perspective coming back to the Company." "These were men who wouldn't believably discuss their inner perspectives with each other in scenes very much," Bork stated. "It would be hard for the audience to know what they were [thinking] otherwise, especially since there were so many characters, and different ones who were central to different episodes."[134] The aim in "The Last Patrol" was to examine Webster's feelings as an outsider, and since the writers felt it would be "hard or unnatural for him to voice his feelings and thoughts through dialogue with others," they used voice-over to clearly convey them instead.[135] "The guys I knew were either gone or very different from what I remembered," Webster narrates at the beginning of the episode. "I was a veteran of D-Day and Market Garden and had been with the company since its formation, but now, because I had missed Bastogne, I was treated as a replacement and felt like I was starting all over again."[136] In "Points," Winters's voice-over narration supplies a sense of unity and cohesion for an episode that otherwise might appear disjointed or sprawling, as it brings the series to a close. It also allows Winters, the central figure of the series and respected leader of Easy, to relate the postwar lives of many of the men in a way that is far more personal and, therefore, meaningful than intertitles could achieve. The viewer has learned over the course of the series that Winters cares about his men, and it comes through in the emotion in his voice and choice of words: "Bull Randleman was one of the best soldiers I ever had; he went into the earth-moving business in Arkansas—he's still there." Sound allows for the expression of intimate thoughts and helps foster a deeper connection between audience and character, generating and developing allegiance.

The distinctly different sound quality of voice-over narration also strengthens the connection between viewer and character. Michel Chion calls the narrating voice the "I-voice" and argues that "sound film has codified the criteria of tone color, auditory space, and timbre to which a voice must conform in order to function as an I-voice." Chion identifies two technical criteria essential in the recording of voice-over, the first being close-miking to create "a feeling of intimacy with the voice, such that we sense no distance between it and our ear."[137] Even choosing the correct microphone for voice-over is a complex endeavor that must take into account the performer's voice and the desired sound, whether it be "crisp and bright, warm but not overly bright, transparent, or silky in the treble range."[138] The second criterion derives from the first and relates to the "dryness" of the voice. Dryness is essentially the absence of reverberation, as reverb situates the voice in a real-world space. Voice-over is usually recorded in a purpose-built studio "offering low reverberation time and background noise" in order to capture the clearest possible sound.[139] If reverb is added to the voice, "it is then no longer a subject with which the spectator identifies, but rather an object-voice, perceived as a body anchored in space," breaking the illusion that the narrator speaks directly into the ear of the listener.[140] This effect is further manipulated in the final sound mix, where it is heavily compressed to enhance its clarity and to stop it being overwhelmed by other sounds, such as music and sound effects.[141] This unique sound quality has become a standard convention, so viewers know when they hear this particular type of voice in conjunction with the use of past tense, they are listening to the character narrate from some (usually) unknown place and time in the future.

Previous chapters have already touched on speech and its narrative function. The writers strive to imitate natural conversation, but, in reality, character dialogue is "designed to communicate certain information to the audience" and differs significantly "from spontaneous everyday speech."[142] The speech of characters—be it through conversations, monologues, lectures, or songs—provides context, assigns meaning to events, explains complex plot points and historical issues, and helps to build character, as outlined in the *Treme* and *Boardwalk Empire* chapters. However, it is worth remembering that the dialogue is the product of not only the writers but the actors, who deliver the words and imbue them with meaning, and the sound department staff, who capture the voice, make it distinct, and manipulate how it sounds to achieve a desired effect. Dialogue once again illustrates the truly collaborative nature of history on-screen that stretches across individuals and various departments.

## Conclusion

Sound is an area that has been overlooked for too long in a range of disciplines. It is pointless to argue for the primacy of the aural over the visual, or vice versa, but as Robynn J. Stilwell states, sound is "easily the equal of such components as lighting, design, camera angles and editing and therefore needs to be integrated into the study of film as these other elements have been."[143] Exactly the same can and should be argued for the place of sound in history-on-screen scholarship. While elements of the image track are considered and critiqued, the soundtrack is often taken for granted and left unexplored. It is vital to remember that just as much time and energy is spent on the soundtrack: songs are carefully chosen and musical scores are composed, sound effects are individually crafted and orchestrated, and actors hone their vocal performances. Looking at each of the three categories of screen sound in *Band of Brothers* demonstrates just how rich an area of examination sound is.

To ascertain how each of these categories of screen sound function and what they add to the narrative, this chapter has been divided into sections, each dealing with a separate category. Such separation is, of course, artificial. The sounds interact and overlap and are designed to work in harmony not only with the image but with each other. Music, sound effects, and speech are the individual elements of sound design, the "total sonic universe" of the series.[144] "Sound design" can be a slippery term with many interconnected meanings, as outlined by Whittington. It can refer to the creation of specific sounds or the "conceptual design of the overall sound track"; it can also relate to how the sounds are designed to be heard in different exhibition spaces. "Sound design" can also refer to and incorporate all of these elements: "Sound design represents the planning and patterns of the film sound track and the meanings that result from its deployment within the exhibition space."[145] No matter how well researched or well executed each of the individual elements of the soundtrack are, they must be able to work together to produce a cohesive whole.

The overall sound design of *Band of Brothers*—with its meticulous attention to detail in the battle scenes, the inclusion of veteran and narrating voices that generate intimacy, and the carefully composed musical scores enhancing the emotions of the soldiers—plays an important part in shaping the Good War and greatest generation interpretation of World War Two promoted by the series. Sound design, Mark S. Ward contends, "is, first and foremost, a form of emotion design. Each set of decisions which goes into the crafting of a sonic element is focused upon the task of designing affect at both the sensory and narrative levels."[146] The way the sound is constructed and organized encourages the viewer not only to care about these soldiers but to appreciate their sacrifices and contributions to the struggle against fascism.

Listening to a sequence from "Part 5: Crossroads" provides just one example of how the different elements of sound are worked together to develop a desired idea or meaning. After shooting the young SS officer at the beginning of the episode, Winters is sent on a forty-eight-hour furlough to Paris, but continues to struggle with his actions that day. We first see him at a busy sidewalk café. The hum of conversation around him, most of it indistinguishable but with some clear snippets from American soldiers behind him, enhances the impression that he feels claustrophobic, confined by all those happy, seemingly lighthearted people around him. After this short scene (fifty seconds), the episode cuts to Winters sitting on a subway car. The sound of the train is loud, coming from all speakers, and the continuous rattling and rumbling of the car as it picks up speed is soon punctuated by the sound of gunfire as Winters experiences brief flashbacks to the battle at the crossroads. The sounds of the car eventually start to slowly decrease in volume as Winters looks behind him and sees a teenage boy who reminds him of the SS officer. The image track cuts back to the scene, only this time, in Winters's imagination, the silence is even more drawn out. Rather than lasting only three seconds, as it had when the event originally occurred, as he remembers it in his mind there is fifteen seconds of silence between the moment he comes across the boy and shoots his gun. The image track returns to the subway and the silence resumes—the train has stopped. The boy speaks kindly and softly to Winters in French, breaking his stupor. Just as the boy stops speaking, gentle music begins and picks up a bit of volume as Winters exits the station, walks along the Seine, and heads back to his hotel. Sound effects (cars, footsteps) and speech (ambient conversation of other people along the Seine) are layered over the music, and the sequence ends as he enters the bathtub with a contented sigh. The final shot of the sequence is through a doorway, looking at Winters as he lies in the tub; the music concludes and is immediately replaced by a unknown male voice talking, providing a sound bridge between this scene and the next one, which takes place as the men of Easy watch a John Wayne film. The sounds and silences in this sequence, constantly shifting in volume and focus (depending on what the audience is supposed to be listening to), and varied use of the surrounds all work to further the impression that Winters is guilt-stricken, is traumatized by war, and is seeking solitude.

The complex sound design of *Band of Brothers* does more than heighten emotion and provide access to the sounds of the past: it has the dual effect of drawing viewers into the narrative and pulling them out of it, especially when experienced in surround sound. As Landsberg argues in her study of the soundscape in *Deadwood,* sound can also lead to cognitive thinking on the part of the audience. Viewers can be both engrossed in the narrative and invested in the characters while also realizing there is something "profoundly different" about what they are watching on-screen. "We oscillate," she states, "between these two poles of mimesis and difference, moving back and forth between the bridge." Viewers' investment and emotional response to the narrative do not necessarily result in facile identification, rather this affective engagement "can lead to new thoughts, ideas, or historical insights."[147] The sound design, issuing from multiple speakers, does not create the simplistic illusion that the viewers are in the narrative, experiencing World War Two as it actually happened. Rather, the incongruity of sitting in a comfortable armchair while surrounded by the sound of bombs, bullets, anguished cries, and heart-wrenching music snaps viewers out of the storyworld. The bodily response they have to the harrowing sounds highlights the stark difference between their own setting and that experienced by the men of Easy Company. Viewers are prompted to reflect upon what war really entails and, in turn, the difficulties of those who lived through it, reinforcing, once again, the series' Good War interpretation.

The soundtrack ultimately adds a dimension to history that just cannot be replicated in written form. It gives history texture and brings the image to life; without sound, even the most impressive visual sequence feels flat and one-dimensional.[148] The addition of sound—of voices, sound effects, and music—surrounding us as we watch is, arguably, that magic ingredient that brings the history on-screen to life. This is why it is so surprising that it has received so little attention. In *Band of Brothers* the visual and the aural complement each other; both have been crafted to present audiences with a gritty and "authentic" window to World War Two and to enhance the creators' interpretation of history. There is potential, though, for filmmakers to play with sound, to experiment with how it is employed and its relationship to the image.

It is worth, perhaps, briefly returning to the issue of the simplistic and problematic historical interpretation of *Band of Brothers*. This was not HBO, Hanks, and Spielberg's last foray into World War Two together. Nine years later, *The Pacific* premiered, putting the $125 million budget of *Band of Brothers* to shame with a $200 million price tag.[149] Like its predecessor, *The Pacific* spared no expense in creating a visually and aurally authentic representation, from the sets, props, and costumes to a meticulously crafted and immersive soundtrack. The historical interpretation of the American experience did, however, evolve. As Debra Ramsay points out, *The Pacific* disrupts and muddies elements of the Good War myth, even while it maintains those of the greatest generation.[150] The subsequent series is significant for two reasons: first, it showcases the importance of HBO's on-going relationships with individuals and production companies (particularly Hanks and his production company, Playtone), and second, it again illustrates the network's willingness to present a variety of histories and interpretations.[151]

# Conclusion

In the years since *Treme* and *Boardwalk Empire* ended, HBO has continued to produce critically acclaimed and buzzworthy historical series. The miniseries *Chernobyl* (2019) explores the 1986 nuclear disaster, illuminating the contributing causes, sequence of events, and consequences of the accident as seen through the eyes of scientists, residents, bureaucrats, and grunts. *Gentleman Jack* (2019–), co-produced with BBC, paints an insightful yet refreshingly lively portrait of nineteenth-century landowner Anne Lister, who secretly wed her female lover. HBO has also dipped its toes into more experimental and unorthodox screen histories with *The Plot Against America* (2020) and *Lovecraft Country* (2020). The former, based on a novel by Philip Roth, presents an alternate version of American history that sees Charles Lindbergh win the 1940 presidential election, setting the United States on a very different path. And while *Lovecraft Country* is ostensibly a science fiction / horror hybrid, the series delivers a powerful historical message about the mid-twentieth-century African American experience.

HBO's lack of advertiser influence, commitment to showrunners' creative freedom, and generous budgets and resources continue to draw in and retain talent who want to tell historical stories. But today it is not the only company offering such benefits; Netflix now entices with similar incentives and is building up a cache of showrunner talent with multimillion-dollar deals.[1] Unsurprisingly, HBO and Netflix have followed similar paths, transforming how content is transmitted and viewed and evolving from movie providers to producers of innovative original content.[2] Netflix was founded in 1997 and initially provided a DVD mail service before moving into streaming content over the internet. Increased access to high-speed wireless internet, along with the proliferation of smartphones and tablets that enabled mobile viewing, meant that Netflix's streaming services soon far outpaced its DVD subscriptions.

With the shift in focus to streaming content, and the later decision to start producing its own original content, Netflix created an "effect" of its own.

The Netflix effect is usually referenced when discussing those aspects that initially separated streaming services from broadcast and cable networks. One element of the Netflix effect is the apparent democratization of entertainment, with viewers able to access a range of content through one source and watch at a time and place of their own choosing.[3] It also refers to the practice of binge-watching entire series in the space of a few days. Binge-watching is not a new phenomenon, but it has become increasingly commonplace with Netflix and other streaming providers (generally) releasing all episodes of a season at the same time, encouraging viewers to consume entire seasons quickly. The success of Netflix's original productions, and particularly its foray into quality drama, has led other streaming services such as Amazon and Hulu to follow suit. Not only is Netflix now at the forefront of original TV programming, but it and other streaming services are also having a profound effect on the film industry, financing and distributing original content and upending standard distribution practices.

The rise of streaming and the dominance of Netflix has prompted major changes in the TV industry, and HBO is having to adapt. Viewers are increasingly moving away from linear TV (for which programming is scheduled) and are streaming content instead. With over two hundred million subscribers globally and a presence in about 60 percent of American homes, Netflix is currently the yardstick against which all other streamers and content providers are measured.[4] Networks are now creating their own streaming platforms or are in the process of doing so in order to attract and maintain audiences. NBC, one of the original Big Three broadcast networks, launched Peacock in April 2020 in an effort to compete. American audiences can stream a selection of content for free, with ads, or can opt for paid subscriptions that allow access to more content without advertisements. Disney Plus has proved thus far to be Netflix's most successful competitor, gaining almost ninety-five million subscriptions since its launch in 2019.[5] The Disney platform gives subscribers access to a vast catalog of films and TV shows, as well as new original content, much of which is based on existing properties, such as *Star Wars* and the Marvel Cinematic Universe. Time Warner (of which HBO is a part) was acquired by AT&T in 2018, and it was announced shortly after the acquisition that the newly named WarnerMedia would launch its own subscription streaming service. HBO Max features thousands of hours of content from the WarnerMedia catalog but, as evidenced by the name, is seeking to attract audiences and subscribers with the HBO brand.[6]

As more and more streaming services launch, creating original content is increasingly vital to attract new subscribers and hold on to current ones, which is once again changing the television landscape. Many media conglomerates are choosing to retain rights to popular legacy TV shows and films rather than selling the rights to other streamers. This means that streamers need to fill out their libraries with original content since they cannot rely on securing (or renewing) licenses to existing titles. This is arguably leading to a shift from quality to quantity in the current TV landscape: in 2009 there were 210 scripted series produced in the US, while in 2019 there were 532.[7] In this era of "peak TV," FX CEO John Landgraf has cautioned that it is "impossible to maintain quality control with too many shows."[8]

The HBO quality brand is not immune to the changes of peak TV.[9] During a company town hall meeting after the acquisition of Time Warner, John Stankey, head of WarnerMedia, indicated that HBO would "have to come up with more content, transforming itself from a boutique operation, with a focus on its signature night line-up, into something bigger and broader."[10] In the wake of leaked audio from the meeting, HBO executives assured the public and critics that AT&T's involvement would not dilute HBO's brand excellence.[11] As of 2021 there has been no sign of this, although there is great potential for brand confusion with the introduction of HBO Max originals. HBO Max originals, created specifically for the streaming service, are more numerous, are skewed to a younger audience, and draw upon WarnerMedia's licensed properties (such as DC Comics). Shows that originally aired on HBO and are closely associated with the network are now appearing as HBO Max originals, and HBO originals are also premiering early on HBO Max. The similarity of the brand names and crossover between properties will likely result in audience confusion and changing expectations about what an HBO show is.[12]

Looking at the wider TV landscape, there are potential pros and cons for long-form historical programming. Quantity could result in histories of hitherto unfilmed historical periods and obscure events, as well as multiple histories of the same event presented from a variety of viewpoints. It could also mean that television histories continue to embrace narrative complexity and become even more experimental. Quantity also potentially opens the door to more diverse showrunners, writers, and production teams, who may approach history through different lenses. (Note that all the showrunners/creators of the series examined in this book were white men.) These trends are already in evidence, so more programming could allow them to flourish further. However, an oversaturation of historical programming and increased narrowcasting could also mean that shows will fail to connect with a wide audience. Even shows with *Treme*'s modest viewership numbers might end up being considered a hit, and historical dramas may become as niche as academic histories. This would, of course, not take away from the historical work they do, but TV's ability to connect with audiences who may not usually engage with history, or particular kinds of history, is a big part of its power.

Regardless of whether peak TV has reached its peak and will start to decline, it is safe to say that history programming will always be a part of the schedule—even when there is no schedule per se. Television histories will not only contribute new historical insights, as this book has shown, but continue to shape how people understand the past, as well as the world they currently live in. "In the contemporary anglophone world," Jerome de Groot reminds us, "the ways in which individuals encounter time, the past, 'history,' and memory mostly fall outside an academic or professional framework."[13] Television, film, music, novels, comics, board games, and video games are just some of the ways people come into contact with the past. For Vivian Sobchack, me, and presumably millions of other viewers, filmic and televisual renderings of the past are the "most compelling accounts" of history. Sobchack eloquently captures the attraction of history on-screen, praising the ability of the moving image "to *tell* me things by *showing* them to me, by their spectacular *narratives of display.*"[14] She is critical of scholars who dismiss both history on-screen and the audiences who watch. This, she argues, is too "elitist a perspective—particularly if we want to understand how historical consciousness emerges in a culture in which we are all immersed in images." Drawing upon her own memories of being a cinematically competent child, Sobchack refuses to see the audience as passive or dumb, suggesting that filmgoers have "learned the lessons of Hayden White's *MetaHistory* even if they've never read it."[15] While I believe this may be an overstatement, I agree that the ability of audiences to understand and read moving images has been underestimated. Historians need to keep up with the viewing public and stay abreast of visual literacy. Historical films and TV shows are often crafted by an incredibly smart, talented, and research-focused team and then viewed by a diverse, media-savvy audience.

By exploring the way history on TV is crafted and attempting to understand the different forms history can take in television shows, this book has sought to appreciate what history on-screen is currently capable of. I do not want to suggest that any one type of history—history on film, history on TV, or traditional academic history—is better than another, but I do believe that each has its own unique capabilities. Traditional written history, the most established form of history, is, of course, going to serve as the benchmark against which these comparatively new forms are measured. Comparing history on-screen to academic written history is not necessarily a bad thing, as it can highlight not only history on TV's shortcomings but its strengths too. The aural and visual elements of history on-screen, aspects that are respectively overlooked and criticized, are its strengths, having the ability to affect viewers in a bodily way, to show rather than tell, and to add to the argument of the text. Moreover, criticisms commonly leveled at history on-screen—that it presents a linear narrative glossing over the complexities of history, ignores opposing interpretations, and fails to comply with rigorous standards of referencing—have also proved to be unfounded.[16] The way history on TV fulfils the requirements of traditional written history can be indirect and requires careful viewing on the part of the audience, but, importantly, these concerns can be addressed. Indeed, it is in addressing these concerns that the long-form series, rather than feature film, reveals its potential as a vehicle for history. As Glen Creeber has pointed out, early historical miniseries such as *Roots* and *Holocaust* "demonstrated the serial's potential to take on large and difficult historical subjects."[17] This potential has only grown in recent years. The longer running time and complex narrative structure of TV series, coupled with recent changes within the TV industry that encourage experimentation, fragmentation, and an invested audience, have resulted in a medium with an incredible ability to tell historical stories.

Not all TV histories are the same, though, and rather than thinking of historical TV dramas as a monolithic category, it is more accurate to recognize the different types of television history that exist. *Band of Brothers* is a synthetic TV history. Gary R. Edgerton has argued that all history on TV is "essentially *synthetic* in nature and should not be judged on whether or not it generates new knowledge as much as it should on how creatively and responsibly it sheds additional light on the existing historical record."[18] Synthetic histories essentially rely upon existing scholarship to shape their narrative and argument. *Band of Brothers,* which closely follows the story laid down in Ambrose's book and crafts a familiar Good War interpretation, fits into this category.

*Band of Brothers* draws heavily from other sources and can be categorized as a synthetic history, but this does not preclude it from having historical value. Although restating data and arguments found elsewhere, the series crafts an interpretation of the Second World War that simply cannot be found in books. The sound, special effects, hair and makeup, costume design, and production design departments fashioned a richly textured "feel" of World War Two that encompasses everything from jumping out of a C-47 above Normandy to the horror of finding a friend's blown-off leg in the snow. The series creates historical space, showing viewers how Easy Company carried out its tactical maneuvers, like those at Brécourt Manor. *Band of Brothers* also exhibits an incredibly complex aural interpretation of World War Two. If we look beyond character and narrative to the unique sights and sounds of television and consider what they alone can offer, we can see that even synthetic histories such as *Band of Brothers* can generate "new knowledge." However, not all history on TV is primarily synthetic; further categories are required to accurately capture the varied approaches to presenting and engaging with history in dramatic series.

*Treme* comes closest to adhering to the standards of academic history and thus can be classified simply as an audiovisual history, a category that surely deserves a place within the discipline. It may at first appear strange that I have identified *Treme,* a show populated with invented characters, as an audiovisual history, while *Band of Brothers,* based on a book by a historian and charting the experiences of real men, has been designated a synthetic history. While *Treme* is centered on invented characters, the show demonstrates a commitment to being faithful in all aspects to the realities of life in post-Katrina New Orleans and also separates itself from synthetic histories by acknowledging debates and presenting opposing arguments on key issues. This approach was shaped by Overmyer and Simon, who, more so than Winter and Milch, felt it was crucial to tell as true a story as possible and were likely influenced by Simon's background as a journalist.[19] Simon and Overmyer ultimately followed many of the same processes as traditional historians when they created *Treme.* They selected aspects of New Orleans culture they believed would best support their overarching argument—that New Orleans is a unique American city that needs to be rebuilt—and incorporated them into the show. Based upon their research, they crafted a narrative they believed accurately reflected post-Katrina New Orleans. With such a recent period in history, the showrunners, along with all of the departments involved in production, could not rely on existing literature and instead had to shape their own interpretations, drawing heavily on firsthand accounts from their consultants and other interviewees.

*Treme*'s approach to history does potentially limit its reach. Compared to HBO's other historical series, the ratings for *Treme* were very small.[20] I believe this was largely down to the fact that Simon and Overmyer privileged telling a "true story" that was often slow and pedagogic over creating a series that prioritized keeping the audience entertained. All the categories of history on TV have their own advantages and drawbacks. The drawback of audiovisual history is that it may only find a modest audience (much like academic history), but presenting a more original and challenging interpretation of history is its advantage. The still-raw wounds of many Americans, especially those in the affected Gulf Coast region, also need to be considered when assessing the series' interpretation of history. With such a traumatic event that many experienced firsthand, it would have surely been a risk for the showrunners to take too much liberty with the documented facts. Viewers, critics, and scholars are likely going to be more open to a TV series that embellishes history and plays with the facts when they have a certain amount of distance from that event or period. Historical series like *Deadwood* and *Boardwalk Empire,* set outside living memory for most people, are not going to come under the same amount of scrutiny as *Treme* and thus have a greater unofficial license to invent freely.

*Deadwood* and *Boardwalk Empire* fit squarely into Alison Landberg's description of historically conscious dramas, the third category of history on TV. Unlike synthetic histories and audiovisual histories, historically conscious dramas are seemingly less tethered to the historical record and are perhaps the most difficult category of history on TV for historians to come to terms with. *Deadwood* and *Boardwalk Empire,* along with other historically conscious dramas, package history in recognizable genres and employ familiar tropes to attract a wider audience. Nonetheless, they produce "a kind of historical knowledge that even an academic historian would recognize as having value." Historically conscious dramas, Landsberg explains, are not generally based around one historical event or figure, but instead function like an experiment in social history. The value of these histories comes from the historical understanding they encourage, conjuring up a more general "period truth" rather than attempting to reconstruct events piece by piece.[21]

The historically conscious drama is the broadest of the three categories and has the greatest capacity for experimentation. *Deadwood* and *Boardwalk Empire* are both similar in that they incorporate real and invented characters and include both real and invented events. But even within these two shows there are differences in how history is employed and the role that it plays in the larger scheme of the narrative. The historical storylines in *Deadwood* involving annexation and the evolution of the camp have a greater bearing on the overall trajectory of the show, whereas in *Boardwalk Empire* personal storylines between the invented characters often have greater weight than the historical threads. Certainly, all historically conscious dramas are not the same, and there is incredible potential within this category to craft historical narratives in ways that are unorthodox yet rewarding. Amazon's *The Man in the High Castle* (2015–19), based loosely on a Philip K. Dick novel, is set in an alternate reality where the Axis powers won World War Two. When the show opens in the early 1960s, the United States as we know it no longer exists; the West Coast has become the Japanese Pacific States, while the eastern and central states have been incorporated in the Greater Nazi Reich (with a neutral buffer zone along the Rocky Mountains). I would argue that this science fiction series could also be categorized as a historically conscious drama. The storylines involving Obergruppenführer John Smith and his family, for example, provide an insight into the policies and propaganda of Nazi Germany. Despite the fact that this is an alternate reality, it summons a "historical sensibility" of life in the Third Reich. That *The Man in the High Castle* is so clearly a fabrication is also potentially an advantage. The past that it presents is undoubtedly a "foreign country" to viewers, a condition that Landsberg stresses must be present to stimulate critical historical thinking on the part of the audience. Transporting an examination of the Nazi regime to an unfamiliar time and place constantly forces viewers out of the narrative. They have to negotiate between what they already know about this very familiar subject and the unconventional interpretation on-screen.

Historically conscious drama is the category of history on TV with the greatest license to invent, but all three types engage in invention. In this, though, it is worth repeating that they are not so far removed from written histories. "'History' can only be imagined and fictively 'formed,'" Alun Munslow tells us. "The authored narrative we call history is never 'found' in the past." Relying on the empirical traces of the past, historians infer the most plausible explanation and craft a narrative they believe represents "the most likely history." While historians are not free to invent and have a responsibility to use data and evidence, writing a history is still "a process of imagination and fictive construal."[22] Ann Curthoys and John Docker likewise argue that history has a dual nature: "It both partakes of the world of literary forms, and at the same time is a rigorous intellectual practice which seeks to achieve historical truth."[23] The revelation that fiction is an inherent part of history is not particularly new, but it is an idea that is currently being embraced and is stimulating a reconsideration of the different forms history can take. The relationship between history and the historical novel is just one area generating exciting new scholarship, with scholars exploring similar issues revolving around history and fiction.[24] I prefer to use the term "invention" rather than "fiction" when discussing the way history is crafted on-screen. "Invention" suggests an almost scientific process that acknowledges the research and reasoning that went into creating the invention, while "fiction" can have an almost arbitrary connotation. This is not to say, though, that "pure fiction" for the sake of adding drama and tension does not have its place in history on TV. Ultimately, the fact that the four TV series invent historical people, dialogue, events, sounds, and sets does not invalidate them as history. More invention can arguably result in a better history.

Invention is unavoidable in all types of history, but for history on-screen especially, it is a tool that enables historical events, arguments, and ideas to be represented effectively. This is clearly demonstrated by *Treme,* which used invented characters and incidents to make a strong argument about the city of New Orleans and the struggles of its residents. The study of character in *Boardwalk Empire* likewise demonstrated that invented characters have the greatest potential to explore a variety of historical issues. The chapter also showcased the possibilities for mixing real and exceptional histories (Capone) with invented and generic histories (Darmody). An exceptional true story told in isolation can potentially mislead an audience by giving a false impression of a period or event.[25] When the invented and the real interact in the same narrative, however, the invented element can have the effect of demythologizing the exceptional, thus creating a more rounded picture. Invention is not only a useful tool in crafting historical narratives and characters; it also makes it possible to film actors in appropriate settings, accompanied by relevant sound effects and with the right clothes, hair, and makeup. Film crews invent the physical and aural traces of the past that are needed to render the past on-screen. Their research and decision-making processes are no less complex than the processes of the writers and showrunners who craft the characters and narrative. Novelist Tim O'Brien perhaps best captured the potential of invention when he wrote: "A thing may happen and be a total lie; another thing may not happen and be truer than the truth."[26]

What is crucial in crafting all types of inventions is that they are based on knowledge rather than ignorance. *Treme* shifted dates and included some anachronisms, but the showrunners and writers made those decisions knowing they were altering the historical record.[27] Changing such relatively minor facts facilitated telling the history more effectively on-screen. It becomes problematic when inventions are based on bad research or when they clash with the empirical data and ignore the discourse of history. The third episode of *Band of Brothers,* for example, focuses on Albert Blithe and charts his struggles coming to terms with what he must do to fulfil his duties as a soldier. By the end of the episode, Blithe has overcome the worst of his fears, but during a volunteer patrol he is badly injured. The postscript closing the episode explains that Blithe never recovered from his wounds and died in 1948. In truth, the real Albert Blithe went on to serve in the US Army for another twenty years and died in 1967.[28] Many young men were obviously petrified by what they experienced and died tragic deaths; this is not a false invention per se. The problem is that *Band of Brothers,* as a synthetic history populated almost exclusively with real historical figures, does not have the license to invent someone's history so freely. The parameters to invent are dictated in part by the type of history that is being created; synthetic histories and audiovisual histories have only a certain amount of leeway, and assessing inventions as either true or false is a relatively straightforward task. When reading and judging the inventions of historically conscious dramas, we need to be more flexible in allowing "pure fiction" that adds drama and conflict. We must first parse out the central focus and objective of the series and judge the inventions accordingly.

*History by HBO* has identified the diverse and distinctive components that compose historical television dramas and has suggested productive ways of reading and assessing this form of history. Indeed, the approaches used in this study can equally be applied to all types of TV programming, as well as feature films and other performative and experiential forms of history. The four HBO case studies have showcased what history on TV is capable of; analysis of other past, present, and future TV shows will surely reveal yet more innovative and unique ways the past is rendered in serial dramas. The fact that history is an "inventive, self-transforming discipline" and that long-form dramas are constantly adapting to changes in the industry and developments in technology means that there will always be new avenues to pursue in this area of study.[29]

# Acknowledgments

This work originated as a PhD thesis, so first and foremost I must thank my supervisors, Jennifer Frost and Allan Cameron, at the University of Auckland (UoA). It was amazing to have a historian and a film and media scholar in my corner; both provided invaluable feedback and helped me shape and develop this project. I am eternally grateful to Jennifer for introducing me to this area of study and, most importantly, for her unwavering support and encouragement over the years.

I am indebted to those professionals—Terence Winter, Maria Caso, James Boyle, and Erik Bork—who took time out of their busy schedules to correspond and talk with me about their time working on the HBO shows under examination. They provided insights that could not have been found anywhere else.

A postdoctoral research award from the Kate Edger Educational Charitable Trust allowed me to continue work on this project, for which I am immensely grateful. I would also like to thank the history department at UoA for granting me an honorary academic appointment and for creating an energizing learning environment. I learned so much from the lecturers I studied under and taught alongside. Finally, thanks to Patricia Bell and Naomi Burge for proofreading early drafts.

# Notes

## Introduction

1. See, for example, the essays contained within Marc Leverette, Brian L. Ott, and Cara Louise Buckley, eds., *It's Not TV: Watching HBO in the Post-Television Era* (New York: Routledge, 2008).

2. Lynn Spigel, "Introduction," in *Television after TV: Essays on a Medium in Transition,* ed. Jan Olsson and Lynn Spigel (Durham, NC: Duke University Press, 2004), 6.

3. Graeme Turner and Jinna Tay, "Introduction," in *Television Studies after TV: Understanding Television in the Post-Broadcast Era,* ed. Graeme Turner and Jinna Tay (New York: Routledge, 2009), 2.

4. Chuck Tryon, *On-Demand Culture: Digital Delivery and the Future of Movies* (New Brunswick, NJ: Rutgers University Press, 2013), 4.

5. Martin Lister et al. define new media as "those methods and social practices of communication, representation, and expression that have developed using the digital, multimedia, networked computer and the ways this machine is held to have transformed work in other media: from books to movies, from telephones to television." Martin Lister et al., *New Media: A Critical Introduction,* 2nd ed. (New York: Routledge, 2009), 2.

6. Amanda D. Lotz, *The Television Will Be Revolutionized,* 2nd ed. (New York: NYU Press, 2014), 3.

7. The length of original TV series produced by cable networks and streaming providers differs immensely, although arguably a ten-episode season is standard. Some series run significantly shorter, others longer, and season lengths are not always consistent for the same show. *The Walking Dead* (AMC, 2010–22), for example, had a first season that consisted of only six episodes, while all future seasons were thirteen to sixteen episodes long, with a two-month midseason hiatus halfway through each season (leading to the use of abbreviations such as season 2a and 2b).

8. John Ellis, *Seeing Things: Television in the Age of Uncertainty* (New York: I. B. Tauris, 2000), 162.

9. Basic cable channels "are the channels that come automatically with a cable subscription," explains Bill Mesce Jr., and most carry advertising. Premium (also known as pay TV) channels are not included in basic cable packages "and need to be specifically requested by the subscriber and require the sub to pay an extra fee." Bill Mesce Jr., *Inside the Rise of HBO: A Personal History of the Company That Transformed Television* (Jefferson, NC: McFarland, 2015), 83.

10. Turner and Tay, "Introduction," 2.

11. Spigel, "Introduction," 1; Lotz, *Television Will Be Revolutionized,* 5; Ethan Thompson and Jason Mittell, "Introduction: An Owner's Manual for Television," in *How to Watch Television,* ed. Ethan Thompson and Jason Mittell (New York: NYU Press, 2013), 5.

12. Lotz, *Television Will Be Revolutionized,* 3.

13. Robin Nelson, "Quality TV Drama: Estimations and Emotions through Time and Space," in *Quality TV: Contemporary American Television,* ed. Janet McCabe and Kim Akass (New York: I. B. Tauris, 2007), 39–40.

14. Different studies offer slightly differing periodization. Here I am drawing primarily upon the work of Mark C. Rogers, Michael Epstein, and Jimmie L. Reeves (TVI/TVII/TVIII) and Amanda D. Lotz (network era / multichannel transition / postnetwork era). For more detail, see Mark C. Rogers, Michael Epstein, and Jimmie L. Reeves, "*The Sopranos* as Brand Equity: The Art of Commerce in the Age of Digital Reproduction," in *This Thing of Ours: Investigating "The Sopranos,"* ed. David Lavery (New York: Columbia University Press, 2002), 43–44; Lotz, *Television Will Be Revolutionized,* 21–32.

15. Roberta Pearson, "Cult Television as Digital Television's Cutting Edge," in *Television as Digital Media,* ed. James Bennett and Niki Strange (Durham, NC: Duke University Press, 2011), 107.

16. Jane Feuer, "HBO and the Concept of Quality TV," in McCabe and Akass, *Quality TV,* 146.

17. Jason Jacobs, "Experimental and Live Television in the US," in *The Television History Book,* ed. Michele Hilmes (London: British Film Institute, 2003), 72–75.

18. For example, see Jane Feuer, Paul Kerr, and Tise Vahimagi, eds., *MTM "Quality Television"* (London: British Film Institute, 1984); Charlotte Brunsdon, "Problems with Quality," *Screen* 31, no. 1 (1990): 67–90; Robert J. Thompson, *Television's Second Golden Age: From "Hill Street Blues" to "ER"* (New York: Continuum, 1996).

19. Thompson, *Television's Second Golden Age,* 98.

20. Robert J. Thompson, "Preface," in McCabe and Akass, *Quality TV,* xvii.

21. John Caughie, *Television Drama: Realism, Modernism, and British Culture* (Oxford: Oxford University Press, 2000), 57.

22. Feuer, "HBO and the Concept of Quality TV," 146, 148.

23. Dean DeFino, *The HBO Effect* (New York: Bloomsbury Academic, 2014), 10. Also see Sean Fuller and Catherine Driscoll for an excellent definition of postnetwork quality TV. Sean Fuller and Catherine Driscoll, "HBO's Girls: Gender, Generation, and Quality Television," *Continuum* 29, no. 2 (2015): 258.

24. For a much more detailed history of the company and its entrepreneurial moves in the TV industry, see DeFino, *HBO Effect,* 4–5, 61–64; Gary R. Edgerton, "Introduction: A Brief History of HBO," in *The Essential HBO Reader,* ed. Gary R. Edgerton and Jeffrey P. Jones (Lexington: University Press of Kentucky, 2008), 1–20; Marc Leverette, Brian L. Ott, and Cara Louise Buckley, "Introduction," in Leverette, Ott, and Buckley, *It's Not TV,* 2–7; George Mair, *Inside HBO: The Billion Dollar War between HBO, Hollywood, and the Home Video Revolution* (New York: Dodd Mead, 1988).

25. Trisha Dunleavy, *Complex Serial Drama and Multiplatform Television* (New York: Routledge, 2017), 20.

26. Rogers, Epstein, and Reeves, "*The Sopranos* as Brand Equity," 46–47.

27. Christopher Anderson, "Producing an Aristocracy of Culture in American Television," in Edgerton and Jones, *Essential HBO Reader,* 31–33; Leverette et al., "Introduction," 3.

28. DeFino, *HBO Effect,* 14.

29. John Mack Faragher, "*Deadwood:* Not Your Typical Western," *Montana: The Magazine of Western History* 57, no. 3 (2007): 62.

30. Edgerton, "A Brief History of HBO," 13.

31. Janet McCabe and Kim Akass, "It's Not TV, It's HBO's Original Programming," in Leverette, Ott, and Buckley, *It's Not TV,* 87.

32. Dunleavy, *Complex Serial Drama,* 24.

33. Leverette et al., "Introduction," 1.

34. Sue Harper, "Bonnie Prince Charlie Revisited: British Costume Film in the 1950s," in *The British Cinema Book,* ed. Robert Murphy (London: British Film Institute, 1997), 133.

35. James Chapman, *Past and Present: National Identity and the British Historical Film* (London: I. B. Tauris, 2005), 3.

36. Natalie Zemon Davis, "'Any Resemblance to Persons Living or Dead': Film and the Challenge of Authenticity," *Historical Journal of Film, Radio and Television* 8, no. 3 (1988): 270.

37. Alison Landsberg, *Engaging the Past: Mass Culture and the Production of Historical Knowledge* (New York: Columbia University Press, 2015), 62.

38. Landsberg, *Engaging the Past,* 85 (italics in original).

39. David Eldridge, *Hollywood's History Films* (London: I. B. Tauris, 2006), 5.

40. As these examples demonstrate, war, and more specifically World War II ("Bomber's Moon," *The Execution of Private Slovik, Hiroshima, Hogan's Heroes,*

*Goodtime Girls, Holocaust,* and *The Winds of War*), has always been a popular period for TV narratives.

41. Gary R. Edgerton, "Television as Historian: A Different Kind of History Altogether," in *Television Histories: Shaping Collective Memory in the Media Age,* ed. Gary R. Edgerton and Peter C. Rollins (Lexington: University Press of Kentucky, 2001), 1.

42. What the authors discovered when crafting the survey questions was that they needed to ask people about the past, not just history. "Our pilot survey showed that three quarters of those we interviewed thought of 'the past' and 'history' as different concepts, with most people defining the past in more inclusive terms and history as something more formal, analytical, official, or distant." Roy Rosenzweig and David Thelen, *The Presence of the Past: Popular Uses of History in American Life* (New York: Columbia University Press, 1998), 210.

43. Rosenzweig and Thelen, *Presence of the Past,* 19–21, 98, 99.

44. "Museums" actually had the highest mean score of 8.4 for trustworthiness, followed by "personal accounts from grandparents or other relatives" with 8.0 and "conversation with someone who was there (witness)" with a mean of 7.8. Rosenzweig and Thelen, *Presence of the Past,* 21, 97.

45. Robert Burgoyne is a particularly important scholar in this area. Burgoyne has explored how Hollywood feature films both reflect and construct American national identity. Studying a range of films from the late 1980s to the mid-2000s, he suggests that a "cinematic rewriting of history [is] currently taking shape, which stands as a particularly conspicuous attempt to rearticulate the cultural narratives that define the American nation." He sees these films as challenging the traditional myths of the nation-state and promoting instead a new national narrative that embraces "civic pluralism." For more see Robert Burgoyne, *Film Nation: Hollywood Looks at U.S. History,* 2nd ed. (Minneapolis: University of Minnesota Press, 2010).

46. Graeme Turner, "Television and the Nation: Does This Matter Anymore?," in Turner and Tay, *Television Studies after TV,* 54.

47. Chapman, *Past and Present,* 6.

48. Mark Connelly, "*Gallipoli* (1981): 'A Poignant Search for National Identity,'" in *The New Film History: Sources, Methods, Approaches,* ed. James Chapman, Mark Glancy, and Sue Harper (Basingstoke, UK: Palgrave Macmillan, 2007), 41.

49. Tessa Morris-Suzuki, *The Past within Us: Media, Memory, History* (New York: Verso, 2005), 153.

50. Alison Landsberg, *Prosthetic Memory: The Transformation of American Remembrance in the Age of Mass Culture* (New York: Columbia University Press, 2004), 2–3.

51. As Glen Creeber points out, both these shows were accused by critics of trivializing the history they presented. Glen Creeber, "'Taking Our Personal

Lives Seriously': Intimacy, Continuity and Memory in the Television Drama Serial," *Media, Culture & Society* 23, no. 4 (2001): 444–50.

52. Morris-Suzuki, *Past within Us,* 147.

53. It is worth noting that the views of those working and publishing within the field of history-on-screen studies may not necessarily reflect the views of the discipline as a whole. Acceptance of film and TV by the wider historical community is moving at a slower pace. For example, while many leading historical journals now include film and TV reviews alongside book reviews, the spectrum of films chosen is generally narrow. The four issues of the *Journal of American History* released in 2016 contained a total of eleven film and TV reviews, six of which were documentaries. The remaining five feature films all centered on real historical figures and included three biopics: *Trumbo* (Roach, 2015), *Born to Be Blue* (Budreau, 2015), and *Miles Ahead* (Cheadle, 2015). The remaining two films, *Spotlight* (McCarthy, 2015) and *The Finest Hours* (Gillespie, 2016) were ensemble dramas that documented real events. Of the five films, only *The Finest Hours,* a big-budget action/adventure/romance Disney film, pushes the boundary of what may be considered a historical film.

54. Robert Rosenstone and Constantin Parvulescu, "Introduction," in *A Companion to the Historical Film,* ed. Robert Rosenstone and Constantin Parvulescu (Malden, MA: Wiley-Blackwell, 2013), 2.

55. These, of course, are not the only early works on history and film. Two other important early works include Paul Smith, ed., *The Historian and Film* (Cambridge: Cambridge University Press, 1976), and Warren Susman, "Film and History: Artifact and Experience," *Film and History* 15, no. 2 (1985): 25–36. For a detailed historiography of history-on-film writing, see Mia M. Treacey, *Reframing the Past: History, Film and Television* (New York: Routledge, 2016).

56. Pierre Sorlin, *The Film in History: Restaging the Past* (Oxford: Blackwell, 1980), vii, 207.

57. Marc Ferro, *Cinema and History,* trans. Naomi Greene (Detroit: Wayne State University Press, 1988), 163.

58. David Herlihy, "Am I a Camera? Other Reflections on Films and History," *American Historical Review* 93, no. 5 (1988): 1191, 1188–90, 1192.

59. Rosenstone's essay, "History in Images / History in Words: Reflections on the Possibility of Really Putting History onto Film," was the lead article that the others were directly responding to. For all articles see the *American Historical Review* 93, no. 5 (1988): 1173–227. O'Connor had already published on the subject of history on film and television before this article and would continue to do so afterwards, editing a prolific number of books (often with Peter C. Rollins) on different periods of American history on film. Toplin would also go on to publish several books on the topic of film and history.

60. Hayden White, "Historiography and Historiophoty," *American Historical Review* 93, no. 5 (1988): 1193.

61. White, "Historiography and Historiophoty," 1193.

62. Davis, "'Any Resemblance to Persons Living or Dead,'" 269–83.

63. The five films Davis looks at are *Spartacus* (Kubrick, 1960), *Burn!* (Pontecorvo, 1969), *The Last Supper* (Gutiérrez Alea, 1976), *Amistad* (Spielberg, 1997), and *Beloved* (Demme, 1998).

64. Natalie Zemon Davis, *Slaves on Screen: Film and Historical Vision* (Cambridge, MA: Harvard University Press, 2000), 15.

65. William Guynn, *Writing History in Film* (New York: Routledge, 2006), 10.

66. In addition to his *AHR* article, Rosenstone's most valuable contributions to the field of history on film include: Robert Rosenstone, "*JFK*: Historical Fact/Historical Film," *American Historical Review* 97, no. 2 (1992): 506–11; Robert Rosenstone, *Visions of the Past: The Challenge of Film to Our Idea of History* (Cambridge, MA: Harvard University Press, 1995); Robert Rosenstone, ed., *Revisioning History: Film and the Construction of a New Past* (Princeton, NJ: Princeton University Press, 1995); Robert Rosenstone, "The Future of the Past: Film and the Beginnings of Postmodern History," in *The Persistence of History: Cinema, Television, and the Modern Event,* ed. Vivian Sobchack (New York: Routledge, 1996), 201–18; Robert Rosenstone, "Oliver Stone as Historian," in *Oliver Stone's USA: Film, History, and Controversy,* ed. Robert Brent Toplin (Lawrence: University Press of Kansas, 2000), 26–39; Robert Rosenstone, *History on Film / Film on History,* 2nd ed. (Harlow, UK: Pearson Education, 2012); Rosenstone and Parvulescu, *Companion to the Historical Film.* Most recently, Rosenstone has written a memoir that chronicles his shifting research interests and the origins of his own involvement in the study of history on film. Robert Rosenstone, *Adventures of a Postmodern Historian: Living and Writing the Past* (London: Bloomsbury, 2016).

67. The article he is referring to was originally published in *Reviews in American History.* Robert Rosenstone, "Reds as History," *Reviews in American History* 10, no. 3 (1982): 299–310.

68. Robert Rosenstone, "The History Film as a Mode of Historical Thought," in Rosenstone and Parvulescu, *Companion to the Historical Film,* 86.

69. Rosenstone, "History Film as a Mode of Historical Thought," 72–73.

70. Useful published tomes on the subject include Tony Barta, ed., *Screening the Past: Film and the Representation of History* (Westport, CT: Praeger, 1998); Dennis Bingham, *Whose Lives Are They Anyway? The Biopic as Contemporary Film Genre* (New Brunswick, NJ: Rutgers University Press, 2010); Tom Brown, *Spectacle in "Classical" Cinemas: Musicality and Historicity in the 1930s* (New York: Routledge, 2016); Burgoyne, *Film Nation;* Robert Burgoyne, *The Hollywood Historical Film* (Malden, MA: Blackwell, 2008); Mike Chopra-Gant, *Cinema and*

*History: The Telling of Stories* (London: Wallflower, 2008); George Custen, *Bio/pics: How Hollywood Constructed Public History* (New Brunswick, NJ: Rutgers University Press, 1992); Eldridge, *Hollywood's History Films;* Leger Grindon, *Shadows on the Past: Studies in the Historical Fiction Film* (Philadelphia: Temple University Press, 1996); Guynn, *Writing History in Film;* Marcia Landy, *Cinematic Uses of the Past* (Minneapolis: University of Minnesota Press, 1996); Trevor McCrisken and Andrew Pepper, *American History and Contemporary Hollywood Film* (Edinburgh: Edinburgh University Press, 2005); Patrick McGee, *Bad History and the Logics of Blockbuster Cinema* (New York: Palgrave Macmillan, 2012); Kathryn Anne Morey, ed., *Bringing History to Life through Film: The Art of Cinematic Storytelling* (Lanham, MD: Rowman & Littlefield, 2014); Bruno Ramirez, *Inside the Historical Film* (Montreal: McGill-Queens University Press, 2014); Philip Rosen, *Change Mummified: Cinema, Historicity, Theory* (Minneapolis: University of Minnesota Press, 2001); Melvyn Stokes, *American History through Hollywood Film: From the Revolution to the 1960s* (London: Bloomsbury Academic, 2013); Jonathan Stubbs, *Historical Film: A Critical Introduction* (New York: Bloomsbury Academic, 2013); Jonathan Stubbs, *Hollywood and the Invention of England: Projecting the English Past in American Cinema, 1930–2017* (New York: Bloomsbury Academic, 2019).

71. See, for example, Kenneth M. Cameron, *America on Film: Hollywood and American History* (New York: Continuum, 1997); Marc C. Carnes, *Past Imperfect: History According to the Movies* (New York: H. Holt, 1995); Joseph Roquemore, *History Goes to the Movies* (New York: Main Street Books, 1999).

72. J. E. Smyth, *Reconstructing American Historical Cinema: From "Cimarron" to "Citizen Kane"* (Lexington: University Press of Kentucky, 2006). See also J. E. Smyth, ed., *Hollywood and the American Historical Film* (New York: Palgrave Macmillan, 2012).

73. Marcia Landy, *Cinema and Counter-History* (Bloomington: Indiana University Press, 2015), x, 251 (emphasis in original).

74. Marnie Hughes-Warrington, *History Goes to the Movies: Studying History on Film* (New York: Routledge, 2007); Marnie Hughes-Warrington, ed., *The History on Film Reader* (New York: Routledge, 2009).

75. Julia Erhart, *Gendering History on Screen: Women Filmmakers and Historical Films* (New York: I. B. Tauris, 2018).

76. For a selection of work see Andrew Higson, "Re-presenting the National Past: Nostalgia and Pastiche in the Heritage Film," *British Cinema and Thatcherism: Fires Were Started,* ed. Lester Friedman (London: University College of London Press, 1993), 109–29; Andrew Higson, *English Heritage, English Cinema: Costume Drama since 1980* (Oxford: Oxford University Press, 2003); Claire Monk and Amy Sargeant, eds., *British Historical Cinema: The History, Heritage and Costume Film* (New York: Routledge, 2001); Julianne Pidduck, *Contemporary*

*Costume Film: Space, Place and the Past* (London: British Film Institute, 2004); Belén Vidal, *Figuring the Past: Period Film and the Mannerist Aesthetic* (Amsterdam: Amsterdam University Press, 2012); Belén Vidal, *Heritage Film: Nation, Genre and Representation* (London: Wallflower, 2012).

77. The works that I have predominantly discussed thus far either are general history-on-film texts or focus more specifically on American history on film. There are, of course, also a variety of books that center on other historical places, periods, and specific events. Medieval Europe is just one period that has generated a vast literature of single-authored works and edited collections that explore how history is presented on-screen.

78. In *The Past within Us,* for example, Tessa Morris-Suzuki examines photographs, films, comic books, and the internet.

79. Cannadine's collection pays the greatest attention to history on TV, with only one essay relating to history on film. David Cannadine, ed., *History and the Media* (New York: Palgrave Macmillan, 2004); Marcia Landy, ed., *The Historical Film: History and Memory in the Media* (New Brunswick, NJ: Rutgers University Press, 2001); Kathleen McDonald, ed., *Americanization of History: Conflation of Time and Culture in Film and Television* (Newcastle upon Tyne, UK: Cambridge Scholars, 2011); Laura Mee and Johnny Walker, eds., *Cinema, Television and History: New Approaches* (Newcastle upon Tyne, UK: Cambridge Scholars, 2014); Vivian Sobchack, ed., *The Persistence of History: Cinema, Television, and the Modern Event* (New York: Routledge, 1996); Sam Edwards, Faye Sayer, and Michael Dolski, eds., *Histories on Screen: The Past and Present in Anglo-American Cinema and Television* (New York: Bloomsbury Academic, 2018).

80. Landsberg, *Engaging the Past.*

81. William Guynn's book on traumatic and catastrophic events in the twentieth century suggests that "film is exceptionally capable of evoking the affective dimension of the past." Jerome de Groot's most recent book argues that the affective nature of films, TV shows, plays, and novels is "fundamental to the historiography of the texts." William Guynn, *Unspeakable Histories: Film and the Experience of Catastrophe* (New York: Columbia University Press, 2016), 1; Jerome de Groot, *Remaking History: The Past in Contemporary Historical Fictions* (New York: Routledge, 2016), 151.

82. Erin Bell and Ann Gray, eds., *Televising History: Mediating the Past in Postwar Europe* (Basingstoke, UK: Palgrave Macmillan, 2010); Ann Gray and Erin Bell, *History on Television* (London: Routledge, 2013). See also Graham Roberts and Philip M. Taylor, eds., *The Historian, Television and Television History: A Collection* (Luton, UK: University of Luton Press, 2001).

83. Edgerton and Rollins, *Television Histories.*

84. Alexander Dhoest, "History in Popular Television Drama: The Flemish Past in *Wij, Heren van Zichem,*" in Bell and Gray, *Televising History,* 182–88.

85. Steve Anderson, "History TV and Popular Memory," in Edgerton and Rollins, *Television Histories,* 26.

86. In a review of Landy's *Cinema and Counter-History,* J. E. Smyth states that she worries "increasingly about how 'history' is defined within film and media studies." J. E. Smyth, review of *Cinema and Counter-History,* by Marcia Landy, *Film Quarterly* 69, no. 4 (2016): 133.

87. Alun Munslow, *Deconstructing History,* 2nd ed. (New York: Routledge, 2006), 80.

88. Rosenstone, "History Film as a Mode of Historical Thought," 84.

89. Rosenstone, *Visions of the Past,* 77.

90. Rosenstone, *History on Film / Film on History,* 44.

91. The film Rosenstone uses, more often than not, to illustrate invention in dramatic feature film is Edward Zwick's *Glory* (1989). Rosenstone, *Visions of the Past,* 68–75.

92. Rosenstone, *Visions of the Past,* 72.

93. Ramirez, *Inside the Historical Film,* 43, 45.

94. Davis insists that historical evidence must be respected. If filmmakers decide to depart from the evidence and engage in invention by "creating a composite character or changing a time frame—then it should be in the spirit of the evidence and plausible, not misleading." If crafting a counterfactual history, or simply experimenting with history in some way, then the film must make this clear to the audience and must not present itself as a "true story." Davis, *Slaves on Screen,* 130–31.

95. McCrisken and Pepper, *Contemporary Hollywood Film,* 6.

96. Brett Martin describes both showrunners and lead characters on postnetwork quality TV serials as "difficult." Brett Martin, *Difficult Men: Behind the Scenes of a Creative Revolution* (New York: Penguin, 2013).

97. Jason Mittell, "Narrative Complexity in Contemporary American Television," *Velvet Light Trap* 58, no. 1 (2006): 29, 32.

## 1. Building a Historical World

1. Jason P. Vest, The Wire, Deadwood, Homicide, *and* NYPD Blue: *Violence Is Power* (Santa Barbara, CA: Praeger, 2011), 136.

2. Anthony N. Smith, *Storytelling Industries: Narrative Production in the 21st Century* (Cham, Switzerland: Palgrave Macmillan, 2018), 75.

3. Trisha Dunleavy, *Complex Serial Drama and Multiplatform Television* (New York: Routledge, 2017), 37–38.

4. William Guynn, *Writing History in Film* (New York: Routledge, 2006), 92.

5. Jonathan Stubbs, *Historical Film: A Critical Introduction* (New York: Bloomsbury Academic, 2013), 39. There are exceptions to this rule. Some foreign and

independent films eschew realist sets and opt instead for stylized and overtly artificial sets (although not a historical film, Lars von Trier's *Dogville,* 2003, is an excellent example). This remains relatively rare, even in feature films, and such experimentation in historical television shows is almost nonexistent.

6. Ed Sikov, *Film Studies: An Introduction* (New York: Columbia University Press, 2010), 8.

7. Tashiro is referring to Sorlin's 1980 book, *The Film in History: Restaging the Past.* C. S. Tashiro, *Pretty Pictures: Production Design and the History Film* (Austin: University of Texas Press, 1998), 64 (italics in original).

8. Stubbs, *Historical Film,* 41.

9. Tashiro, *Pretty Pictures,* 64.

10. Stubbs, *Historical Film,* 46.

11. Roland Barthes, *Mythologies,* trans. Annette Lavers (London: Vintage, 1993), 26.

12. Anne Hollander, "The 'Gatsby Look' and Other Costume Movie Blunders," *New York Magazine,* May 27, 1974, 58.

13. This is, of course, a generalization about the discipline as a whole. Burke recognizes that there have always been some historians who have utilized visual sources to their full potential. He also identifies the start of a shift in attitude towards the visual beginning in the 1980s. Peter Burke, *Eyewitnessing: The Uses of Images as Historical Evidence* (London: Reaktion Books, 2001), 10–13.

14. Michael L. Wilson, "Visual Culture: A Useful Category of Historical Analysis," in *The Nineteenth-Century Visual Culture Reader,* ed. Jeannene M. Przyblyski and Vanessa R. Schwartz (New York: Routledge, 2004), 29.

15. Burke, *Eyewitnessing,* 14–15.

16. Wilson, "Visual Culture," 30.

17. Robert Rosenstone, *Visions of the Past: The Challenge of Film to Our Idea of History* (Cambridge, MA: Harvard University Press, 1995), 59.

18. Robert Rosenstone, *History on Film / Film on History,* 2nd ed. (Harlow, UK: Pearson Education, 2012), 19.

19. Alison Landsberg, *Engaging the Past: Mass Culture and the Production of Historical Knowledge* (New York: Columbia University Press, 2015), 93 (italics in original).

20. Sikov, *Film Studies,* 5; John Gibbs, *Mise-en-scène: Film Style and Interpretation* (London: Wallflower, 2002), 100.

21. Adrian Martin, *Mise en Scène and Film Style: From Classical Hollywood to New Media Art* (Basingstoke, UK: Palgrave Macmillan, 2014), xiv.

22. Gibbs, *Mise-en-scène,* 1.

23. Martin, *Mise en Scène and Film Style,* 4.

24. David Bordwell, Kristin Thompson, and Jeff Smith, *Film Art: An Introduction,* 11th ed. (New York: McGraw-Hill Higher Education, 2012), 113. Other

definitions are broader and more inclusive. For Gibbs, the physical elements noted in Bordwell, Thompson, and Smith's definition provide only half the equation, which are the contents of the frame. Also included in Gibbs's concept of mise-en-scène is how these contents are organized: "framing, camera movement, the particular lens employed and other photogenic decisions." Gibbs, *Mise-en-scène,* 1.

25. Oscar-winning production designer Richard Sylbert, quoted in Peter Ettedgui, *Production Design and Art Direction* (Woburn, MA: Focal Press, 1999), 40.

26. Tashiro, *Pretty Pictures,* xvi.

27. Maria Caso, email to author, June 22, 2016.

28. Jeremy G. Butler, "Smoke Gets in Your Eyes: Historicizing Visual Style in *Mad Men,*" in *Mad Men: Dream Come True TV,* ed. Gary R. Edgerton (London: I. B. Tauris, 2010), 55–56.

29. Sue Harper, quoted in Butler, "Smoke Gets in Your Eyes," 56.

30. Eve Stewart, quoted in Fionnuala Halligan, *Production Design* (Lewes, UK: Ilex, 2012), 161.

31. Antxón Gómez, quoted in Halligan, *Production Design,* 109.

32. Tim Bergfelder, Sue Harris, and Sarah Street, *Film Architecture and the Transnational Imagination: Set Design in 1930s European Cinema* (Amsterdam: Amsterdam University Press, 2007), 14.

33. Léon Barsacq, *Caligari's Cabinet and Other Grand Illusions: A History of Film Design* (Boston: New York Graphic Society, 1976).

34. Charles Affron and Mirella Jona Affron, *Sets in Motion: Art Direction and Film Narrative* (New Brunswick, NJ: Rutgers University Press, 1995).

35. Jane Barnwell, *Production Design: Architects of the Screen* (London: Wallflower, 2004); Bergfelder, Harris, and Street, *Film Architecture;* Ettedgui, *Production Design and Art Direction;* Halligan, *Production Design;* Vincent LoBrutto, *The Filmmaker's Guide to Production Design* (New York: Allworth, 2002); Juan Antonio Ramírez, *Architecture for the Screen: A Critical Study of Set Design in Hollywood's Golden Age* (Jefferson, NC: McFarland, 2004).

36. Jane Barnwell charts the various terms used within the US industry: technical director, interior decorator, art director, and production designer. These changing terms "reflect the changing complexity and focus of the role over time." Barnwell, *Production Design,* 7–9.

37. Janie Bryant is credited on *Deadwood* as Katherine Jane Bryant. However, she now uses the professional name Janie Bryant, which is what I will be using throughout the chapter.

38. Deborah Thomas, *Reading Hollywood: Spaces and Meanings in American Film* (London: Wallflower, 2001), 10.

39. I recognize that many scholars writing about history on-screen (including Rosenstone and Toplin) refer positively to the "look and feel" created by film

and do not use it in a derogative sense. My argument is that this statement often obscures and undersells what history on-screen is capable of.

40. Bergfelder, Harris, and Street, *Film Architecture,* 15.

41. William S. Greever, *The Bonanza West: The Story of the Western Mining Rushes, 1848–1900* (Norman: University of Oklahoma Press, 1963), 316–17.

42. Watson Parker, *Deadwood: The Golden Years* (Lincoln: University of Nebraska Press, 1981), 219.

43. Jason Jacobs, *Deadwood* (London: British Film Institute, 2012), 23.

44. Horace Newcomb, "*Deadwood,*" in *The Essential HBO Reader,* ed. Gary R. Edgerton and Jeffrey P. Jones (Lexington: University Press of Kentucky, 2008), 99.

45. Steven Peacock, "Borders and Boundaries in *Deadwood,*" in *Genre and Performance: Film and Television,* ed. Christine Cornea (Manchester: Manchester University Press, 2010), 96.

46. Ramírez, *Architecture for the Screen,* 81–89.

47. Parker, *Deadwood,* 192.

48. Kelly J. Dixon, "Siding up to the Archaeology of Western Saloons: Historical Archaeology Takes on the Wild of the West," *World Archaeology* 38, no. 4 (2006): 581.

49. Elliott West, *The Saloon on the Rocky Mountain Mining Frontier* (Lincoln: University of Nebraska Press, 1979), 96, 80.

50. West, *Saloon on the Rocky Mountain Mining Frontier,* 79–80.

51. West, *Saloon on the Rocky Mountain Mining Frontier,* 96.

52. The humor comes from the fact that Wu initially speaks only two words of English: "Sweargen," for Swearengen, and "cocksucker." Their interactions involve drawings and a slow and confused process of deduction.

53. Parker, *Deadwood,* 144–48.

54. William Whyte, "How Do Buildings Mean? Some Issues of Interpretation in the History of Architecture," *History and Theory* 45, no. 2 (2006): 156, 177.

55. Duane A. Smith, *Rocky Mountain Mining Camps: The Urban Frontier* (Bloomington: Indiana University Press, 1967), 65.

56. Ramírez, *Architecture for the Screen,* 206.

57. West, *Saloon on the Rocky Mountain Mining Frontier,* 43.

58. Greever, *Bonanza West,* 318.

59. David Milch, *Deadwood: Stories of the Black Hills* (New York: Bloomsbury, 2006), 135.

60. Episode 7 of season 1, for example, has quite a different structure. It starts with Bullock and Charlie Utter tracking down Jack McCall at a fort and deciding to take him to Yankton, which is a few days' ride away. The episode then cuts back to camp, where several days have passed and Bullock and Utter return to the camp.

61. Smith, *Rocky Mountain Mining Camps,* 75.

62. It is worth noting here as well that all these sets serve dual functions. As Caso explains, the set design of the Ellsworth house enhances elements of Alma Garret's storyline (the stone around her bedroom and its tiny window speak to her unhappiness). Set design has to serve dramatic functions as well as historical ones. "Deadwood 360° Tour," bonus disc, *Deadwood: The Complete Series* (HBO, 2013), DVD.

63. Smith, *Rocky Mountain Mining Camps,* 118; Parker, *Deadwood,* 185.

64. Smith, *Rocky Mountain Mining Camps,* 118.

65. Michelle Pierson, "A Production Designer's Cinema: Historical Authenticity in Popular Films Set in the Past," in *The Spectacle of the Real: From Hollywood to "Reality" TV and Beyond,* ed. Geoff King (Bristol: Intellect, 2005), 147, 146.

66. Bruno Ramirez, *Inside the Historical Film* (Montreal: McGill-Queens University Press, 2014), 39.

67. As Pierson states, sepia has "come to function as the color of history in all sorts of popular cultural contexts." Pierson, "Production Designer's Cinema," 145.

68. Maria Caso, email to author, June 22, 2016.

69. Robert Rosenstone, "History in Images / History in Words: Reflections on the Possibility of Really Putting History onto Film," *American Historical Review* 93, no. 5 (1988): 1177.

70. I have chosen to primarily utilize these two popular entertainment websites (the AV Club and HitFix) throughout this book. In November 2016, HitFix became part of Uproxx, but as the site was called HitFix at the time all the episode reviews and posts were made, I will continue to refer to it as HitFix. Recaps and reviews of individual episodes are posted by critics after each show airs, and from that point on fellow viewers are invited to post comments, questions, and critiques. *Band of Brothers* and *Deadwood* both originally aired before this practice was common, but given their popularity and cult status, both shows have been subject to what are often called "rewind" reviews.

71. Rosenstone, *Visions of the Past,* 59.

72. Landsberg, *Engaging the Past,* 8.

73. Landsberg, *Engaging the Past,* 15–18.

74. This scene of grief in *Deadwood* contrasts greatly with a scene of grief in *Treme.* In the latter, before Toni Bernette is notified by the police that her missing husband has been found dead, the scene jumps from inside the Bernette residence with Toni and the police to outside. We do not get to witness the actual news being imparted and see and share Toni's grief at such close quarters.

75. Landsberg, *Engaging the Past,* 28, 92.

76. *OED Online,* 3rd ed. s.v. "feel, v.," accessed October 10, 2016.

77. Victoria Kelley, "A Superficial Guide to the Deeper Meanings of Surface," in *Surface Tensions: Surface, Finish and the Meaning of Objects,* ed. Glenn Adamson and Victoria Kelley (Manchester: Manchester University Press, 2013), 13 (italics in original).

78. Vivian Sobchack, *Carnal Thoughts: Embodiment and Moving Image Culture* (Berkeley: University of California Press, 2004), 63.

79. Laura U. Marks, *Touch: Sensuous Theory and Multisensory Media* (Minneapolis: University of Minnesota Press, 2002), 2.

80. Laura U. Marks, *The Skin of the Film: Intercultural Cinema, Embodiment, and the Senses* (Durham, NC: Duke University Press, 2000), 162.

81. Thomas Elsaesser and Malte Hagener, *Film Theory: An Introduction through the Senses,* 2nd ed. (New York: Routledge, 2015), 134.

82. Alicia Annas, "The Photogenic Formula: Hairstyles and Makeup in Historical Films," in *Hollywood and History: Costume Design in Film,* ed. Edward Maeder (London: Thames and Hudson, 1987), 52–54.

83. Janie Bryant, "Janie Bryant Interview Part 1 of 3," interview by Bonnie Datt, Archive of American Television, August 9, 2012, video, https://interviews.televisionacademy.com/interviews/janie-bryant?clip=65603#interview-clips.

84. Parker, *Deadwood,* 151.

85. Maria Caso, email to author, June 22, 2016.

86. Sarah Gilligan, "Long Coats, Flowing Fabrics: Fashioning Masculinity and Desire in Film and Television," in Adamson and Kelley, *Surface Tensions,* 134.

87. LoBrutto, *Filmmaker's Guide to Production Design,* 89.

88. Sobchack, *Carnal Thoughts,* 76.

89. Landsberg, *Engaging the Past,* 27, 65.

90. Sarah Street, *Costume and Cinema: Dress Codes in Popular Film* (London: Wallflower, 2001), 23.

91. Christine Sprengler, *Screening Nostalgia: Populuxe Props and Technicolor Aesthetics in Contemporary American Film* (New York: Berghahn Books, 2009), 123.

92. Natalie Zemon Davis worked on *The Return of Martin Guerre* (Vigne, 1982). Davis, "'Any Resemblance to Persons Living or Dead': Film and the Challenge of Authenticity," *Historical Journal of Film, Radio and Television* 8, no. 3 (1988): 270–71.

93. Hannah Greig worked on *The Duchess* (Dibb, 2008). Hannah Greig, "As Seen on the Screen: Material Culture, Historical Accuracy and the Costume Drama," in *Writing Material Culture History,* ed. Anne Gerritsen and Giorgio Riello (London: Bloomsbury, 2015), 314.

94. Edward Maeder, "The Celluloid Image: Historical Dress in Film," in Maeder, *Hollywood and History,* 11; Ramírez, *Architecture for the Screen,* 48.

95. Jane Gaines and Charlotte Herzog, "Which Body Too Much? Norma Shearer as Marie Antoinette," in *Fashioning Film Stars: Dress, Culture, Identity,* ed. Rachel Moseley (London: British Film Institute, 2005), 24.

96. Maeder, "Celluloid Image," 42, 9.

97. LoBrutto, *Filmmaker's Guide to Production Design,* 111–12.

98. Bryant, "Interview."

99. Rosenstone, *Visions of the Past,* 72.

100. Margaret Ponsonby, "Textiles and Time: Conservation and Public Response," in Adamson and Kelley, *Surface Tensions,* 72.

101. Leslie Ellis Miller, "Europe 1600–1800 in a Thousand Objects," in Gerritsen and Riello, *Writing Material Culture History,* 245.

102. Miller, "Europe 1600–1800 in a Thousand Objects," 247.

103. Philippe Perrot, *Fashioning the Bourgeoisie: A History of Clothing in the Nineteenth Century* (Princeton, NJ: Princeton University Press, 1994), 12.

104. The same is also true for sets. Specially built sets are designed with light, equipment, and potential camera angles in mind and can be constantly altered during shooting as needed and desired. However, if shooting on location in a historic building, no such changes can be made to the structure to facilitate the optimal film shot.

105. On the Terrence Malick film *The New World* (2005), production designer Jack Fisk built the Jamestown settlement set using the same methods as the original inhabitants. As Fisk points out, this gave those working on the film a unique insight and wonderful appreciation of the colonists. However, the authentic method of building Jamestown does not affect what viewers see or their understanding of the historical narrative on-screen. Halligan, *Production Design,* 96.

106. Maeder, "Celluloid Image," 15.

107. Janie Bryant, quoted in Sam Molineaux, "Art Dept: Evoking Period on *Deadwood*—Costume," *Below the Line,* September 1, 2005, http://www.btlnews.com/crafts/art-dept-evoking-period-on-deadwood-costume/.

108. Of course, as noted earlier, none of these departments operate in isolation. What the viewer sees is also shaped by how the sets and costumes are lit and captured on camera by the director of photography and how they are edited together.

109. Christopher Anderson, "Producing an Aristocracy of Culture in American Television," in Edgerton and Jones, *Essential HBO Reader,* 37.

110. Dunleavy, *Complex Serial Drama,* 81.

111. Alun Munslow, *A History of History* (New York: Routledge, 2012), 118, 6, 120, 119.

112. E. H. Carr, *What Is History?* (1961; repr., London: Penguin, 2008), 22, 23.

113. See, for example, Robert Brent Toplin, ed., *Oliver Stone's USA: Film, History, and Controversy* (Lawrence: University Press of Kansas, 2000); and Willem Hesling, "Oliver Stone's *Nixon:* The Rise and Fall of a Political Gangster," in *A Companion to the Historical Film,* ed. Robert Rosenstone and Constantin Parvulescu (Malden, MA: Wiley-Blackwell, 2013), 179–98. Other works that focus on the idea of the director as cinematic historian include Yosefa Loshitzky, ed., *Spielberg's Holocaust: Critical Perspectives on Schindler's List* (Bloomington: Indiana University Press, 1997); and Franz Weiser, "The Conventions of Unconventionality:

Reconsidering the Cinematic Historian in *Even the Rain,*" *Rethinking History* 19, no. 2 (2015): 268–84.

114. Natalie Zemon Davis, *Slaves on Screen: Film and Historical Vision* (Cambridge, MA: Harvard University Press, 2000), x–xi, 12.

115. Having worked on historical films undoubtedly provides scholars with a unique perspective from which to explore history on-screen. Ramírez's insights are based largely on his own experience on film sets and his interactions with cast and crew, which have given him the opportunity to understand, in great detail, how filmic language operates. "My awareness," Ramírez states, "of filmic language, of its 'rules' and of its narrative potential, grew also from my understanding of how various film-making crafts bring their own special artistic talents and imagination to the construction of the moving image." Ramirez, *Inside the Historical Film,* 33, 37–39.

116. According to Alisa Perren and Thomas Schatz, "showrunner" was first used in *Variety* in 1990 and appeared approximately a hundred times over the 1990s. There were more than five hundred references to showrunners from 2000 to 2011 in the same publication. Alisa Perren and Thomas Schatz, "Theorizing Television's Writer-Producer: Re-viewing *The Producer's Medium,*" *Television & New Media* 16, no. 1 (2014): 87.

117. Jason Mittell, *Complex TV: The Poetics of Contemporary Television Storytelling* (New York: NYU Press, 2015), 89–90.

118. Miranda J. Banks, "*I Love Lucy:* The Writer-Producer," in *How to Watch Television,* ed. Ethan Thompson and Jason Mittell (New York: NYU Press, 2013), 245.

119. Mark Singer, "The Misfit: How David Milch Got from *NYPD Blue* to *Deadwood* by Way of an Epistle of St. Paul," *New Yorker,* February 14, 2005, http://www.newyorker.com/magazine/2005/02/14/the-misfit-2.

120. Some showrunners, such as Matthew Weiner of *Mad Men*, insist on adding their names to script credits to acknowledge their creative input. Brett Martin, *Difficult Men: Behind the Scenes of a Creative Revolution* (New York: Penguin, 2013), 71, 258.

121. Sean Bridgers, quoted in Milch, *Deadwood,* 160.

122. Over three years (2011–13) TV reviewer Alan Sepinwall ran summer DVD "rewinds" of *Deadwood* on HitFix, where he posted a review/recap each week. A number of actors from the series also followed along and posted lengthy comments in the comments blogs. Jim Beaver (Ellsworth) posted something for almost every episode, giving behind-the-scenes stories and insights into how the show was made as well as righting the occasional incorrect fact from Sepinwall. He was joined by Keone Young (Mr. Wu) and once or twice by W. Earl Brown (Dority) and Garret Dillahunt (Jack McCall/Francis Wolcott). Their comments on this blog proved to be a particularly rich source. Earl (Guest), August 13, 2013

(8:39 p.m.), comment on Alan Sepinwall, "'Deadwood' Rewind: Season 3, Episode 10: 'A Constant Throb,'" HitFix, August 9, 2013, https://uproxx.com/sepinwall/deadwood-rewind-season-3-episode-10-a-constant-throb/. All HitFix posts have since been migrated to the Uproxx website.

123. Mittell, *Complex TV,* 90.

124. Bianchi directed eight episodes of *Deadwood* across the three seasons (two season 1 episodes, four season 2 episodes, and two season 3 episodes) and was also credited as producer for season 2.

125. "Making of Episode 12, 'Boy-the-Earth-Talks-To': The Wedding Celebration," disc 6, *Deadwood: The Complete Second Season* (HBO, 2013), DVD.

126. See, for example, the comments from Ian McShane, Robin Weigert, Titus Welliver, and Sean Bridgers in Milch, *Deadwood,* 22, 70, 138, 160.

127. Michael Z. Newman and Elana Levine, *Legitimating Television: Media Convergence and Cultural Status* (New York: Routledge, 2012), 39.

128. Newcomb, "*Deadwood,*" 92.

129. Tobias Steiner, "Steering the Author Discourse: The Construction of Authorship in Quality TV, and the Case of *Game of Thrones,*" *Series* 1, no. 2 (2015): 183.

130. The early to mid 2000s was the period of the "Davids" for HBO, with David Chase (*The Sopranos*), David Simon (*The Wire,* 2002–8), and David Milch (*Deadwood*) in the area of dramatic original programming and Larry David (*Curb Your Enthusiasm,* 2000–) in comedy.

131. "Making of Episode 12, 'Boy-the-Earth-Talks-To': Trusting the Process with David Milch," disc 6, *Deadwood: The Complete Second Season* (HBO, 2013), DVD.

132. Newman and Levine, *Legitimating Television,* 53.

133. As noted previously, this can be difficult to judge accurately because the networks tend to "push" the role of the showrunner in their marketing and promotional materials. However, based on comments from cast and crew during and after the series was completed, I firmly believe that Milch did have an incredibly strong influence on many areas of production and on the day-to-day running of the set.

134. Maria Caso, email to author, June 22, 2016.

135. One such request was that Wild Bill Hickok be wearing a red sash (as he is shown wearing in at least one photograph) on the night of his death. Bryant, "Interview."

136. Maria Caso, email to author, June 22, 2016.

137. Here I am drawing upon Juan Antonio Ramírez, who asks similar questions: How many people have ever found themselves "trapped inside a burning skyscraper or entombed within an Egyptian pyramid," or who has "passed any time inside a Shanghai brothel or the airborne ballroom of a zeppelin"? Ramírez, *Architecture for the Screen,* 5.

138. Earl (Guest), comment on Sepinwall, "'Deadwood' Rewind."

139. Halligan, *Production Design,* 9.

140. Terence Winter, quoted in Noel Murray, "*Boardwalk Empire* Creator Terence Winter on Raising the Stakes in Season Two (Part 1 of 4)," *AV Club,* August 27, 2012, http://www.avclub.com/articles/boardwalk-empire-creator-terence-winter-on-raising,84239/.

141. Terence Winter, quoted in Jennifer Vineyard, "Terence Winter on What's Next for *Boardwalk Empire,*" *Vulture,* December 3, 2012, http://www.vulture.com/2012/12/terence-winter-on-whats-next-for-boardwalk.html.

142. That Paramount partially owned the show ate into HBO's profits. For a discussion of some of the reasons behind the cancelation, see Alan Sepinwall, *The Revolution Was Televised,* 2nd ed. (New York: Gallery Books, 2015), 128–32. For a response to Sepinwall's comments from W. Earl Brown, see Earl (guest), July 30, 2013 (4:27 p.m.), comment on Alan Sepinwall, "Programming Note: 'Deadwood' Review Delayed Again," HitFix, July 26, 2013, https://uproxx.com/sepinwall/programming-note-deadwood-review-delayed-again/.

143. Robert Ito, "Rebuilding 'Deadwood,' Plank by Plank," *New York Times,* May 15, 2019, https://www.nytimes.com/2019/05/15/arts/television/deadwood-the-movie-hbo.html.

144. Maria Caso, quoted in Wendy Wilkinson, "Behind the Scenes of Deadwood: The Movie," *Cowboys & Indians,* April 12, 2019, https://www.cowboysindians.com/2019/04/behind-the-scenes-of-deadwood-the-movie/.

## 2. Constructing and Inventing Historical Characters

1. Terence Winter, quoted in Angela Watercutter, "TV Fact-Checkers: Ginning Up *Boardwalk Empire*'s Boozy Gangster Paradise," *Wired,* September 14, 2012, http://www.wired.com/underwire/2012/09/tv-fact-checkers-boardwalk-empire/.

2. Terence Winter, quoted in Noel Murray, "*Boardwalk Empire* Creator Terence Winter on Raising the Stakes in Season Two (Part 2 of 4)," AV Club, August 28, 2012, http://www.avclub.com/articles/boardwalk-empire-showrunner-terence-winter-dissect,84300/.

3. Terence Winter, quoted in Maureen Ryan, "An Interview with 'Boardwalk Empire' Creator Terence Winter," *AolTV,* September 10, 2010, http://www.aoltv.com/2010/09/10/boardwalk-empire/ (website no longer active).

4. Ryan, "Interview with 'Boardwalk Empire' Creator."

5. Terence Winter, foreword to *Boardwalk Empire: The Birth, High Times, and Corruption of Atlantic City,* by Nelson Johnson (London: Ebury, 2011), xii.

6. David Bordwell, Janet Staiger, and Kristin Thompson, *The Classical Hollywood Cinema: Film Style and Mode of Production to 1960* (New York: Columbia University Press, 1985), 12.

7. Timothy Corrigan and Patricia White, *The Film Experience: An Introduction* (Boston: Bedford/St Martin's, 2004), 224.

8. Murray Smith, "*Engaging Characters:* Further Reflections," in *Characters in Fictional Worlds: Understanding Imaginary Beings in Literature, Film and Other Media,* ed. Jens Eder, Fotis Jannidis, and Ralf Schneider (New York: De Gruyter, 2010), 234, 236.

9. David C. Giles, "Parasocial Relationships," in Eder, Jannidis, and Schneider, *Characters in Fictional Worlds,* 447.

10. Jason Mittell, *Complex TV: The Poetics of Contemporary Television Storytelling* (New York: NYU Press, 2015), 127.

11. The potential of the TV serial as a form of history is the focus of the next chapter on *Treme.*

12. John Fiske, *Television Culture* (London: Methuen, 1987), 149–50.

13. Michael Z. Newman, "From Beats to Arcs: Toward a Poetics of Television Narrative," *Velvet Light Trap* 58, no. 1 (Fall 2006): 23.

14. Brett Martin, *Difficult Men: Behind the Scenes of a Creative Revolution* (New York: Penguin, 2013), 4.

15. James Wolcott, "Prime Time's Graduation," *Vanity Fair,* April 3, 2012, http://www.vanityfair.com/hollywood/2012/05/wolcott-television-better-than-movies.

16. "The Crooked Timber of Humanity: How HBO Is Redefining Storytelling: An Interview with Richard Plepler," *Fletcher Forum of World Affairs* 42, no. 2 (Summer 2018): 233.

17. Anthony N. Smith, *Storytelling Industries: Narrative Production in the 21st Century* (Cham, Switzerland: Palgrave Macmillan, 2018), 76.

18. Jens Eder, Fotis Jannidis, and Ralf Schneider, "Characters in Fictional Worlds: An Introduction," in Eder, Jannidis, and Schneider, *Characters in Fictional Worlds,* 5.

19. Henriette Heidbrink, "Fictional Characters in Literary and Media Studies: A Survey of the Research," in Eder, Jannidis, and Schneider, *Characters in Fictional Worlds,* 73.

20. Smith, "*Engaging Characters:* Further Reflections," 232–35.

21. Jens Eder, "Understanding Characters," *Projections* 4, no. 1 (2010): 37.

22. Terence Winter, interview by author, May 22, 2012.

23. Terence Winter, interview by author, May 22, 2012.

24. John McCarty, *Bullets over Hollywood: The American Gangster Picture from the Silents to "The Sopranos"* (Cambridge, MA: Da Capo, 2004), 111; J. E. Smyth, *Reconstructing American Historical Cinema: From "Cimarron" to "Citizen Kane"* (Lexington: University Press of Kentucky, 2006), 75.

25. Capone once again became a popular screen figure in the late 1950s and 1960s, beginning with *The Scarface Mob* (Karlson, 1959), based on the exploits of

Special Agent Eliot Ness and his squad of "Untouchables." The success of *The Scarface Mob* led to the creation of the television series *The Untouchables* (ABC, 1959–63), which featured Capone as a recurrent character. While Capone graced TV screens, he also received attention on the silver screen in *Al Capone* (Wilson, 1959) and *The St. Valentine's Day Massacre* (Corman, 1967), two films that centered on the Chicago mobster without any of the pretenses employed by the early gangster films. These examples are only the best-known portrayals of Capone on film; there have been many more direct portrayals of Capone, as well as characters that have been based on him. Most recently Capone was played by Jon Bernthal in the children's movie *Night at the Museum: Battle of the Smithsonian* (Levy, 2009) and by Tom Hardy in *Capone* (Trank, 2020), which charts his final years in Florida after his prison sentence.

26. Robert J. Schoenberg, *Mr. Capone: The Real and Complete Story of Al Capone* (New York: William Morrow, 1993), 8.

27. Laurence Bergreen, *Capone: The Man and the Era* (New York: Simon & Schuster, 1994), 20.

28. The first four seasons were made up of twelve episodes, approximately fifty-two minutes long, while the fifth and final season consisted of eight episodes.

29. Roberta E. Pearson and Máire Messenger Davis, "'You're Not Going to See That on TV': *Star Trek: The Next Generation* in Film and Television," in *Quality Popular Television: Cult TV, the Industry and Fans,* ed. Mark Jancovich and James Lyons (London: British Film Institute, 2003), 114.

30. "Making *Boardwalk Empire,*" disc 5, *Boardwalk Empire: The Complete First Season* (HBO, 2012), DVD.

31. Laura Beshears, "Honorable Style in Dishonorable Times: American Gangsters of the 1920s and 1930s," *Journal of American Culture* 33, no. 3 (2010): 197.

32. Corrigan and White, *Film Experience,* 229.

33. The event took place on May 8, 1924, approximately a year after the episode is set. Capone walked into a bar owned by Heine Jacobs and shot a man named Joe Howard six times in front of at least three witnesses. Howard had beaten Capone's close friend and associate Jake "Greasy Thumb" Guzik, although different biographers provide various motives for Capone's seemingly drastic actions.

34. Winter, quoted in Watercutter, "TV Fact-Checkers."

35. In *Scarface,* Capone has a relationship with a woman initially involved with the Johnny Torrio character (Johnny Lovo in the film), as well as an uncomfortable relationship with his sister.

36. Capone's love of family continues to be shown in season 4 when his brothers are introduced. Capone is seen playfully roughhousing with his brothers and is completely devastated when his brother Frank is killed.

37. Viewers have appreciated the fully rounded portrait, with one commentator on the AV Club website posting: "It's great to see such a layered human version of Capone. I'm so used to seeing him as a one role loud mouth gangster like Robert De Niro in the Untouchables." The Silent 1, October 8, 2012 (3:30 p.m.), comment on Noel Murray, "*Boardwalk Empire:* 'Blue Bell Boy,'" AV Club, October 7, 2012, http://www.avclub.com/articles/blue-bell-boy,86002/.

38. Smyth, *Reconstructing American Historical Cinema,* 64–65.

39. Edward Behr, *Prohibition: The 13 Years That Changed America* (London: BBC Books, 1997), 180.

40. Schoenberg, *Mr. Capone,* 62.

41. John Kobler, *Capone: The Life and World of Al Capone,* 2nd ed. (New York: Da Capo, 2003), 72.

42. Bergreen, *Capone,* 84.

43. Terence Winter, commentary, "Pilot: Boardwalk Empire," disc 1, *Boardwalk Empire: The Complete First Season* (HBO, 2012), DVD.

44. Winter, quoted in Watercutter, "TV Fact-Checkers."

45. In this, the writers are aided by the actors, most of whom have done a significant amount of research on their character.

46. Robert Rosenstone, *Visions of the Past: The Challenge of Film to Our Idea of History* (Cambridge, MA: Harvard University Press, 1995), 72.

47. Robert Berkhofer, *Beyond the Great Story: History as Text and Discourse* (Cambridge, MA: Harvard University Press, 1997), 117.

48. In season 3, set in 1923, events in Chicago are moved forward approximately a year so that Capone's career can advance and he can continue to evolve as a character. During Torrio's 1924 trip to Europe, Capone was left in charge of the running of Torrio's illegal business ventures and showed what an effective leader he could be. In the show this trip and transfer of power take place a year earlier, but again, it does not radically upset or alter Capone's known history.

49. Winter, quoted in Watercutter, "TV Fact-Checkers."

50. Comments posted on the AV Club and HitFix weekly reviews were generally very favorable in regards to Capone's character. "Can we get a Capone spin off series when this is all done please?" one viewer asked. Cultstatus, November 26, 2012 (5:32 a.m.), comment on Alan Sepinwall "Review: Boardwalk Empire—'Two Imposters,'" HitFix, November 25, 2012, https://uproxx.com/sepinwall/review-boardwalk-empire-two-imposters-youll-be-a-man-my-son/. All HitFix posts have since been migrated to the Uproxx website.

51. In this section I am putting a lot of emphasis on Winter as showrunner and decision maker. This is not to ignore the contributions of the other writers and various departments in crafting the character of Thompson, but Winter was responsible for writing the pilot, establishing the characters, and deciding on the different character types (at least for season 1).

52. Terence Winter, quoted in Susan Dormady Eisenberg, "An Interview with Terence Winter: Executive Producer, Writer, and Creator of HBO's *Boardwalk Empire* (Part 1)," *Huffington Post,* February 7, 2012, http://www.huffingtonpost.com/susan-dormady-eisenberg/terence-winter-boardwalk-empire_b_1254667.html.

53. Terence Winter, quoted in David Bianculli, "Down on the 'Boardwalk' with Terence Winter," *NPR,* September 28, 2010, http://www.npr.org/templates/transcript/transcript.php?storyId=130184684.

54. This is by far the most detailed portrait of Johnson currently available, although it does not add anything significantly new to the existing interpretation of Johnson, and is padded out with facts about Atlantic City. Frank J. Ferry, *Nucky: The Real Story of the Atlantic City Boardwalk Boss* (Margate, NJ: ComteQ, 2013).

55. Nelson Johnson, *Boardwalk Empire: The Birth, High Times, and Corruption of Atlantic City* (London: Ebury, 2011), 79, xvi.

56. Johnson, *Boardwalk Empire,* 93.

57. Jonathan Van Meter, *The Last Good Time: Skinny DÁmato, the Notorious 500 Club, the Rat Pack and the Rise and Fall of Atlantic City* (New York: Bloomsbury, 2003), 45.

58. Other incidental facts about Nucky Johnson are also featured on the show, including that he owned a powder-blue Rolls-Royce. An actual 1920s Rolls-Royce was procured for the show and repainted to make it the same color as Johnson's.

59. Van Meter, *Last Good Time,* 42.

60. Murray Smith, *Engaging Characters: Fiction, Emotion, and the Cinema* (Oxford: Clarendon, 1995), 83.

61. Assistant Attorney General Esther Randolph is based on Assistant Attorney General Mabel Walker Willebrandt. Like her real-life inspiration, Randolph is a dedicated, hardworking woman and an anomaly of the time, a high-ranking woman within the federal government.

62. Nelson Johnson, *The Northside: African Americans and the Creation of Atlantic City* (Medford, NJ: Plexus, 2010).

63. Terence Winter, interview by author, May 22, 2012.

64. Lisa Padovani, quoted in Chris Laverty, "*Boardwalk Empire* Costume Q&A: John Dunn and Lisa Padovani," *Clothesonfilm,* September 21, 2011, http://clothesonfilm.com/boardwalk-empire-costume-qa-john-dunn-lisa-padovani/22114/.

65. For example, multiple characters based on the same historical figure in a narrative could allow storytellers to explore the alternative paths their lives may have taken.

66. Terence Winter, quoted in Christina Radish, "Martin Scorsese and Terence Winter Interview," *Collider,* September 14, 2010, https://collider.com/boardwalk-empire-interview-martin-scorsese-terrence-winter/.

67. Although Johnson's position as county treasurer did not bring in a pay check, he did not really need one with the $500,000 a year he made from protection money from the Atlantic City vice rackets. Johnson, *Boardwalk Empire,* 98.

68. *Oxford English Dictionary,* 3rd ed., s.v. "racketeer" and "gangster."

69. In order to keep FBI agent Nelson Van Alden off his back, Thompson arranges for another man to take the fall for the hijacking and murders in the pilot. It is Thompson's brother Eli, the sheriff of Atlantic City, and his deputy who beat the fall guy, Hans Schroeder, to a bloody pulp before dumping him over the side of a boat into the Atlantic Ocean. Nucky undoubtedly gives the order but distances himself from the actual violence.

70. George S. Larke-Walsh, *Screening the Mafia: Masculinity, Ethnicity and Mobsters from "The Godfather" to "The Sopranos"* (Jefferson, NC: McFarland, 2010), 82.

71. Murray Smith, "Just What Is It That Makes Tony Soprano Such an Appealing, Attractive Murderer?," in *Ethics at the Cinema,* ed. Ward E. Jones and Samantha Vice (New York: Oxford University Press, 2011), 74.

72. While he shares many of the same characteristics, Thompson is arguably not the appealing antihero that Tony Soprano is. He has often divided viewers and elicited a number of negative responses on the internet, but nonetheless he fits into the same mold. These criticisms are often directed at Steve Buscemi, as many do not see him as an engaging leading man, and others simply do not find Thompson to be the most compelling character on the show.

73. Smith, *Engaging Characters,* 142.

74. Smith, "Just What Is It," 84.

75. Smith, *Engaging Characters,* 194.

76. "Partial allegiance refers to cases in which we find ourselves sympathetic to some actions and attitudes of the character, but antipathetic to others," Smith explains. "Perverse allegiance captures those cases where a film seeks to turn around aspects of our normal evaluation, eliciting our sympathy for actions and attitudes, which, on reflection, we realize we ought not endorse." Smith, "*Engaging Characters:* Further Reflections," 244–45.

77. Terence Winter, interview by author, May 22, 2012.

78. These three elements of character tend to get stressed in screenwriting guides. For example, see Linda Seger, *Advanced Screenwriting: Raising Your Script to Academy Award Level* (Los Angeles: Silman-James, 2003), 138–47.

79. Richard Dyer, *Stars,* with a supplementary chapter and bibliography by Paul McDonald (London: British Film Institute, 1998), 107.

80. Even before the viewer really gets to know Darmody, parts of his history are revealed through the signs of character that also prefigure his place and relationships on the show. His name, James Darmody, is clearly of Irish origin, and, as Dyer points out, names can suggest class and ethnic background as well as character traits. Organized crime in the 1920s, and even still today, is grouped by

ethnic identity, with Jewish, Irish, and Italian gangs being the most predominant in the 1920s. There did exist, however, a considerable amount of crossover, and the gangs were not rigidly exclusive. Some gangsters, such as Rothstein, ran an ethnically diverse operation, and even the Torrio-Capone gang in Chicago employed non-Italians, such as the Jewish Jake Guzik. In film and television, though, ethnically categorized crime syndicates have remained a staple of the gangster genre, and from this viewers will likely understand the significance of Darmody's name. Dyer, *Stars,* 109; Marc Mappen, *Prohibition Gangsters: The Rise and Fall of a Bad Generation* (New Brunswick, NJ: Rutgers University Press, 2013), 32.

81. Dyer, *Stars,* 106.

82. Roberta Pearson, "Anatomising Gilbert Grissom: The Structure and Function of the Televisual Character," in *Reading CSI: Crime TV under the Microscope,* ed. Michael Allen (London: I. B. Tauris, 2007), 55–56.

83. Smyth, *Reconstructing American Historical Cinema,* 197, 219.

84. Armitage Trail, *Scarface* (London: Bloomsbury Paperbacks, 1997), 41.

85. George Browne, *An American Soldier in World War I,* ed. David L. Snead (Lincoln: University of Nebraska Press, 2006), 128.

86. Jennifer Keene notes that it is extremely difficult to generalize about wartime experiences, or even to identify just who a typical soldier was. Only about 40 percent of American troops served in combat roles, while the remaining 60 percent worked in organizational and supply roles, often far back from the front lines. Jennifer Keene, *The United States and the First World War* (Harlow, UK: Longman, 2000), 60.

87. Jeremy G. Butler, *Television: Critical Methods and Applications,* 4th ed. (New York: Routledge, 2012), 56–57.

88. Beth Linker, *War's Waste: Rehabilitation in World War I America* (Chicago: University of Chicago Press, 2011), 8.

89. Nancy Gentile Ford, *The Great War and America: Civil-Military Relations during World War I* (Westport, CT: Praeger, 2008), 101.

90. Richard Severo and Lewis Milford, *The Wages of War: When America's Soldiers Came Home—from Valley Forge to Vietnam* (New York: Open Road Integrated Media, 1989), 240.

91. Butler, *Television,* 58.

92. Jeffrey Kirkwood, introduction to *Haunted by Combat: Understanding PTSD in War Veterans Including Women, Reservists and Those Coming Back from Iraq,* by Daryl S. Paulson and Stanley Krippner (Westport, CT: Praeger Security International, 2007), xvi, xix.

93. Patrick Phillips, *Understanding Film Texts: Meaning and Experience* (London: British Film Institute, 2000), 62.

94. Dyer, *Stars,* 125.

A number of comments on HitFix conveyed concerns over Buscemi's ability to carry the lead role of a show, some of them in part influenced by his prior roles. "I'm still having trouble seeing Buscemi in this role," Sareeta commented after the pilot episode. "I am so used to him playing a background sort of wimpy character." Sareeta, September 21, 2010 (2:04 a.m.), comment on Alan Sepinwall, "Boardwalk Empire—'Pilot,'" HitFix, September 19, 2010, https://uproxx.com/sepinwall/boardwalk-empire-pilot-the-day-the-drinking-died/.

95. DC, December 12, 2011 (5:09 a.m.), comment on Alan Sepinwall, "Boardwalk Empire—'To the Lost,'" HitFix, December 11, 2011, https://uproxx.com/sepinwall/boardwalk-empire-to-the-lost-nucky-get-your-gun/.

96. mike_c, December 12, 2011 (3:20 p.m.), comment on Sepinwall, "Boardwalk Empire—'To the Lost.'"

97. C1, December 12, 2011 (6:57 p.m.) and Stravu9, December 12, 2011 (3:27 a.m.), comments on Sepinwall, "Boardwalk Empire—'To the Lost.'"

98. William Guynn, *Writing History in Film* (New York: Routledge, 2006), 36.

99. Guynn, *Writing History in Film*, 38.

100. Terence Winter, interview by author, May 22, 2012.

101. Robert Rosenstone, "Oliver Stone as Historian," in *Oliver Stone's USA: Film, History, and Controversy*, ed. Robert Brent Toplin (Lawrence: University Press of Kansas, 2000), 26.

102. Ever, December 12, 2011 (11:46 p.m.), comment on Sepinwall, "Boardwalk Empire—'To the Lost.'"

103. Brian, November 29, 2010 (4:05 p.m.), comment (since deleted on Uproxx site) on Alan Sepinwall, "Boardwalk Empire—'Paris Green,'" HitFix, November 28, 2010, https://uproxx.com/sepinwall/boardwalk-empire-paris-green-baptism-by-fire/.

104. Anonymous, November 22, 2010 (10:16 p.m.), comment (since deleted on Uproxx site) on Alan Sepinwall, "Boardwalk Empire—'Emerald City,'" HitFix, November 21, 2010, https://uproxx.com/sepinwall/boardwalk-empire-emerald-city-with-great-power-comes-great-responsibility/.

105. Gridlock, November 9, 2010 (3:37 a.m.), comment on Alan Sepinwall, "Boardwalk Empire—'Hold Me in Paradise,'" HitFix, November 7, 2010, https://uproxx.com/sepinwall/boardwalk-empire-hold-me-in-paradise-first-in-war/.

106. Greg Grant, September 17, 2012 (2:15 a.m.), comment (since deleted on Uproxx site) on Alan Sepinwall, "Season Premiere Review: Boardwalk Empire—'Resolution,'" HitFix, September 16, 2012, https://uproxx.com/sepinwall/season-premiere-review-boardwalk-empire-resolution-walk-like-an-egyptian/.

107. Dr. Gross, October 8, 2012 (1:30 p.m.), comment on Sepinwall, "Review: Boardwalk Empire—'Blue Bell Boy,'" HitFix, October 7, 2012, https://uproxx.com/sepinwall/review-boardwalk-empire-blue-bell-boy-cellars-market/.

108. ficus, November 2, 2012 (8:51 p.m.), comment on Alan Sepinwall, "Review: Boardwalk Empire—'Sunday Best,'" HitFix, October 28, 2012, https://uproxx.com/sepinwall/review-boardwalk-empire-sunday-best-house-of-the-bathing-son/.

109. Dyer, *Stars,* 122.

110. Phillips, *Understanding Film Texts,* 88.

111. Dyer, *Stars,* 118.

112. Gary Alan Fine, *Difficult Reputations: Collective Memories of the Evil, Inept and Controversial* (Chicago: University of Chicago Press, 2001), 7.

113. Jonathan Eig, quoted in Katherine Don, "How Real Is Boardwalk Empire's Al Capone?," *Salon,* October 11, 2010, http://www.salon.com/2010/10/11/boardwalk_empire_al_capone/.

114. Phillips, *Understanding Film Texts,* 62.

115. Jean-Louis Comolli, "Historical Fiction: A Body Too Much," *Screen* 19, no. 2 (1978): 44.

116. In online discussions following episodes, numerous commenters often referenced or questioned how history matches up with what happened on the show. For example, commenter r1186 posted: "In reality, Nucky Thompson was convicted of tax evasion, fraud etc and sent to jail," obviously confusing Nucky Johnson with the fictional Nucky Thompson. Ben Kabak set him straight with the reply: "Nucky Thompson is NOT a real person. Nucky Johnson was real." This discussion took place after an episode midway through season 4, demonstrating that even after a number of seasons this confusion still existed. r11856, October 14, 2013 (1:52 p.m.) and Ben Kabak, October 14, 2013 (2:46 p.m.), comments on Alan Sepinwall, "Review: Boardwalk Empire—'The North Star,'" HitFix, October 13, 2013, https://uproxx.com/sepinwall/review-boardwalk-empire-the-north-star-just-another-girl-on-the-irt/.

117. Although we do not actually see Swearengen die in the last moments of *Deadwood: The Movie,* it is clearly implied that this is the end of the road for the Gem's proprietor.

118. Johnny C., "Is Jimmy Darmody Based on a Real Person?," *A Boardwalk Empire Blog* (blog), September 28, 2010, http://theboardwalkempire.blogspot.co.nz/2010/09/was-jimmy-darmody-based-on-real-person.html.

119. "Getting to Know the Characters of Boardwalk Empire," *Efficient Drinker* (blog), September 21, 2010, https://www.efficientdrinker.com/blog/boardwalk-empire-characters/ (website no longer active).

120. For example, Agent Nelson Van Alden's real-life inspiration is supposedly William Frank, who investigated Nucky Johnson's operation in the 1930s. Apart from both investigating Nucky, there is no correlation between the two, or even between their investigations.

121. Each of these areas of history, particularly biography, has come under attack, especially since historians moved away from the "great man" approach to history. Historian John Tosh points out that "biographical narrative encourages a simplified, linear interpretation of events" and notes that "an exclusive focus on the thoughts and actions of individuals is likely to find no shape and to see instead only a chaotic sequence of accident and blunder." John Tosh, *The Pursuit of History: Aims, Methods, and New Directions in the Study of Modern History,* 5th ed. (New York: Longman/Pearson, 2010), 120, 224.

## 3. Crafting Complex Historical Narratives in Serial Television

1. Simon and Overmyer worked together on *Homicide: Life on the Street* (NBC, 1993–99), which was when they first began talking about a New Orleans–set television series. However, their plans would always dissolve when they tried to imagine selling a show about New Orleans culture to a Los Angeles executive. David Simon and Eric Overmyer, "After *The Wire,* Taking on New Orleans in *Treme,*" interview by Terry Gross, *NPR,* April 5, 2010, http://www.npr.org/2010/04/05/125364838/after-the-wire-taking-on-new-orleans-in-treme.

2. Creeber's discussion of historical series focuses on *Roots* and *Holocaust,* which are both from the late 1970s. Glen Creeber, "'Taking Our Personal Lives Seriously': Intimacy, Continuity and Memory in the Television Drama Serial," *Media, Culture & Society* 23, no. 4 (2001): 443–49.

3. Kristin Thompson, *Storytelling in Film and Television* (Cambridge, MA: Harvard University Press, 2003), 37.

4. For example, Creighton's YouTube rants are based upon the blogs of Ashley Morris, with snippets, including Morris's trademark "fuck you, you fucking fucks," borrowed directly from the source. While both are also university professors (Morris, computer science; Creighton, English), other parts of Creighton's character are drawn from additional sources or completely invented. His suicide is not informed by Morris, who died of a heart attack in 2008, but by the spike in the suicide rate that, after Hurricane Katrina, reached four times higher than before the storm. Simon notes that for this scenario he and his staff took inspiration from Stevenson Palfi, a New Orleans–based filmmaker who committed suicide in December 2005. Davis McAlary perhaps comes closest to repeating the problems of "based-on characters," sharing a similar name with his real-life inspiration, Davis Rogan.

5. Catherine Dessinges, Dominique Gendrin, and Wendy Hajjar, "Fiction and Reality in HBO's *Treme:* A Narrative Alchemy in the Service of Political Truth," *TV/Series* 1, no. 1 (2012): 186.

6. Jeremy G. Butler, *Television: Critical Methods and Applications,* 4th ed. (New York: Routledge, 2012), 41.

7. In order to avoid confusion, from this point on I will refer to this type of television narrative as an "episodic series" rather than just a "series" due to the multiple uses and meanings of the word.

8. Jason Mittell, "Narrative Complexity in Contemporary American Television," *Velvet Light Trap* 58, no. 1 (Fall 2006): 29–40; Thomas Schatz, "*St Elsewhere* and the Evolution of the Ensemble Series," in *Television: The Critical View,* 4th ed., ed. Horace Newcomb (New York: Oxford University Press, 1987), 85–100; Jeffrey Sconce, "What If? Charting Television's New Textual Boundaries," in *Television after TV: Essays on a Medium in Transition,* ed. Jan Olsson and Lynn Spigel (Durham, NC: Duke University Press, 2004), 93–112; Sarah Kozloff, "Narrative Theory and Television," in *Channels of Discourse, Reassembled: Television and Contemporary Criticism,* ed. Robert C. Allen (Chapel Hill: University of North Carolina Press, 1992), 67–100.

9. Kozloff, "Narrative Theory and Television," 92.

10. *Law and Order* (NBC, 1990–2010) is an example of an episodic series that remained true to the form. Shows like *CSI: Crime Scene Investigation* (CBS, 2000–2015) and *House* (Fox, 2004–12), while appearing like episodic series with a case solved every week, contain serial elements involving the main characters and their interpersonal relationships.

11. Alun Munslow, *Narrative and History* (Basingstoke, UK: Palgrave Macmillan, 2007), 1.

12. Hayden White, "The Structure of Historical Narrative," in *Hayden White, the Fiction of Narrative: Essays on History, Literature and Theory, 1957–2007,* ed. Robert Doran (Baltimore: Johns Hopkins University Press, 2010), 120–21.

13. "Historians' traditional understanding of the nature, epistemological grounding, truth-value, and goals of research and writing faced a significant challenge beginning in the late 1960s and 1970s," explains Gabrielle M. Spiegel, "with the emergence of what came to be known as the 'linguistic turn,' the notion that language is the constitutive agent of human consciousness and the social production of meaning, and that our apprehension of the world, both past and present, arrives only through the lens of language's precoded perceptions." For a more thorough explanation of the linguistic turn, see Gabrielle M. Spiegel, "Introduction," in *Practicing History: New Directions in Historical Writing after the Linguistic Turn,* ed. Gabrielle M. Spiegel (New York: Routledge, 2005), 2–6.

14. Geoffrey Roberts, "The History and Narrative Debate," in *The History and Narrative Reader,* ed. Geoffrey Roberts (New York: Routledge, 2001), 2. For more on historians' turn away from narrative (and then their return to it), see Lawrence Stone, "The Revival of Narrative: Reflections on a New Old History," *Past & Present,* no. 85 (1979): 3–24.

15. Hayden White, "Storytelling: Historical and Ideological," in Doran, *Hayden White, the Fiction of Narrative,* 273.

16. Paul Ricoeur, *Time and Narrative: Volume 1,* trans. Kathleen McLaughlin and David Pellauer (Chicago: University of Chicago Press, 1984), 91; Alun Munslow, *Routledge Companion to Historical Studies,* 2nd ed. (New York: Routledge, 2006), 182.

17. Elizabeth A. Clark, *History, Theory, Text: Historians and the Linguistic Turn* (Cambridge, MA: Harvard University Press, 2004), 94; Eileen Ka-May Cheng, *Historiography: An Introductory Guide* (London: Continuum, 2012), 129.

18. Clark, *History, Theory, Text,* 86.

19. Munslow, *Narrative and History,* 4 (italics in original).

20. Munslow, *Narrative and History,* 64.

21. Robert Rosenstone, "History in Images / History in Words: Reflections on the Possibility of Really Putting History onto Film," *American Historical Review* 93, no. 5 (1988): 1174, 1178.

22. Jason Mittell is not the only television scholar to note changes in narrative structure on TV, but he has been influential in charting changes and developments. Mittell, "Narrative Complexity," 29.

23. Mittell uses *Breaking Bad* (AMC, 2008–13) and *The Wire* to demonstrate "stark contrasts among the range of options within the realm of serialised primetime dramas." Both are examples of narrative complexity despite their obvious structural and stylistic differences. Jason Mittell, "The Qualities of Complexity: Vast versus Dense Seriality in Contemporary Television," in *Television Aesthetics and Style,* ed. Jason Jacobs and Steven Peacock (New York: Bloomsbury Academic, 2013), 45–56.

24. Jason Mittell, "Previously On: Prime Time Serials and the Mechanics of Memory," in *Intermediality and Storytelling,* ed. Marina Grishakova and Marie-Laure Ryan (New York: De Gruyter, 2010), 78.

25. Mittell, "Narrative Complexity," 37.

26. For an example, see Rossend Sánchez-Baró's article on the "formidable" confusion caused by *Breaking Bad*'s cold opens. Rossend Sánchez-Baró, "Uncertain Beginnings: *Breaking Bad*'s Episodic Openings," in *Breaking Bad: Critical Essays on the Contexts, Politics, Style, and Reception of the Television Series,* ed. David P. Pierson (Lanham, MD: Lexington Books, 2014), 139–54.

27. Mittell, "Narrative Complexity," 37; Michael Z. Newman, "From Beats to Arcs: Toward a Poetics of Television Narrative," *Velvet Light Trap* 58, no. 1 (Fall 2006): 22.

28. For a more detailed explanation of some of the key changes in the industry resulting in the "postnetwork era," see Amanda D. Lotz, *The Television Will Be Revolutionized,* 2nd ed. (New York: NYU Press, 2014), 25–34.

29. Anthony N. Smith, *Storytelling Industries: Narrative Production in the 21st Century* (Cham, Switzerland: Palgrave Macmillan, 2018), 88.

30. Smith, *Storytelling Industries,* 89 (italics in original).

31. For example, *Boardwalk Empire* premiered the same year and did not drop below 2.5 million in live-plus-same-day viewings during the first season. *True Blood*'s third season, airing in 2010, regularly posted ratings above 5 million.

32. Richard Plepler, quoted in Dave Walker, "With 'Treme' Renewed for a Third Season, Its Writers Focus on Stories Left to Tell," *Times-Picayune,* August 14, 2011, http://www.nola.com/treme-hbo/index.ssf/2011/08/with_treme_renewed_for_a_third.html (article no longer stored on site).

33. Both HitFix and AV Club reviewers regularly reminded readers to utilize Walker's guide. Echoing similar sentiments, viewer Far Ceide posted on Walker's blog, "Dave, your explainers really enrich my appreciation of 'Treme.' Thanks again for this work." Far Ceide, October 1, 2012, comment on Dave Walker, "'Treme' Explained: 'Saints,'" *Times-Picayune,* September 30, 2012, http://www.nola.com/treme-hbo/index.ssf/2012/09/treme_explained_saints.html (article no longer stored on site).

34. David Herman, "Introduction," in *The Cambridge Companion to Narrative,* ed. David Herman (Cambridge: Cambridge University Press, 2007), 13.

35. David Simon, "HBO's *Treme* Creator David Simon Explains It All for You," *Times-Picayune,* April 11, 2010, http://www.nola.com/treme-hbo/index.ssf/2010/04/hbos_treme_creator_david_simon.html (article no longer stored on site).

36. Charles McGrath, "The Triumph of the Prime-Time Novel," *New York Times,* October 22, 1995, http://www.nytimes.com/1995/10/22/magazine/the-prime-time-novel-the-triumph-of-the-prime-time-novel.html.

37. Greg Metcalf, *The DVD Novel: How the Way We Watch Television Changed the Television We Watch* (Santa Barbara, CA: Praeger, 2012).

38. Sean O'Sullivan, "Broken on Purpose: Poetry, Serial Television, and the Season," *Storyworlds: A Journal of Narrative Studies* 2 (2010): 60.

39. Brett Martin, *Difficult Men: Behind the Scenes of a Creative Revolution* (New York: Penguin, 2013), 6.

40. Mittell, "Narrative Complexity," 30.

41. Jason Mittell, "Film and Television Narrative," in Herman, *Cambridge Companion to Narrative,* 162.

42. Hayden White, "Historiography and Historiophoty," *American Historical Review* 93, no. 5 (1988): 1193.

43. David Simon, quoted in Matt Zoller Seitz, "Hot Seat: David Simon Explains 'Treme,'" *Salon,* July 5, 2011, http://www.salon.com/2011/07/04/treme_season_2_david_simon_interview/.

44. Simon stated that he is not interested in sensational TV tropes—a gun being put to a person's head, a car being wrecked: "those are not the stakes of post-Katrina New Orleans, and I'm interested in post-Katrina New Orleans." David Simon, quoted in Alan Sepinwall, "Interview: 'Treme' Co-creator David

Simon Post-mortems Season One," HitFix, June 20, 2010, https://uproxx.com/sepinwall/interview-treme-co-creator-david-simon-post-mortems-season-one/. All HitFix posts have since been migrated to the Uproxx website.

45. Simon himself has admitted that the live viewing numbers for his HBO serials (both *The Wire* and *Treme*) are "appalling" and notes that *The Wire* did not become a cult hit until all five seasons had been aired. Angela Watercutter, "David Simon on *Treme,* the CIA and Why TV Isn't Journalism," *Wired,* November 24, 2012, http://www.wired.com/2012/11/david-simon-tv-journalism-cia/4/ (article no longer stored on site).

46. Seymour Chatman, *Story and Discourse: Narrative Structure in Fiction and Film* (Ithaca, NY: Cornell University Press, 1978), 19 (italics in original).

47. Maria Pramaggiore and Tom Wallis, *Film: A Critical Introduction,* 3rd ed. (London: Laurence King, 2011), 69.

48. David Bordwell, *Poetics of Cinema* (New York: Routledge, 2008), 98, 110.

49. Anthony N. Smith, "TV or Not TV? *The Sopranos* and Contemporary Episode Architecture in US Network and Premium Cable Drama," *Critical Studies in Television* 6, no. 1 (2011): 36–38.

50. Newman explains that networks prefer beats that are under two and a half minutes, as they believe the audience's attention may be lost. Cable networks, on the other hand, are more flexible with this rule, allowing scenes to linger and slowly play out. Newman, "From Beats to Arcs," 17; Smith, "TV or Not TV?," 39.

51. Smith, "TV or Not TV?," 46.

52. Thompson, *Storytelling in Film and Television,* 54; Smith, "TV or Not TV?," 41–44.

53. Some shows with a large ensemble cast, such as *Game of Thrones,* focus on a selection of the characters and locations from week to week, but on *Treme* most of the characters appear every week, at least for the first three seasons.

54. Steven Johnson, *Everything Bad Is Good for You: How Today's Popular Culture Is Actually Making Us Smarter* (New York: Riverhead Books, 2005), 65–72.

55. Indeed, some writers use this formula when planning a show. David Chase, for example, works with a rough formula of thirteen beats each for the A and B story, five or six for the C story, and a couple for a D story. O'Sullivan, "Broken on Purpose," 63.

56. In a previous episode Antoine, a trombone player by trade, was unjustly assaulted and arrested by the police and his instrument lost in police evidence. His lawyer, Toni, is trying to track down his trombone for him and alerts him to how Japanese jazz fans are funding musicians through Tipitina's Foundation. Toni is also LaDonna's lawyer, and together the two are working to find out what has become of LaDonna's brother Daymo, who is suspected to have been in police custody on the day of the hurricane and has not been seen since.

57. Robin Nelson, *TV Drama in Transition: Forms, Values, and Cultural Change* (New York: St. Martin's, 1997), 24.

58. Nelson states that multiple storylines incorporating a variety of characters and storylines help keep viewers interested. Even if there is one storyline or set of characters that does not interest a segment of the audience, a different narrative thread will be taken up in the next beat. Nelson, *TV Drama in Transition,* 33.

59. I call the scenes where Janette cooks for the famous chefs—Tom Colicchio, Wylie Dufresne, Eric Ripert, and David Chang—a vignette because it is only dealt with in these three closely spaced beats and serves more as a short character piece or short story than really continuing or developing Janette's longer-running restaurant woes.

60. Adam Nossiter, "New Orleans Crime Swept Away, with Most of the People," *New York Times,* November 10, 2005.

61. Michael Leitner et al., "The Impact of Hurricane Katrina on Reported Crimes in Louisiana: A Spatial and Temporal Analysis," *Professional Geographer* 63, no. 2 (2011): 258.

62. For a full report on crime statistics, not just in Orleans Parish but also neighboring parishes that took in Katrina evacuees, see Leitner et al., "Impact of Hurricane Katrina," 244–61.

63. Although difficult to pinpoint exact numbers due to conflicting census estimates, VanLandingham concludes that the 2006 murder rate increased by at least 49 percent over recorded numbers for 2004. Mark J. VanLandingham, "Murder Rates in New Orleans, La, 2004–2006," *American Journal of Public Health* 97, no. 9 (2007): 1614–15.

64. Eloise Dunlap, Jennifer Graves, and Ellen Benoit, "Stages of Drug Market Change during Disaster: Hurricane Katrina and Reformulation of the New Orleans Drug Market," *International Journal of Drug Policy* 23, no. 6 (2012): 477.

65. Nona Ivey, quoted in Nossiter, "New Orleans Crime Swept Away."

66. Amanda Ripley et al. highlight some of the problems in the New Orleans justice system both before and after the storm, including the peculiar "sixty-day homicide" rule that Colson mentions. Amanda Ripley et al., "What Happened to the Gangs of New Orleans?," *Time,* May 22, 2006, 54–61.

67. Bordwell, *Poetics of Cinema,* 100.

68. A cold open is a scene or sequence that appears before the opening credits. Not all shows use this device; *Boardwalk Empire* is an example of a show that starts straight into the title sequence and then begins the weekly narrative.

69. Creighton watched part of Bush's Jackson Square speech on YouTube during the previous episode.

70. Spencer S. Hsu, "Post-Katrina Promises Unfulfilled: On the Gulf Coast, Federal Recovery Effort Makes Halting Progress," *Washington Post,* January 28,

2006; Tracie L. Washington et al., *NAACP Reports Housing in New Orleans: Policy Recommendations for Equitable Rebuilding* (n.p.: NAACP, Gulf Coast Advocacy Center, Opportunity Agenda, and Kirwan Institute for the Study of Race and Ethnicity, 2006).

71. Creighton's references to San Francisco as "an overpriced cess pool with hills" and declaration that "anything that's any good in Chicago comes from someplace else" clearly demonstrate his extremely biased point of view.

72. Local council authorities insisted they could not open the housing projects, despite the fact they were relatively undamaged, because they were under federal control. The debate over public housing in New Orleans and the fate of the Big Four developments remained a contentious issue for a number of years after the storm. Displaced residents filed lawsuits in 2006 and 2007 in an attempt to halt demolition.

73. Sheryl Gay Stolberg, "Year after Katrina, Bush Still Fights for 9/11 Image," *New York Times,* August 28, 2006.

74. A *USA Today*/Gallup poll was conducted in September and October 2005 with a sample of 1,510 participants. In August 2006, 602 of those individuals were recontacted and asked to participate in another poll with updated questions. Frank Newport, "Follow-up on Katrina Victims: One Year Later," Gallup, August 21, 2006, http://www.gallup.com/poll/24208/FollowUp-Katrina-Victims-One-Year-Later.aspx#4.

75. Munslow, *Routledge Companion to Historical Studies,* 180.

76. Peter Burke, "History of Events and the Revival of Narrative," in *The History and Narrative Reader,* ed. Geoffrey Roberts (New York: Routledge, 2001), 310.

77. Given Toni's vexed relationship with the NOPD, the fact that she has a friendly rapport with Colson serves to show the audience that he is one of the "good guys" and that his assessment of crime can be taken as accurate. Still, the fact he is dressed as a police officer may incline some in the audience to think his sympathies lie with his fellow officers.

78. Watercutter, "David Simon on *Treme.*"

79. Smith, *Storytelling Industries,* 93.

80. Robert Rosenstone, *Visions of the Past: The Challenge of Film to Our Idea of History* (Cambridge, MA: Harvard University Press, 1995), 60.

81. Murray Smith, *Engaging Characters: Fiction, Emotion, and the Cinema* (Oxford: Clarendon, 1995), 142, 188 (italics in original).

82. Murray Smith, "*Engaging Characters:* Further Reflections," in *Characters in Fictional Worlds: Understanding Imaginary Beings in Literature, Film and Other Media,* ed. Jens Eder, Fotis Jannidis, and Ralf Schneider (New York: De Gruyter, 2010), 244.

83. Being the Big Chief of a Mardi Gras Indian tribe, Albert is a culture bearer of New Orleans culture. Delmond, although a part of the Indian tradition, is

more open to change and is a successful modern jazz musician splitting his time between New Orleans and New York. Delmond is first introduced to the jazz center idea by developer Will Branson, who argues there should be a world-class jazz performance center in New Orleans. Now is the time to move ahead, he suggests, with so much of the city being rebuilt after the storm.

84. Manning Marable, for example, argues that the storm was "perceived as a golden opportunity by corporate and conservative political elites who had long desired to 'remake' the historic city." Manning Marable, "Introduction," in *Seeking Higher Ground: The Hurricane Katrina Crisis, Race and Public Policy Reader,* ed. Manning Marable and Kristen Clarke (New York: Palgrave Macmillan, 2008), xi; Juliette Landphair, "'The Forgotten People of New Orleans': Community, Vulnerability, and the Lower Ninth Ward," *Journal of American History* 94, no. 3 (2007): 844.

85. Kevin Fox Gotham, "Tourism Gentrification: The Case of New Orleans' Vieux Carre (French Quarter)," *Urban Studies* 42, no. 7 (2005): 1105.

86. Gotham, "Tourism Gentrification," 1105. Numbers, of course, do not tell the full story. As Kevin Fox Gotham points out, "The transition to a tourism-dominated economy has paralleled population decline, white flight to the suburbs, racial segregation, poverty and a host of other social problems" in New Orleans. Furthermore, many jobs in the tourism industry are seasonal, have a high turnover, are low paid, and do not make up for the loss of jobs in other sectors of the New Orleans economy. Kevin Fox Gotham, "Marketing Mardi Gras: Commodification, Spectacle and the Political Economy of Tourism in New Orleans," *Urban Studies* 39, no. 10 (2002): 1740, 1743.

87. When Liguori first mentions the jazz center plan to Nelson, he describes a proposal very similar to one headed by the owner of the New Orleans Hyatt Regency to create a twenty-acre jazz district that would include a national jazz center and new city government buildings. It was estimated that this new tourist center would create 6,500 permanent jobs and "generate more than $6 billion in economic benefits over 20 years." "Hyatt-Superdome Area to Be Redeveloped into New Hyatt Jazz District: Finished Site to Generate More than 6,500 Permanent Jobs," press release, May 30, 2006, https://www.hospitalitynet.org/news/4027606.html.

88. Michael L. Dolfman, Solidelle Fortier Wasser, and Bruce Bergman, "The Effects of Hurricane Katrina on the New Orleans Economy," *Monthly Labor Review* 130, no. 6 (2007): 7.

89. "Report of the Cultural Committee: Mayor's Bring New Orleans Back Commission," January 17, 2006, 12, https://nolaplans.com/plans/BNOB/Culture%20Committee%20Report%20Attachment%20C.pdf.

90. Anna Hartnell, "Katrina Tourism and a Tale of Two Cities: Visualizing Race and Class in New Orleans," *American Quarterly* 61, no. 3 (2009): 723–47;

Lynell L. Thomas, "'Roots Run Deep Here': The Construction of Black New Orleans in Post-Katrina Tourism Narratives," *American Quarterly* 61, no. 3 (2009): 749–68.

91. Hartnell, "Katrina Tourism," 724.

92. Jonathan Mark Souther, *New Orleans on Parade: Tourism and the Transformation of the Crescent City* (Baton Rouge: LSU Press, 2006), 209.

93. Joyce Williams, quoted in Lolis Eric Elie, "Armstrong Park Planning Exclusionary, Treme Residents Complain," *Times-Picayune*, August 18, 2009, http://www.nola.com/politics/index.ssf/2009/08/armstrong_park_planning_exclus.html (article no longer stored on site).

94. Katy Reckdahl, "Locked-Up Armstrong Park Lamented as 'Neglected Jewel' of Treme, French Quarter Area," *Times-Picayune*, August 17, 2011, http://www.nola.com/politics/index.ssf/2011/08/locked-up_armstrong_park_lamen.html (article no longer stored on site).

95. Mtangulizi Sanyika, "Katrina and the Condition of Black New Orleans: The Struggle for Justice, Equity, and Democracy," in *Race, Place, and Environmental Justice after Hurricane Katrina*, ed. Robert D. Bullard and Beverly Wright (Boulder, CO: Westview, 2009), 104.

96. Vincanne Adams, *Markets of Sorrow, Labors of Faith: New Orleans in the Wake of Katrina* (Durham, NC: Duke University Press, 2013); Rita J. King, "Post-Katrina Profiteering: The New Big Easy," in Bullard and Wright, *Race, Place, and Environmental Justice*, 169–82.

97. Bruce Eggler, "Inspector General Urges City Council to Reject Municipal Auditorium Deal," *Times-Picayune*, November 11, 2009, http://www.nola.com/politics/index.ssf/2009/11/post_134.html (article no longer stored on site).

98. Karl F. Seidman, *Coming Home to New Orleans: Neighborhood Rebuilding after Katrina* (New York: Oxford University Press, 2013), 8–9.

99. Antoine's home in Mid-City was flooded, and he and Desiree have to rent outside of the city where it is difficult for him to get to his music gigs; the bottom floor of Janette's home, as well as the roof, was badly damaged and she receives her Road Home payout only in season 3; Albert's home was also badly damaged, and season 1 documented his struggles with the insurance company over the payout; Colson is still living in his FEMA trailer through season 3.

100. For scholarly texts that discuss the Road Home Program, see Adams, *Markets of Sorrow*, 74–97; Lisa K. Bates and Rebekah A. Green, "Housing Recovery in the Ninth Ward: Disparities in Policy, Process and Prospects," in Bullard and Wright, *Race, Place, and Environmental Justice*, 229–45; Christina Finch, Christopher T. Emirich, and Susan L. Cutter, "Disaster Disparities and Differential Recovery in New Orleans," *Population and Environment* 31, no. 4 (2010): 179–202.

101. Gadbois's *Squandered Heritage* blog posts have been archived on *The Lens*, a nonprofit, nonpartisan public-interest newsroom cofounded by Gadbois

in 2010. Karen Gadbois, "What Is up with This?," *The Lens,* June 28, 2008, http://thelensnola.org/2008/06/28/what-is-up-with-this/.

102. David Simon, quoted in Watercutter, "David Simon on *Treme.*"

103. David Simon and Eric Overmyer, commentary, "Do You Know What It Means," disc 1, *Treme: The Complete First Season* (HBO, 2011), DVD.

104. "I'm looking forward to going back and watching earlier episodes again after having seen them all," commented Jan on HitFix at the end of season 1. Jan, June 21, 2010 (1:19 p.m.), comment (since deleted on Uproxx site) on Alan Sepinwall, "'Treme'—'I'll Fly Away': Stormy Weather," HitFix, June 20, 2010, https://uproxx.com/sepinwall/treme-i-11-fly-away-stormy-weather/.

105. Jill Lepore, "Historians Who Love Too Much: Reflections on Microhistory and Biography," *Journal of American History* 88, no. 1 (2001): 133.

106. This is how Creighton describes New Orleans while being interviewed by a British reporter who questions the rebuilding of New Orleans in the pilot episode.

107. Burke, "History of Events and the Revival of Narrative," 310; Gordon S. Wood, *The Purpose of the Past: Reflections of the Uses of History* (New York: Penguin, 2008), 127.

108. Katy Reckdahl, "Mardi Gras Indians' Suits Stitched with Help of Invisible Hands," *Times-Picayune,* February 20, 2012, http://www.nola.com/mardigras/index.ssf/2012/02/mardi_gras_indians_suits_stitc.html (article no longer stored on site).

109. "I will say that as a native, caucasian New Orleanian, I have learned more about the Mardi Gras Indians by watching Treme than I have by living in the city for over 40 years," Ybnorma11 posted partway through season 1. "I knew they existed and little else." Ybnorma11, June 22, 2010, comment on Dave Walker, "'Treme' Explained: 'I'll Fly Away,'" *Times-Picayune,* June 20, 2010, http://www.nola.com/treme-hbo/index.ssf/2010/06/treme_explained_ill_fly_away.html (article no longer stored on site).

110. For example, see Reid Mitchell, *All on a Mardi Gras Day: Episodes in the History of New Orleans Carnival* (Cambridge, MA: Harvard University Press, 1995), 113–30; Michael P. Smith, "Buffalo Bill and Mardi Gras Indians," in *Mardi Gras, Gumbo, and Zydeco: Readings in Louisiana Culture,* ed. Marcia G. Gaudet and James C. McDonald (Jackson: University Press of Mississippi, 2003), 16–25; Richard Brent Turner, *Jazz Religion, the Second Line, and Black New Orleans* (Bloomington: Indiana University Press, 2009), 39–68.

111. Mitchell, *All on a Mardi Gras Day,* 116, 122.

112. Cherice Harrison-Nelson, quoted in Clyde Woods, "Upholding Community Traditions: An Interview with Cherice Harrison-Nelson," *American Quarterly* 61, no. 3 (2009): 645, 642.

113. Smith, *Storytelling Industries,* 79–84.

114. Martha P. Nochimson, *Television Rewired: The Rise of the Auteur Series* (Austin: University of Texas Press, 2019), 141.

115. James F. Brooks, Christopher R. N. DeCorse and John Walton, "Introduction," in *Small Worlds: Method, Meaning, and Narrative in Microhistory,* ed. James F. Brooks, Christopher R. N. DeCorse, and John Walton (Santa Fe: School for Advanced Research, 2008), 4.

116. Here I am referencing Ladurie's work as well as two other well-known microhistories that appeared in the 1980s: Natalie Zemon Davis, *The Return of Martin Guerre* (Cambridge, MA: Harvard University Press, 1983); and Robert Darnton, *The Great Cat Massacre and Other Episodes in French Cultural History* (New York: Basic Books, 1984).

117. Stone's examples of "new" narrative history include works by Ladurie, Zemon Davis, Darnton, Ginzburg, and E. P. Thompson. Stone, "Revival of Narrative," 19.

118. Stone, "Revival of Narrative," 15; István Szijártó, "Four Arguments for Microhistory," *Rethinking History* 6, no. 2 (2002): 210.

119. Richard D. Brown, "Microhistory and the Postmodern Challenge," *Journal of the Early Republic* 23, no. 1 (2003): 11.

120. Looking at press coverage of post-Katrina New Orleans, Robin Andersen concludes that the plight of New Orleans was quickly forgotten in the American press. And when the city did receive media attention, it was often focused on violence perpetrated by the poor. Robin Andersen, "HBO's *Treme:* Exposing the Fractured Press Coverage of the Storm and Post-Katrina New Orleans," in *Censored 2012: Sourcebook for the Media Revolution,* ed. Mickey Huff (New York: Seven Stories, 2011), 423–36.

121. Brown, "Microhistory and the Postmodern Challenge," 18.

122. Burke, "History of Events and the Revival of Narrative," 307.

123. Lepore, "Historians Who Love Too Much," 133.

124. Brown, "Microhistory and the Postmodern Challenge," 15.

125. David Simon, "David Simon on What HBO's *Treme* Meant to Him and What He Hopes It Meant to New Orleans," *Times-Picayune,* December 27, 2013, http://www.nola.com/treme-hbo/index.ssf/2013/12/david_simon_on_what_hbos_treme.html (article no longer stored on site).

126. John Tosh, *The Pursuit of History: Aims, Methods, and New Directions in the Study of Modern History,* 5th ed. (New York: Longman/Pearson, 2010), 82.

127. Gordon Wood opines that sometimes the "sheer intensity and interest of particular stories overwhelm their larger significance, turning them into little trees in search of a forest." Wood, *Purpose of the Past,* 128.

128. Gérard Genette, *Paratexts: Thresholds of Interpretation,* trans. Jane E. Lewin (Cambridge: Cambridge University Press, 1997), 2, 4–5.

129. Jonathan Gray, *Show Sold Separately: Promos, Spoilers, and Other Media Paratexts* (New York: NYU Press, 2010), 6, 23.

130. Craig Hight, "Making-of Documentaries on DVD: *The Lord of the Rings* Trilogy and Special Editions," *Velvet Light Trap* 56 (Fall 2006): 5; Aaron Barlow, *The DVD Revolution: Movies, Culture and Technology* (Westport, CT: Praeger, 2004), 76.

131. Hight, "Making-of Documentaries on DVD," 7.

132. Debra Ramsay, "Flagging Up History: The Past as a DVD Bonus Feature," in *A Companion to the Historical Film,* ed. Robert Rosenstone and Constantin Parvulescu (Malden, MA: Wiley-Blackwell, 2013), 59, 68.

133. Ramsay, "Flagging Up History," 68.

134. At one point during the commentary for the pilot episode, Simon and Overmyer suggest viewers google Mardi Gras Indians to learn more about them. However, over the course of this commentary and others for season 1 episodes (Overmyer for episode 8, Simon for episode 10), they do relate a lot more useful information about Mardi Gras Indians that complements what is happening on-screen.

135. Given that the Criterion Collection provided the blueprint for DVD special features, it is unsurprising that the Criterion Channel streaming library continues to provide a vast array of special features for its catalog of films and offers an example of how special features can be incorporated on streaming platforms.

136. For example, a weekly podcast for the historical series *Chernobyl* (HBO, 2019), featuring showrunner Craig Mazin in discussion with host Peter Segal, was made available on a number of platforms, including Spotify and YouTube.

137. In January 2021, Hulu released a commentary cut of the film *Palm Springs* (Barbakow, 2020) featuring the director, writer, and stars. This opens up another potential avenue for film and TV commentaries if other streaming services follow suit.

138. For a thoughtful consideration of the special features included on the *Deadwood* DVD box set and how they present and address history, see Allison Perlman, "*Deadwood,* Generic Transformation and Televisual History," *Journal of Popular Film and Television* 39, no. 2 (2011): 110–12.

139. Simon, "David Simon on What HBO's *Treme* Meant to Him."

140. Similarly, Michael Samuel argues that *Treme* is a "social, cultural and historical document of life in New Orleans post Hurricane Katrina" that is informed and shaped by Simon's background as a journalist. For more, see Michael Samuel, "'The Storm': Spatial Discourses and Katrina Narratives in David Simon's *Treme* (2010–2013)," in *Ten Years after Katrina: Critical Perspectives of the Storm's Effect on American Culture and Identity,* ed. Mary Ruth Marotte and Glenn Jellenik (Lanham, MD: Lexington Books, 2014), 33–56.

141. Burke, "History of Events and the Revival of Narrative," 314, 311.

142. Simon, "David Simon on What HBO's *Treme* Meant to Him."

143. Thomas J. Billard, "Experimental Evidence for Differences in the Prosocial Effects of Binge-Watched Versus Appointment-Viewed Television Programs," *Journalism & Mass Communication Quarterly* 96, no. 4 (2019): 1025–51.

144. Jared C. Horvath et al., "The Impact of Binge Watching on Memory and Perceived Comprehension," *First Monday* 22, no. 9 (2017): https://doi.org/10.5210/fm.v22i9.7729.

145. David Simon, quoted in Alan Sepinwall, "*Treme* Co-creator David Simon on the Series' End and His Career's Future," HitFix, December 29, 2013, https://uproxx.com/sepinwall/treme-co-creator-david-simon-on-the-series-end-and-his-careers-future/.

146. Alan Sepinwall, "HBO Renews 'Treme' for Abbreviated Fourth and Final Season," HitFix, September 22, 2012, https://uproxx.com/sepinwall/hbo-renews-treme-for-abbreviated-fourth-and-final-season/.

147. Mittell, "Narrative Complexity," 31.

## 4. Listening to History

1. This is something that I am also guilty of, choosing to use such terms as "history on-screen" and "history on television" and referring to audiences *watching* at home. However, as James Buhler, Rob Deemer, and David Neumeyer point out, there is not (yet) "an easy way to point in language to this complex interplay of hearing and seeing in the experience of a film." So for now these terms will have to suffice, and it should be understood that to watch history on-screen means to both see what is on-screen and listen to what issues from the speakers. James Buhler, Rob Deemer, and David Neumeyer, *Hearing the Movies: Music and Sound in Film History* (New York: Oxford University Press, 2010), xxii.

2. Herbert Zettl, *Sight, Sound, Motion: Applied Media Aesthetics,* 5th ed. (Belmont, CA: Thomson/Wadsworth, 2007), 331.

3. Gianluca Sergi, "The Sonic Playground: Hollywood Cinema and Its Listeners," in *Hollywood Spectatorship: Changing Perceptions of Cinema Audiences,* ed. Melvyn Stokes and Richard Maltby (London: British Film Institute, 2001), 121.

4. Producer Tony To describes this "filmmaking language" as the shaky, handheld, subjective point of view. Tony To, quoted in Thomas Schatz, "Old War / New War: *Band of Brothers* and the Revival of the WWII War Film," *Film & History* 32, no. 1 (2002): 76.

5. Tom Hanks, quoted in Bill Carter, "HBO Bets Pentagon-Style Budget on a World War II Saga," *New York Times,* September 3, 2001.

6. Jeff Bewkes, quoted in Carter, "HBO Bets Pentagon-Style Budget."

7. Mike Dowson, quoted in Blair Jackson, "Surround Mixing for *Band of Brothers*," *Mix Online*, November 1, 2001, http://www.mixonline.com/news/profiles/surround-mixing-band-brothers/365073.

8. John Orloff, "Why 'Band of Brothers' Lasts: A Perspective from One of Its Writers," *Task & Purpose*, August 3, 2018, https://taskandpurpose.com/band-brothers-lasts-perspective-one-writers.

9. Dolby, "Dolby Digital 5.1 Programming Takes Off," press release, April 1, 2003, http://investor.dolby.com/news-releases/news-release-details/dolby-digital-51-programming-takes; Dolby, "HBO's *The Wire* Broadcast in Dolby Digital 5.1," press release, June 12, 2003, http://investor.dolby.com/news-releases/news-release-details/hbos-wire-broadcast-dolby-digital-51; Dolby, "HBO's *Carnivale* to Be Broadcast in Dolby Digital 5.1 Audio," press release, August 25, 2003, http://investor.dolby.com/news-releases/news-release-details/hbos-carnivale-be-broadcast-dolby-digital-51-audio (webpages no longer active).

10. Vincent LoBrutto, *Sound on Film: Interviews with Creators of Film Sound* (Westport, CT: Praeger, 1994), xi.

11. For an overview of postproduction sound process, see Elizabeth Weis, "Sync Tanks: The Art and Technique of Postproduction Sound," *Cineaste* 21, nos. 1–2 (1995): 56–61.

12. Gary Rydstrom, quoted in Gianluca Sergi, *The Dolby Era: Film Sound in Contemporary Hollywood* (Manchester: Manchester University Press, 2004), 170.

13. Ben Burtt, quoted in David Sonnenschein, *Sound Design: The Expressive Power of Music, Voice, and Sound Effects in Cinema* (Studio City, CA: Michael Wiese, 2001), 197.

14. George H. Roeder Jr., "Coming to Our Senses," *Journal of American History* 81, no. 3 (1994): 1112.

15. David W. Samuels et al., "Soundscapes: Toward a Sounded Anthropology," *Annual Review of Anthropology* 39 (2010): 338.

16. Kara Keeling and Josh Kun, "Introduction: Listening to American Studies," *American Quarterly* 63, no. 3 (2011): 446.

17. Alain Corbin, *Village Bells: Sound and Meaning in the Nineteenth-Century French Countryside* (New York: Columbia University Press, 1998); Richard Cullen Rath, *How Early America Sounded* (Ithaca, NY: Cornell University Press, 2003); Mark M. Smith, *Listening to Nineteenth-Century America* (Chapel Hill: University of North Carolina Press, 2001); Mark M. Smith, ed., *Hearing History: A Reader* (Athens: University of Georgia Press, 2004); Les Back and Michael Bull, eds., *The Auditory Culture Reader*, 2nd ed. (New York: Routledge, 2015); Kara Keeling and Josh Kun, eds., "Sound Clash: Listening to American Studies," special issue, *American Quarterly* 63, no. 3 (2011).

18. Robert Rosenstone, *History on Film / Film on History*, 2nd ed. (Harlow, UK: Pearson Education, 2012), 44.

19. J. E. Smyth, "*Julia*'s Resistant History: Women's Historical Films in Hollywood and the Legacy of *Citizen Kane,*" in *A Companion to the Historical Film,* ed. Robert Rosenstone and Constantin Parvulescu (Malden, MA: Wiley-Blackwell, 2013), 100; Guy Westwell, "In Country: Narrating the Iraq War in Contemporary US Cinema," in Rosenstone and Parvulescu, *Companion to the Historical Film,* 388–95.

20. Alison Landsberg, *Engaging the Past: Mass Culture and the Production of Historical Knowledge* (New York: Columbia University Press, 2015), 27, 70–84.

21. Winfried Pauleit, "Sonic Icons: Prominent Moments of Cinematic Self-Reflexivity," *Research in Film and History* (2018): https://doi.org/10.25969/mediarep/14812; Mattias Frey, "The Authenticity Feeling: Language and Dialect in the Historical Film," *Research in Film and History* (2018): https://doi.org/10.25969/mediarep/14811; Rasmus Greiner, "Sonic Histospheres: Sound Design and History," *Research in Film and History* (2018): https://doi.org/10.25969/mediarep/14810.

22. Sergi, *Dolby Era,* 4.

23. For a more detailed overview of sound scholarship until 2004, see the chapter "Critical Receptions of Sound" in Sergi, *Dolby Era,* 56–90.

24. There are, of course, some exceptions. A recent edited collection on the series *Mad Men* included a section on "Visual and Aural Stylistic Influences." The essay, included by Tim Anderson, thoughtfully explores the use of music both during episodes and over the closing credits, although Maurice Yacowar's piece on "suggestive silences" has little to do with the series' soundscape. Gary R. Edgerton, ed., *Mad Men: Dream Come True TV* (London: I. B. Tauris, 2010).

25. Hilmes considers various types of TV programming (fiction and nonfiction, not just the dramatic series I am focused on) and explores why TV sound has largely been neglected. Michele Hilmes, "Television Sound: Why the Silence?," *Music, Sound and the Moving Image* 2, no. 2 (2008): 153.

26. For an overview of exhibition practices relating to movie theater sound, see Rick Altman, "The Sound of Sound: A Brief History of the Reproduction of Sound in Movie Theatres," *Cineaste* 21, nos. 1–2 (1995): 67–71.

27. Buhler, Deemer, and Neumeyer, *Hearing the Movies,* 395.

28. Mark Kerins, *Beyond Dolby (Stereo): Cinema in the Digital Sound Age* (Bloomington: Indiana University Press, 2011), 320–21.

29. The music used in television programs—played over opening and closing credit sequences and during the shows themselves—is one area that has started to generate scholarship, although the soundtrack as a whole remains largely unexplored. See, for example, James Andrew Deaville, ed., *Music in Television: Channels of Listening* (New York: Routledge, 2011); Kevin Donnelly and Philip Hayward, eds., *Music in Science Fiction Television: Tuned to the Future* (New York: Routledge, 2013); Ronald W. Rodman, *Tuning In: American Narrative Television Music* (New York: Oxford University Press, 2010).

30. Mike Dowson, quoted in Jackson, "Surround Mixing for *Band of Brothers.*"

31. Claudia Gorbman, *Unheard Melodies: Narrative Film Music* (London: British Film Institute, 1987), 22.

32. Gorbman, *Unheard Melodies,* 3.

33. Robynn J. Stilwell, "Sound and Empathy: Subjectivity, Gender and the Cinematic Soundscape," in *Film Music: Critical Approaches,* ed. Kevin J. Donnelly (New York: Continuum, 2001), 169.

34. Soundtracks Kamen scored over his career include *Die Hard* (McTiernan, 1988), *Robin Hood: Prince of Thieves* (Reynolds, 1991), *Mr. Holland's Opus* (Herek, 1995), and the series *From the Earth to the Moon* (HBO, 1998).

35. I am using the names provided on the *Band of Brothers* soundtrack released by Sony in 2001.

36. For a much more detailed explanation of the Good War and greatest generation myths, see Michael C. C. Adams, *The Best War Ever,* 2nd ed. (Baltimore: Johns Hopkins University Press, 2015); Philip D. Beidler, *The Good War's Greatest Hits: World War Two and American Remembering* (Athens: University of Georgia Press, 1998); Kenneth D. Rose, *Myth and the Greatest Generation: A Social History of Americans in World War II* (New York: Routledge, 2008).

37. Adams, *Best War Ever,* xv.

38. John Bodnar, *The "Good War" in American Memory* (Baltimore: Johns Hopkins University Press, 2010), 213–14.

39. John Bodnar, "*Saving Private Ryan* and Postwar Memory in America," *American Historical Review* 106, no. 3 (2001): 806.

40. Tanine Allison, "Virtue through Suffering: The American War Film at the End of Celluloid," *Journal of Popular Film and Television* 45, no. 1 (2017): 51.

41. Anne Mork, "'Will This Picture Help Win the War'? *Band of Brothers* and the Mythology of World War II," *American Studies in Scandinavia* 43, no. 2 (2012): 68.

42. Rodman, *Tuning In,* 57.

43. Rodman, *Tuning In,* 34.

44. Rodman, *Tuning In,* 24.

45. Rodman, *Tuning In,* 42 (italics in original).

46. Rodman, *Tuning In,* 25.

47. Gorbman, *Unheard Melodies,* 32, 58.

48. Anahid Kassabian, *Hearing Film: Tracking Identifications in Contemporary Hollywood Film Music* (New York: Routledge, 2001), 56.

49. Rodman, *Tuning In,* 15.

50. Gorbman, *Unheard Melodies,* 85.

51. Gorbman, *Unheard Melodies,* 85; Kassabian, *Hearing Film,* 17.

52. Kassabian, *Hearing Film,* 21.

53. Tagg and Clarida's study asked for verbal-visual associations when the *Miami Vice* (NBC, 1984–90) theme music was played. Kassabian, *Hearing Film,* 20.

54. For more on the color manipulation of *Band of Brothers,* see Damian Sutton, "The DreamWorks Effect: The Case for Studying the Ideology of Production Design," *Screen* 45, no. 4 (2004): 383–90.

55. Wesley J. O'Brien, *Music in American Combat Films: A Critical Study* (Jefferson, NC: McFarland, 2012), 140.

56. O'Brien, *Music in American Combat Films,* 138.

57. Gorbman, *Unheard Melodies,* 16–18.

58. William Smith, review of "Main Titles for the HBO Miniseries *Band of Brothers* (Instrumental)," Amazon, July 14, 2008, http://www.amazon.com/Main-Titles-Miniseries-Brothers-Instrumental/dp/B00136NLFQ/ref=sr_1_2?ie=UTF 8&qid=1441409192&sr=8-2&keywords=band+of+brothers+soundtrack.

59. John O "peacemover," review of "*Band of Brothers:* Original Motion Picture Soundtrack," Amazon, December 4, 2001, http://www.amazon.com/Band-Brothers-Original-Picture-Soundtrack/dp/B00136LYPA/ref=cm_cr_pr_product_top?ie=UTF8.

60. Bram Janssen, review of "*Band of Brothers:* Original Motion Picture Soundtrack," Amazon, October 27, 2003, http://www.amazon.com/Band-Brothers-Original-Picture-Soundtrack/dp/B00136LYPA/ref=cm_cr_pr_product_top?ie=UTF8.

61. Unnamed reviewer, review of "*Band of Brothers:* Original Motion Picture Soundtrack," Amazon, November 15, 2002, http://www.amazon.com/Band-Brothers-Original-PictureSoundtrack/dp/B00136LYPA/ref=cm_cr_pr_product_top?ie=UTF8.

62. Mork, "*Band of Brothers,*" 67.

63. Dick Winters, quoted in Stephen Ambrose, *Band of Brothers* (London: Pocket Books, 2001), 263.

64. Gorbman, *Unheard Melodies,* 81.

65. John Orloff, July 1, 2009 (7:15 p.m.), comment on Alan Sepinwall, "Band of Brothers Rewind, Episode 9: 'Why We Fight,'" *What's Alan Watching?* (blog), June 29, 2009, http://sepinwall.blogspot.co.nz/2009/06/band-of-brothers-rewind-episode-9-why.html.

66. A number of viewers picked up on this very subtle and nuanced message, carried in large part through the choice of music. On the AV Club website, one commenter posted: "It's not just that Beethoven is beautiful German music, it's that Beethoven in a lot of ways is the strongest symbol along with Goethe of the German humanist principle, which in a lot of ways was the polar opposite of Hitler's racism." Another posted on Alan Sepinwall's blog about recognizing the music in the first scene, but then coming to appreciate its significance during the second: "The juxtaposition of Beethoven's music with what Nixon (and the others) had seen at the camp was just devastating." Matropoli catropoli, May 29, 2014 (6:15 a.m.), comment on Emily Todd VanDerWerff, "*Band of Brothers:*

'Why We Fight,'" AV Club, May 28, 2014, http://www.avclub.com/tvclub/band-brothers-why-we-fight-205104; Jeanne, June 29, 2009 (10:33 p.m.), comment on Sepinwall, "Band of Brothers Rewind, Episode 9."

67. Ambrose, *Band of Brothers,* 68, 104.

68. Stanley Alten, *Audio in Media,* 10th ed. (Boston: Wadsworth Cengage Learning, 2014), 319.

69. Alten, *Audio in Media,* 332.

70. Alun Munslow, *Narrative and History* (Basingstoke, UK: Palgrave Macmillan, 2007), 9.

71. James Lastra, "Reading, Writing, and Representing Sound," in *Sound Theory, Sound Practice,* ed. Rick Altman (New York: Routledge, 1992), 67 (italics in original).

72. Masha Shpolberg, "The Din of Gunfire: Rethinking the Role of Sound in World War II Newsreels," *NECSUS: European Journal of Media Studies* 3, no. 2 (Autumn 2014): 123, https://doi.org/10.5117/NECSUS2014.2.SHPO.

73. Munslow, *Narrative and History,* 9.

74. James Boyle, email to author, June 3, 2015.

75. Primary sources like diaries and legal documents are archived so that, ideally, all scholars can have access to them. These aural primary sources are likewise utilized by other sound teams: Tom Hanks gave Ken Burns access to the *Band of Brothers* sound library for the creation of his documentary series *The War* (PBS, 2007).

76. Sonnenschein, *Sound Design,* 190.

77. Alten, *Audio in Media,* 319.

78. Thomas Doherty, *Projections of War: Hollywood, American Culture, and World War II* (New York: Columbia University Press, 1999), 270.

79. Shpolberg, "Din of Gunfire."

80. Thomas Elsaesser and Malte Hagener, *Film Theory: An Introduction through the Senses,* 2nd ed. (New York: Routledge, 2015), 155.

81. James Boyle, email to author, June 3, 2015.

82. Mike Dowson quoted in Jackson, "Surround Mixing for *Band of Brothers.*"

83. Gary Rydstrom, the sound designer for *Ryan,* was happy that the artificially created sounds resonated with veterans who told him after viewing the movie that the sound had been captured correctly. Sergi, *Dolby Era,* 168.

84. Tomlinson Holman, *Surround Sound: Up and Running* (Boston: Focal Press, 2008), 1.

85. Sergi, *Dolby Era,* 20.

86. Sergi, *Dolby Era,* 24–29; Kerins, *Beyond Dolby* (*Stereo*), 31–32.

87. Sergi, *Dolby Era,* 31; Kerins, *Beyond Dolby* (*Stereo*), 41.

88. Barbara Klinger, *Beyond the Multiplex: Cinema, New Technologies, and the Home* (Berkeley: University of California Press, 2006), 22.

89. "Dolby Digital 5.1," Dolby Professional, accessed May 5, 2021, https://professional.dolby.com/tv/dolby-digital/.

90. Kerins, *Beyond Dolby (Stereo)*, 47.

91. Gary Rydstrom, quoted in Holman, *Surround Sound,* 197.

92. Kerins, *Beyond Dolby (Stereo)*, 54.

93. For a full explanation of the dynamic range of digital surround sound and how it compares to previous systems, see Kerins, *Beyond Dolby (Stereo)*, 4–65.

94. Gary Rydstrom, quoted in Holman, *Surround Sound,* 196.

95. Kerins, *Beyond Dolby (Stereo)*, 65.

96. Mike Dowson, quoted in Jackson, "Surround Mixing for *Band of Brothers.*"

97. William Whittington, *Sound Design and Science Fiction* (Austin: University of Texas Press, 2007), 126.

98. Elsaesser and Hagener, *Film Theory,* 154, 148.

99. Lucy Fife Donaldson, *Texture in Film* (New York: Palgrave Macmillan, 2014), 114.

100. Varying use of the surrounds is also important; heavy use of the surrounds in battle sequences such as those in "The Breaking Point" can become draining on audiences and lose their impact if not balanced with equally effective subtle use of the surrounds.

101. Nicolas J. Cull, "Film Reviews: *Band of Brothers,*" *American Historical Review* 107, no. 3 (2002): 992.

102. Alison Landsberg, *Prosthetic Memory: The Transformation of American Remembrance in the Age of Mass Culture* (New York: Columbia University Press, 2004), 48.

103. Whittington, *Sound Design and Science Fiction,* 122.

104. The Directors Guild of America considers sound a technical category, and therefore head credits cannot be given to sound. Sergi, *Dolby Era,* 144.

105. Arnt Maasø, "The Proxemics of the Mediated Voice," in *Lowering the Boom: Critical Studies in Film Sound,* ed. Jay Beck and Tony Grajeda (Urbana: University of Illinois Press, 2008), 36.

106. Michel Chion, *The Voice in Cinema,* trans. Claudia Gorbman (New York: Columbia University Press, 1999), 6–7 (italics in original).

107. Buhler, Deemer, and Neumeyer, *Hearing the Movies,* 9.

108. Charles Hardy III and Pamela Dean, "Oral History in Sound and Moving Image Documentaries," in *Handbook of Oral History,* ed. Thomas L. Charlton, Lois E. Myers, and Rebecca Sharples (Lanham, MD: Altamira, 2006), 512.

109. Brien R. Williams, "Doing Video Oral History," in *The Oxford Handbook of Oral History,* ed. Donald A. Ritchie (New York: Oxford University Press, 2011), 268.

110. Mork, "*Band of Brothers,*" 61.

111. "One of my favorite parts of watching the series for the first time was figuring out over the course of the series that the interview segments at the

beginning of episodes were the characters in the series, and then trying to figure out who was who," posted CaliThunderbird. CaliThunderbird, April 3, 2014 (8:48 a.m.), comment on Emily Todd VanDerWerff, "*Band of Brothers:* 'Currahee,'" AV Club, April 2, 2014, http://www.avclub.com/tvclub/band-brothers-currahee-202958.

112. The other "signs of performance" that Butler identifies are gestural, facial, and corporeal (the body). Jeremy G. Butler, *Television: Critical Methods and Applications,* 4th ed. (New York: Routledge, 2012), 65–67.

113. Theo van Leeuwen, "Voice: A Semiotics of the Voice," in *Sound and Music in Film and Media: An Overview,* ed. Graeme Harper, Ruth Doughty, and Jochen Eisentraut (New York: Bloomsbury Academic, 2009), 427.

114. Jody Kreiman and Diana Sidtis, *Foundations of Voice Studies: An Interdisciplinary Approach to Voice Production and Reception* (Malden, MA: Wiley-Blackwell, 2011), 303–5.

115. David Schwimmer was the biggest "star" in *Band of Brothers,* especially when it first aired in 2001. While he still sounds very similar to his character Ross Geller on *Friends* (NBC, 1994–2004), his vocal performance on the sitcom is often faster paced and higher pitched with a whinier inflection to match his neurotic character on that show.

116. Ambrose, *Band of Brothers,* 163.

117. Donald Malarkey with Bob Welch, *Easy Company Soldier: The Legendary Battles of a Sergeant from World War II's "Band of Brothers"* (New York: St. Martin's, 2008), 190.

118. Ambrose, *Band of Brothers,* 23–27.

119. William Guarenere and Edward Heffron with Robyn Post, *Brothers in Battle, Best of Friends* (New York: Berkley Caliber, 2007), 18.

120. Tom McArthur, ed., *Concise Oxford Companion to the English Language* (Oxford: Oxford University Press, 1998), 6.

121. Peter Trudgill, *Sociolinguistics: An Introduction to Language and Society,* 4th ed. (London: Penguin, 2000), 2.

122. For more on the use of accents and different languages in Hollywood films, see Lukas Bleichenbacher, *Multilingualism in the Movies: Hollywood Characters and Their Language Choices* (Tübingen, Germany: Francke, 2007).

123. Jeanine Basinger, *The World War II Combat Film: Anatomy of a Genre* (Middletown, CT: Wesleyan University Press, 2003), 46, 259.

124. Caryn James, "TV Weekend: An Intricate Tapestry of a Heroic Age," *New York Times,* September 7, 2001. Multiple online commenters went further by commending his regional accent. For example, Sister T posted that she was "stunned" when she watched the DVD extras and heard Lewis's British accent. "I could have sworn he had a Lancaster County, PA accent. He had the demeanor and tonal inflections that I associate with older folks in Lancaster County and

other parts of PA." Sister T, June 1, 2009 (9:31 p.m.), comment on Alan Sepinwall, "Band of Brothers Rewind, Episode 1: 'Currahee,'" *What's Alan Watching?* (blog), June 1, 2009, http://sepinwall.blogspot.co.nz/2009/06/band-of-brothers-rewind-episode-1.html.

125. Roe was born and raised in Louisiana but did not have the strong Cajun heritage that he claims in the series. In "Part Six: Bastogne," he tells a fellow medic that his grandmother was a Cajun traiteurs (healer), but this is an invention.

126. Emily Todd VanDerWerff, "*Band of Brothers:* 'Bastogne,'" AV Club, May 7, 2014, http://www.avclub.com/tvclub/band-brothers-bastogne-204326.

127. TV critic Alan Sepinwall ranked Warren "the worst" when it came to accents on the show. Alan Sepinwall, "Band of Brothers Rewind, Episode 1, 'Currahee,'" *What's Alan Watching?* (blog), June 1, 2009, http://sepinwall.blogspot.co.nz/2009/06/band-of-brothers-rewind-episode-1.html.

128. Shane Taylor, "Ross Owen's Band of Brothers Cast Interviews: Shane Taylor," *Black Sky Radio* (blog), July 28, 2010, http://bandofbrotherswherearetheynow.blogspot.co.nz/2010/07/shane-taylor.html.

129. This is possible for American history but becomes much more difficult when it comes to the histories of other nations and very distant time periods. Adopting the language and accents of ancient Rome for the HBO series *Rome* would be almost impossible and, if attempted, would likely alienate the audience.

130. Stephanie Hoth, "The Female Voice in *Sex and the City* and *Desperate Housewives:* Voice-Over Narration in Contemporary American Television Series," in *Gendered (Re)Visions: Constructions of Gender in Audiovisual Media,* ed. Marion Gymnich, Kathrin Ruhl, and Klaus Scheunemann (Göttingen, Germany: V&R Unipress, 2010), 79.

131. Sarah Kozloff, *Invisible Storytellers: Voice-Over Narration in American Fiction Film* (Berkeley: University of California Press, 1988), 44–45.

132. Hoth, "Female Voice," 82.

133. Alan Sepinwall, "Band of Brothers Rewind, Episode 7, 'The Breaking Point,'" *What's Alan Watching?* (blog), June 22, 2009, http://sepinwall.blogspot.co.nz/2009/06/band-of-brothers-rewind-episode-7.html. A number of people responding to Sepinwall's review concurred with his critique: "I agree, Alan," posted Carolyn. "The narration drove me nutty and at least 85% of the time seemed to be explaining something that was already perfectly obvious." Carolyn, July 1, 2009 (1:11 p.m.), comment on Sepinwall, "Band of Brothers Rewind, Episode 7"

134. Erik Bork, email to author, March 15, 2015.

135. Erik Bork, email to author, March 15, 2015.

136. David Kenyon Webster did participate in D-Day and Market Garden (where he was injured). However, he had not been with the company since its formation but transferred to Easy after D-Day and before Market Garden.

137. Chion, *Voice in Cinema,* 50–51.

138. Alten, *Audio in Media,* 220.

139. Tomlinson Holman, *Sound for Film and Television* (Boston: Focal Press, 1997), 186.

140. Chion, *Voice in Cinema,* 51.

141. Alten, *Audio in Media,* 221.

142. Sarah Kozloff, *Overhearing Film Dialogue* (Berkeley: University of California Press, 2000), 14, 18.

143. Stilwell, "Sound and Empathy," 168.

144. Michel Rabiger and Mick Hubris-Cherrier, *Directing: Film Techniques and Aesthetics,* 5th ed. (Burlington, MA: Focal Press, 2013), 128.

145. Whittington, *Sound Design and Science Fiction,* 2–3.

146. Mark S. Ward, "Art in Noise: An Embodied Simulation Account of Cinematic Sound Design," in *Embodied Cognition and Cinema,* ed. Maarten Coegnarts and Peter Kravanja (Leuven, Belgium: Leuven University Press, 2015), 163–64.

147. Landsberg, *Engaging the Past,* 77, 16.

148. Playing one of the battle sequences in *Band of Brothers* with the sound off clearly illustrates this point. The scenes do not have the immediacy and tension that they do when played with sound.

149. Alex Ben Block, "How HBO Spent $200 Million on 'The Pacific,'" *Hollywood Reporter,* August 26, 2010, https://www.hollywoodreporter.com/news/how-hbo-spent-200-million-27133.

150. Debra Ramsay, *American Media and the Memory of World War II* (London: Routledge, 2015), 148–52.

151. As another example, HBO has produced four historical shows with David Simon as showrunner or co-showrunner (*Treme, Show Me a Hero, The Deuce,* and *The Plot against America*). The histories presented in what could be called Simon's historical oeuvre tend to be bottom-up histories that challenge traditional American narratives of progress and exceptionalism, while Playtone's series tend to hew closer to dominant and master narratives.

## Conclusion

1. Prolific TV writer-producers Shonda Rhimes and Ryan Murphy have both signed five-year deals with Netflix for $150 million and $300 million, respectively. Since completing *Game of Thrones* for HBO, showrunners David Benioff and Dan Weiss have also signed a multimillion-dollar deal with the streamer.

2. Kevin McDonald and Daniel Smith-Rowsey, "Introduction," in *The Netflix Effect: Technology and Entertainment in the 21st Century,* ed. Kevin McDonald and Daniel Smith-Rowsey (New York: Bloomsbury Academic, 2016), 5.

3. Chuck Tryon, *On-Demand Culture: Digital Delivery and the Future of Movies* (New Brunswick, NJ: Rutgers University Press, 2013), 2.

4. Todd Spangler, "Netflix Tops 200 Million Streaming Customers, Handily Beats Q4 Subscriber Forecast," *Variety,* January 19, 2021, https://variety.com/2021/digital/news/netflix-q4–2020-earnings-200-million-subscribers-1234887784/.

5. Todd Spangler, "Disney Plus Pops to 95 Million Paid Subscribers," *Variety,* February 11, 2021, https://variety.com/2021/digital/news/disney-plus-pops-to-95-million-paid-subscribers-1234906356/.

6. In May 2021 it was announced that WarnerMedia would be merging with Discovery and forming Warner Bros. Discovery. The deal is set to close mid-2022, so it remains to be seen what these latest business developments will mean for HBO.

7. Scripted programming did decline 7 percent in 2020 (to 493 shows), most likely due to the COVID-19 pandemic. Lesley Goldberg, "Peak TV Update: Scripted Originals Dip 7% in 2020, FX Says," *Hollywood Reporter,* January 29, 2021, https://www.hollywoodreporter.com/tv/tv-news/peak-tv-update-scripted-originals-dip-7-in-2020-fx-says-4124718/.

8. Lacey Rose and Marisa Guthrie, "FX Chief John Landgraf on Content Bubble: 'This Is Simply Too Much Television,'" *Hollywood Reporter,* August 7, 2015, https://www.hollywoodreporter.com/tv/tv-news/fx-chief-john-landgraf-content-813914/.

9. For more on the concept of peak TV and the streaming revolution, see Amanda Lotz, *We Now Disrupt This Broadcast: How Cable Transformed Television and the Internet Revolutionized It All* (Cambridge, MA: MIT Press, 2018).

10. John Stankey, quoted in Edmund Lee and John Koblin, "HBO Must Get Bigger and Broader, Says Its New Overseer," *New York Times,* July 8, 2018, https://www.nytimes.com/2018/07/08/business/media/hbo-att-merger.html.

11. Casey Bloys, HBO programming chief (now promoted to chief content officer of HBO and HBO Max), has repeatedly stated in interviews and during Television Critics Association press tours that the AT&T merger will not negatively impact the HBO brand. For example, see Daniel Holloway and Elaine Low, "HBO's Casey Bloys on Scaling Up under AT&T, Streaming Plans and 'Big Little Lies 2,'" *Variety,* February 8, 2019, https://variety.com/2019/tv/news/hbo-casey-bloys-emmys-att-programming-1203133367/.

12. The *Sex and the City* reboot, titled *And Just Like That,* is going to be an HBO Max original, despite the fact that *Sex* was an HBO show. Two special episodes of *Euphoria* (2019–), an HBO show, premiered on HBO Max before they were released on the cable channel.

13. Jerome de Groot, *Remaking History: The Past in Contemporary Historical Fictions* (New York: Routledge, 2016), 7.

14. Vivian Sobchack, "The Insistent Fringe: Moving Images and Historical Consciousness," *History and Theory* 36, no. 4 (1997): 16, 14 (italics in original).

15. Sobchack, "Insistent Fringe," 5.

16. Of course, I am not suggesting that all historical drama series adhere to the standards of academic history; there are many TV shows to which these common criticisms would apply. I only wish to argue that historians must not automatically assume that all historical TV series and films share the same shortcomings.

17. Glen Creeber, "'Taking Our Personal Lives Seriously': Intimacy, Continuity and Memory in the Television Drama Serial," *Media, Culture & Society* 23, no. 4 (2001): 444.

18. Gary R. Edgerton, "Introduction: A Different Kind of History Altogether," in *Television Histories: Shaping Collective Memory in the Media Age,* ed. Gary R. Edgerton and Peter C. Rollins (Lexington: University Press of Kentucky, 2001), 9 (italics in original).

19. Simon worked as a journalist for the *Baltimore Sun* for twelve years and wrote the book *Homicide: A Year on the Killing Streets,* on which the TV series *Homicide: Life on the Street* was based.

20. *Boardwalk* averaged around five million viewers in its first season, and *Deadwood* around 4.5 million. The ratings for *Band of Brothers* varied greatly, starting with around ten million viewers for the first episode and then dropping to five million for the finale. *Band of Brothers* achieved much greater success on DVD, generating over $700 million in revenue and becoming HBO's best-selling DVD within its first eight years of release. Claude Brodesser-Akner, "HBO's Choppy Waters on Hanks and Spielberg's *The Pacific,*" *Vulture,* February 3, 2010, http://www.vulture.com/2010/02/the_pacific_hbo_250_million.html.

21. Alison Landsberg, *Engaging the Past: Mass Culture and the Production of Historical Knowledge* (New York: Columbia University Press, 2015), 63, 64.

22. Alun Munslow, "Fiction, Imagination and the Fictive: The Literary Aesthetics of Historying," in *The Fiction of History,* ed. Alexander Lyon Macfie (New York: Routledge, 2015), 35, 32.

23. Ann Curthoys and John Docker, "The Boundaries of History and Fiction," in *The SAGE Handbook of Historical Theory,* ed. Nancy Partner and Sarah Foot (London: SAGE Publications, 2013), 203.

24. See, for example, Sara J. Brenneis, *Genre Fusion: A New Approach to History, Fiction, and Memory in Contemporary Spain* (West Lafayette, IN: Purdue University Press, 2014); Jerome de Groot, *The Historical Novel* (London: Routledge, 2010); Beverley Southgate, *"A New Type of History": Fictional Proposals for Dealing with the Past* (London: Routledge, 2015).

25. Here I am drawing upon a criticism of *Schindler's List* by Jacob Epstein included in Creeber, "'Taking Our Personal Lives Seriously,'" 448.

26. Tim O'Brien, *The Things They Carried* (London: Flamingo, 1990), 79.

27. David Simon addressed the many inventions of *Treme* in a piece for the *Times-Picayune* before the first show aired. As he put it, "We are likely to be at our best in those instances in which we are entirely aware of our deceits, just as we are likely to fail when we proceed in ignorance of the facts. Technically speaking, when we cheat and know it, we are 'taking creative liberties,' and when we cheat and don't know it, we are 'screwing up.'" David Simon, "HBO's *Treme* Creator David Simon Explains It All for You," *Times-Picayune,* April 11, 2010, http://www.nola.com/treme-hbo/index.ssf/2010/04/hbos_treme_creator_david_simon.html (article no longer stored on site).

28. Gordon Blithe, the son of Albert Blithe, has recounted his struggles in trying set the record straight about his father's death. After watching the series and figuring out the Albert Blithe depicted was meant to be his father (confirmed when he matched their RA numbers), Gordon attempted to find out how and why it had happened. Some of the surviving Easy Company soldiers had apparently told Ambrose that Blithe died in 1948 and that they had attended his funeral. Neither Ambrose nor anyone involved in the series checked this information. Marcus Brotherton, *A Company of Heroes: Personal Memories about the Real Band of Brothers and the Legacy They Left Us* (New York: Berkley Caliber, 2010), 3–10.

29. Curthoys and Docker, "Boundaries of History and Fiction," 203.

# Index